LADY
COLIN
CAMPBELL

Victorian 'Sex Goddess'

LADY
COLIN
CAMPBELL

Victorian 'Sex Goddess'

G·H·FLEMING

THE WINDRUSH PRESS · GLOUCESTERSHIRE

First published in Great Britain by
The Windrush Press,
Windrush House,
Main Street,
Adlestrop, Moreton-in-Marsh,
Gloucestershire
1989

British Library Cataloguing in Publication Data
Fleming, G. H.
  Lady Colin Campbell: Victorian 'sex
  goddess'
  1. Great Britain. Divorce, 1837–1900
  I. Title
  306.89'0941

  ISBN 0–900075–11–2

Typeset by DP Photosetting, Aylesbury, Bucks
Printed and bound in Great Britain by
Biddles Ltd, Guildford

Picture Credits
Portrait of Lady Colin Campbell: The National Portrait Gallery; George Lewis: The National Portrait Gallery; Sir Charles Russell and Sir Richard Webster: by permission of the Benchers of Lincoln's Inn (Photos: The Courtauld Institute); Robert Finlay: by permission of the Middle Temple (Photo: The Courtauld Institute); The Illustrated Police News and the Penny Illustrated Paper: The British Library, Newspaper Library.

Contents

Acknowledgements

At the British Newspaper Library, in the London suburb of Colindale, I obtained detailed reports of the Campbell trial from more than forty newspapers. For supplementary materials I used the Library of the Guildhall, in London, and the London Library. To become familiar with the Victorian legal milieu, I was permitted by Frederick Walker to examine the holdings in the Lincoln's Inn Library.

I also used the facilities of the British Library, in the British Museum; the Hackney Public Library; the Kensington and Chelsea Libraries; the Newham Public Library; the Library of the Royal College of Surgeons; the Wandsworth Public Library; the Westminster Research Library; the Bristol Central Library; the Bristol University Library; and the public library at Gray's, in Essex. Additionally, I visited the Leigh Court Mental Hospital, through the kindness of L. H. Burton and his staff, and the Royal Purfleet Hotel, thanks to the hospitality of its manager, Richard White. At 79 Cadogan Place, the focal point of this book, Dr John Creightmore, Dr J. R. Gaynor, and Hilary Hiscocks were extremely hospitable to me and graciously allowed me to examine, almost literally, every square inch of the house.

This book was written in the Newberry Library, Chicago, where I was a steady beneficiary of numerous members of its staff, most particularly Karen Skubish.

My literary agent, Shelley Power, provided me with encouragement and several valuable suggestions.

All of the foregoing deserve my appreciation and thanks.

For Mey

Introduction

The longest, most sensational divorce trial in British history was Campbell v. Campbell, which consumed eighteen court days in London during the final weeks of 1886. Since no official record exists, I collated reports from more than forty newspapers to create my own transcript. This book is based upon that transcript.

Campbell v. Campbell was the story of a failed marriage. But it was more than that. Much more. More than fifty witnesses gave evidence. They covered the entire spectrum of society, from the nobility to the least significant servant. The trial was microcosmically Victorian, the picture of an era.

Campbell v. Campbell calls to mind William Frith's *Railway Station*. Just as Frith presented life as he saw it on a Paddington platform, so I have invented nothing. Nor did I distort or exaggerate anything. I didn't have to. The story that unfolded in the witness box contained drama, mystery, suspense, love, sex, jealousy, revenge, anger, irony, humour, and pathos. My role was to rearrange the material into a pattern that is logical, chronological, and non-repetitive. Although I have painted in the background and have inserted occasional *ex cathedra* observations, the narrative is carried by the participants and observers. Unless otherwise stated, every quoted passage was taken verbatim from statements and questions of barristers and from sworn testimony of witnesses.

Because of the many speakers, the effect seems reminiscent of Kurosawa's classic film *Rashomon*. Again and again the same event is seen through the eyes of more than one person. Again and again the reports of an incident are contradictory. In each instance the reader is left to speculate on just what really did happen.

Through it all, the dominating figure is the woman who has given this book its title. To those who sat in the press gallery and publicized her activities she was, as one of them put it, a 'sex goddess.' One reporter said that she possessed 'the unbridled lust of Messalina and the indelicate readiness of a common harlot.' In another paper her life story was characterized as one of 'immorality and obscenity without parallel.'

Even if these comments had not been gross exaggerations, they would have given an incomplete, one-sided view of Lady Colin Campbell. She was a most remarkable person. She was talented, creative, and brilliant at a time when women weren't supposed to be talented, creative, and brilliant. As I comment later, 'The traditional female role [was] one that Lady Colin Campbell did not choose to play. In many ways, the story of her life is that of a woman trying to elude the nets which had been put in place by society.' Herein, I submit, lies the significance of her life, and herein, I hope, is a legitimate *raison d'être* for this book.

CHAPTER 1

Excitement on the Strand

On Friday, 26 November, 1886 the London *Morning Post's* Judicial Calendar included this entry: 'Probate, Divorce and Admiralty Division, Court I. Before Mr. Justice Butt. At 10 1/2 Divorce Cause, with a special jury. Campbell v. Campbell, and Campbell v. Campbell, Marlborough, Shaw, Butler, and Bird.'

Thirty years earlier there could not have been a Campbell v. Campbell. Until 1857, a British divorce could be acquired only through a bill in Parliament. Then the Matrimonial Causes Act created a divorce court. A husband had one cause of action, adultery. A wife had to prove adultery plus desertion or cruelty.

Lady Colin Campbell charged her husband with adultery plus cruelty. He accused her of having had sex with a Duke, a General, a surgeon, and London's fire chief.

The Probate, Divorce and Admiralty Division, Court I, popularly known as Divorce Court No. 1, was, like London's other high civil courts, located in the imposing four-year-old Gothic structure at the east end of the Strand, the Royal Courts of Justice. On the morning of 26 November, the scene outside the building was unheard-of. The pavement and streets were packed with people. This was not the Old Bailey, with titillating criminal trials. Only civil actions were tried here. But for three weeks this would be the most exciting legal place in town.

Inside, there was more turmoil. Corridors were jammed, and the western wing of the first floor provided an exceptional sight. Wooden barriers were in use for the first time since the building had opened in January 1883. They shielded the swinging-door entrance to Divorce Court No. 1. Three uniformed guards admitted only those who held valid credentials, mostly young barristers and newspaper reporters. Anyone in a barrister's robe could normally enter any court – part of a young trial lawyer's education was watching his elders in action. But on this occasion a minor fraction of those who turned up gained entrance. It was almost unprecedented for begowned barristers to be prevented from entering a courtroom. As for the newsmen, they represented journals from all over the nation.

Inside, the reporters' gallery was to the right of the judge's bench. The young barristers sat or stood in the rear, beneath a small public gallery, which just before ten o'clock was opened to fifty men. (Because much of the evidence was expected to be morally repulsive, females were denied admission.)

A few minutes after ten, a side door opened. Four women and two men entered and walked over to the first row of seats, ten chairs behind an elongated desk. This was the solicitors' table.

Most noticeable, and most noticed, was one of the women. She was 28-years-old, five feet ten inches tall, and fashionably slender. She had black hair, dark eyes, and an olive complexion. Her face was remarkable for beauty and for intellectuality. She wore a plum-coloured velvet dress and jacket, a black bonnet, and turquoise earrings. As she proceeded to her seat, she typified self-possession and self-confidence. She was one of the parties to the action, Lady Colin Campbell.

Lady Colin was accompanied by her small, careworn mother; her distinguished-looking father, called by one newspaper 'an aristocratic version of Mr Gladstone'; her shorter but otherwise strikingly similar sister Francesca; her highly attractive older cousin, Lady Miles; and the group's escort, Lady Colin's solicitor, George Lewis.

Then as now, the richest and most famous members of the legal profession were barristers, but one solicitor kept up with the best of them, George Lewis. He had been involved in most of high society's recent *causes célèbres*, and it was natural for him to be part of this case.

Just after Lady Colin had sat down, Lord Colin arrived with *his* solicitor, William Humphreys, and two of his four brothers, Lords Archibald and Walter Campbell. Lord Colin's solicitor actually was William Humphrey's father Charles, well known for his work in criminal trials, who because of illness had been replaced for the trial by his junior associate. A man in his early thirties, William Humphreys was twenty years younger than Lewis.

After brushing by his wife, Lord Colin casually removed his muffler and overcoat and took his seat. Not quite as tall as she, he was moderately handsome with delicate, refined features, dark brown hair combed straight back, and a carefully-tended moustache. He looked pensive, haggard and sickly, the antithesis of his charmingly arrogant wife.

In court, the Campbells were physically separated by two chairs, occupied by their solicitors.

[4]

Immediately behind them were two rows for barristers. At 10.10, carrying leather valises, they began to arrive.

Barristers fall into two groups, much the smaller of which have their names followed by the initials QC. They are the cream of the profession, the Queen's Counsel. When a QC represents a client, a barrister without the initials also must be retained. In Campbell v. Campbell, each party was represented by two QC's. Four additional QC's would appear for the co-respondents. Along with the six ordinary counsel, fourteen barristers would be in court.

The QC's sat in one row, with the others behind them. Elsewhere they would have been like other people. But not here. Their costumes, providing a link with the past, transformed them into an élite corps above the common rank of men, such as the solicitors in their street clothes, and, taking their places just before 10.30, the twelve jurors.

Jury duty was required of most property-holding males between 21 and 60. There were two categories of jurors, common and special. Special jurors owned property of greater value than held by common jurors, or, according to the statute, were 'persons of higher degree,' such as bankers, merchants, and holders of a degree from Oxford or Cambridge. Whereas common jurors were unpaid, special jurors generally received one guinea for each case on which they served. Either party could ask for a special jury and would bear the expense. In the current case, Lady Colin made the request. (Special juries were abolished for most cases in 1949, and they disappeared entirely in 1971.)

The jury box was to the judge's left. At 10.20 a clerk read from a list of names, and twelve men came down from a small gallery and entered the box. As in all civil trials, they could not be challenged. Well dressed, they ranged in age from the late twenties to the late fifties. Four wore beards, three had bushy sideburns, and they were all moustached.

The twelfth juror was in place at 10.28. Promptly at 10.30 a curtain behind the bench parted; somebody shouted something unintelligible, and everyone arose. In a fur-tipped cape and red gown, the judge had arrived. He made several bows, which were returned by solicitors, barristers, and court personnel, and then all were again seated.

The judge was 56-year-old Sir Charles Parker Butt, QC, who had presided over this court since 1883. He was tall, lean, erect, with a high forehead, long, straight nose, beard turning white, and eyes which seen through bifocal glasses were bright blue and twinkling. An American observer said he looked Lincolnesque.

A clerk then swore in the jurors. Holding a Bible, each one read aloud the oath printed on a card, to render a verdict upon the evidence.

Now the trial could begin.

When two or more barristers represent a client, one manages the case and is the leader. The other advocate, or advocates, regardless of age, are designated juniors and follow his instructions. Traditionally, the most junior counsel for the plaintiff (or petitioner) reads the pleadings, a formal statement of facts. Normally nothing is more routine. But not in the Campbell case. Judge Butt called for the pleadings, and two juniors – Charles Mathews for Lady Colin and Richard Searle for Lord Colin – rose and began reading simultaneously. There was loud laughter.

Judge Butt demanded, 'What is the meaning of this?'

The leaders – Sir Charles Russell for Lady Colin and Robert Finlay for Lord Colin – stood, and the juniors sat down. Finlay contended that his client should begin because his petition had been drawn up and was about to be filed when George Lewis, hearing about it, hurriedly dashed off a petition which was filed minutes before Lord Colin's. Sir Charles said that because Lady Colin's petition was filed first, she was the petitioner.

This was no academic exercise. The party that began a case also ended it, with the last, unanswered words.

On the principle of first come first served, Judge Butt gave Lady Colin the right to begin. It was another victory for George Lewis.

Charles Mathews again got up. He was short, 36-years-old, a stepson of the famous comedian Charles James Mathews. He was rapidly becoming known for his work in criminal trials and notorious civil actions. The presence in the case of Mathews on the floor and Charles Humphreys behind the scenes, two Old Bailey regulars, was perhaps a commentary on Campbell v. Campbell.

After Mathews had done his duty, Sir Charles Russell rose to deliver the opening statement.

Sir Charles was the best barrister of his time, perhaps of the century, 'the king,' said the *Evening News*, 'almost the autocrat, of the front benches of the bar.' He routinely dominated everyone in court, even the judge. The nation's foremost trial lawyer was also the best paid. His income was about £25,000.

Russell had often been allied with George Lewis, almost the only solicitor for whom he showed respect. He was barely polite, seldom even civil, to solicitors, but they eagerly briefed him.

He was a strongly-built, chubby-faced, square jawed, clean shaven Irishman in his early fifties. He spoke with a rich Irish brogue. Advised that giving up his brogue could mean another £1000 a year, he said that he would not part with it for the £1000.

'Gentlemen of the jury,' Russell said, 'this is a painful case which began in September 1880, when Lady Colin, then Gertrude Blood, was staying with friends in Scotland, where she met Lord Colin Campbell ...'

CHAPTER 2

A Whirlwind Courtship

Early in September 1880, while visiting friends in Inveraray, Scotland, Gertrude Blood met Lord Colin Campbell.

Lord Colin was born in 1853, the fifth and last son of Scotland's most prominent nobleman, George John Douglas Campbell, eighth Duke of Argyll. The Duke's wealth was overpowering: his land holdings comprised 175,000 acres, and his Castle of Inveraray was one of Britain's grandest estates. He was not an idle rich man. Since inheriting his title in 1847 at the age of 24, he had been Chancellor of the University of St Andrews, Lord Privy Seal, Lord Rector of Glasgow University, President of the Royal Society of Edinburgh, Hereditary Master of the Queen's Household in Scotland, Keeper of the Great Seal of Scotland, Postmaster General, and Secretary of State for India. He delivered eloquent speeches in the House of Lords; he contributed provocative letters to *The Times*; and, as a fellow of the Royal Society and of the Geological Society, he wrote solid scientific articles.

Little of Argyll's intellect and diligence had passed to Colin, a typical young aristocrat. He had studied without distinction at Eton, St Andrews University, and Trinity College, Cambridge, where he received a pass degree. He was a director of several companies in the city; he belonged to the Brooks's Club; he had been an officer in the first Argyllshire Volunteers; and, since graduating from Cambridge in 1878, he had held the Liberal Party's safe Parliamentary seat of Argyllshire, which would be his until 1885. His only noteworthy political action came in September 1879, when he voted against a bill, favoured by most of his constituents, to abolish flogging in the army. He refused to avoid going on record by leaving the House during the vote.

After leaving Cambridge, Lord Colin thought of becoming a surgeon and spent a few months studying at the Royal College of surgeons. This was too arduous, and lately he decided on an easier course of professional action. He would attend the requisite number of dinners which would lead to his enrolment as a barrister.

Illustriously named but modestly gifted. This epitome of Lord Colin Campbell would hardly characterize Gertrude Elizabeth Blood.

Gertrude's parents were Mr and Mrs Edmund Maghlin Blood, of London by way of County Clare, Ireland. In her youth, Mary, Gertrude's mother, had been noted for her beauty. At 18 she married Timothy O'Beirne, and at 19 she was a moderately well-to-do widow. Her second, and current, husband, was a member of the Reform Club, a connoisseur of painting, and a gentleman of leisure. The Bloods were respectable, financially secure, and unremarkable except for rearing their three daughters. They had not been brought up merely to be living room adornments but had received a liberal education in Italy and France and had been encouraged to develop their talents.

Gertrude, the second daughter and third child, born in 1857, was the most accomplished of the Bloods. Her intellectual and artistic gifts were multifarious. When she met Lord Colin, she was a singer who had often given recitals and a painter who had frequently exhibited her work. Her first talent, however, was that of writing. She had grown up in the Mediterranean area, where the family lived because of Mr Blood's health, and her early writings reflected this background. Her literary career began at the age of 14 with an article in *Cassell's Magazine,* 'A Turkish Bath in Cairo.' Two years later she had a published volume for children on the pleasures of travelling abroad. She followed this with several articles, and then, in 1878 her first work of fiction appeared, a short novel, *Topo, a Tale About English Children in Italy.* With pictures by the young, soon-to-be famous illustrator Kate Greenaway, it tells the story of an English family who lived in Italy because of their mother's physical condition. It was one of the most popular juvenile books of its time and went through seven printings. For *Topo,* Gertrude used a pen name, 'G. B. Brunefille.' This was an 'inside joke.' In her family, Gertrude had the darkest skin. Hence her *nom de plume* Brunefille, 'brown girl.'

Gertrude's brownness was due in part to time spent under the Mediterranean sun. She was a great outdoors woman. As a swimmer she had demonstrated her expertise in the Nile and off Byron's favourite beach at the Lido. As a horsewoman she loved the challenge of mounting and taming animals noted for their ferocity. She was also proficient with a fencing foil, a fishing rod, and a bicycle. She could do many things, and whatever she did she did well.

Gertrude Blood was also charming and beautiful.

Two days after they had met, Colin proposed marriage, and Gertrude at once accepted the offer. Neither of them knew how old the other was.

His impetuousness is understandable, but why did she rush into this? Was she blinded by the Argyll lustre? Did she like the idea of becoming a Lady? Did she need a husband whom she could dominate? Did she, like a Browning heroine, fall in love at first sight? Whatever the reason, the decision was apparently her own.

'The engagement between my daughter and Lord Colin,' Mary Ann Blood said, 'was made without my knowledge. The first thing I heard was that it had been made.' Nor did the Campbells have prior knowledge. Colin wanted to wait to break the news to his father. The Duke held strong views on marriage, especially within his family. He expected his children to make 'good' matches, and they had not yet failed him. One daughter was in line to become a duchess; another was the wife of an Anglican bishop; his eldest son was the husband of the Queen's fourth daughter, Princess Louise.

The Duke would hardly welcome an engagement to a woman whom his son had known for less than three days and came from a family without eminence or wealth. Gertrude nevertheless insisted that he be informed at once. She then left for London.

On the next day, Colin wrote to her, 'My own darling – I have made up my mind to tell my father. I shall never forget that your first request was that I should do something because it was right.'

Argyll refused to recognize the engagement.

This didn't discourage the young couple. They planned to marry during the Christmas holiday season.

CHAPTER 3

A Mysterious Ailment

In Kensington, near the Victoria and Albert Museum, lies Thurloe Square. Like much of the area, it was built in the middle of the nineteenth century. The central garden is surrounded by four- and five-storey red brick houses with rusticated stucco facings, white pillars on either side of the front door, and wrought-iron first floor balconies. It is pleasant, attractive, comfortably middle class. In 1880 the residents included an artist, a physician, an MP, a countess, a lieutenant general, a Fellow of the Chemical Society, a Fellow of the Linnaean Society, and a Fellow of the Royal Microscopical Society. Two of the homes were occupied by private girls' schools. The end houses of each of the four blocks which make up the eastern and western sides of the square have an added embellishment, stucco pilasters rising from the first floor. One of the end houses, number 6 in 1880 (46 today) was the home of the Blood family.

In October 1880, Lord Colin visited Thurloe Square for the first time. He told his future mother-in-law about something that he had not mentioned to Gertrude.

'Mrs Blood,' he said, 'I have to undergo a slight operation for fistula. I am going to Sir Henry Thompson's private hospital on account of the good nursing there.'

Sixty-year-old Sir Henry Thompson, whose small hospital was at 35 Wimpole Street, was one of the world's foremost specialists in genito-urinary surgery. He had been a pioneer in removing tumours from urinary bladders. His patients had included Belgium's King Leopold I and Emperor Napoleon III.

Thompson was an unlikely surgeon for someone who was suffering only from fistula. But was his ailment really fistula? The coming operation would be Thompson's second on Lord Colin. And he was not the only one whom Lord Colin had consulted. Since 1871, because of this problem he had seen six medical men on at least eleven different occasions. They included the eminent surgeon Sir Preston Hewitt, who had operated on him twice.

Gertrude and her parents knew nothing about this medical history. As far as they were concerned, the treatment began in October 1880 in Sir Henry Thompson's hospital.

After the surgery, Lord Colin was bed-ridden for more than a month. This was rather unusual for 'a slight operation.' He said that the long period of recovery was 'on account of the mental anxiety I suffered with regard to the engagement.' This explanation didn't satisfy Gertrude's father, who confronted the patient in his hospital room.

'I want you to tell me frankly and truthfully,' Mr Blood asked, 'if you are in fact suffering from a loathsome disease.'

'I solemnly assure you,' Colin said, 'that there is no foundation for that suggestion. My ailment is of no consequence.'

Mrs Blood meanwhile was concerned about plans for the marriage. She wrote to Colin and said that because of the uncertainty surrounding the date of the wedding, 'Gertrude is in a state of nervous tension.'

The wedding, it will be remembered, had been scheduled for the Christmas season, but on 22 December, Colin wrote to Mrs Blood and said that because of his health 'the end of July will be the best time for the marriage.'

Responding to his doctor's advice, in January he left on a sea voyage to the Cape of Good Hope.

He was gone for more than two months, during which time, he said, he received letters from Gertrude 'by every mail.'

He returned to London late in March and moved into living quarters at 24 Pont Street, near Thurloe Square. Having gained no great benefits from his journey, he immediately called upon middle-aged, grey-haired John Propert, a general surgeon. Propert at once referred him to a specialist, William Allingham.

Allingham was one of the most distinguished Fellows of the Royal College of Surgeons. After winning prizes in medical school, and serving with distinction as a battlefield surgeon in the Crimean War, he became one of the first doctors to concentrate on the rectum. He wrote articles and books on rectal ailments, including the classic work, *On Diseases of the Rectum, Their Diagnosis and Treatment*. He was a senior surgeon at St Mark's Hospital for Fistula, Piles, and Other Diseases of the Rectum, and was probably the world's premier authority on the anus.

Allingham performed surgery on Lord Colin in April 1881. It was not successful. The failure, Lord Colin said, was due to 'anxiety of my mind consequent on my father's opposition to the engagement.' He did not explain why other surgeons had been unsuccessful for nearly ten years.

What actually was Lord Colin's malady?

Sir Charles Russell asked Mrs Blood, 'Had you the slightest idea of the nature of Lord Colin's illness?'

'Not the slightest.'

And Lady Colin said, 'I never did know what his complaint was.'

The advocates were not reluctant to offer their opinions.

Lord Colin's team of barristers was led by a 44-year-old Scotsman, Robert Finlay, QC. Finlay was noted for his work in commercial actions and had seldom appeared in *causes célèbres* or in divorce cases of any kind. He had a scholarly interest in classical literature and a medical degree from the University of Edinburgh. He gave up medicine because of an abrasive personality, an obvious handicap in an era when doctors had close personal relationships with patients. He was handsome and still abrasive, a man who never hesitated to call a spade a spade.

'For many years,' Finlay said, 'Lord Colin suffered from a stricture of the urethra, and the result of constant irritation was an abscess, ending in a fistula. True, his illness resulted from an indiscretion committed at Cambridge. But his symptoms would have been the same if the stricture had come from a blow or other external injury.'

Russell said, 'Lord Colin's disease was originally of peculiar virulence or it became serious through neglect, and when it passed its active stage, it left behind severe effects which affected the sufferer's health and inflamed his private parts. An operation was necessary to make an artificial passage in the urethral passage. In this state of affairs it is highly probable that a disease would be communicated by contact. In saying that he suffered from fistula Lord Colin could only have intended to mislead his fiancée. He was not suffering from fistula. He suffered from a disease quite different from fistula. Plainly and simply, this disease was syphilis.'

CHAPTER 4

Pre-Marital Problems

For a few weeks after Allingham's operation, Lord Colin lay bed-ridden in the home of his brother Lord George Campbell, Argyll's fourth son. A retired lieutenant in the Royal Navy, he was a member of a prominent firm of corn dealers. His residence was in fashionable Bryanston Square, just north of Marble Arch. While recuperating in his brother's home, Lord Colin was under the constant supervision of a surgical nurse, 35-year-old Elizabeth Wright.

Meanwhile, on 24 May Mrs Blood wrote for the first time to the groom's father:

'I wish to explain our position. We had nothing to do with the engagement. It was made without our consent being asked, but when our daughter returned from Scotland we saw that it was useless to try to induce her to change her mind. I think you have had the same experience with your son. They have certainly been true to each other for the eight months during which they have been engaged, and we have determined to make the best of what cannot be changed, as, according to my old-fashioned ideas, it would be a scandal and a breach of honour if either of them were to draw back, which there appears to be not the smallest inclination to do.

'Gertrude is brave, but there are limits to what a girl can bear. If anyone had prophesied to me a year ago that I should consent to such a marriage as this I should have laughed at the very idea. I should have expected her to be received with pride and joy in any family. She is well-born, beautiful, of a most noble character, and exceptionally gifted. Her only defect is that she has but the portion of a gentlewoman. Therefore she has been treated with slender courtesy by every member of your grace's family.

'She marries a man who cannot settle sixpence on her. We wish to leave £4000 of Gertrude's money entirely unsettled in order that Lord Colin may be so much assured of capital in his future career; but this depends on your grace's consenting to settle Lord Colin's younger son's portion as a jointure upon his wife. This with £2000 secured to her as a mortgage on her further property would be a small provision, but it would be certain. If your grace refuses this arrangement, it will make no difference as to the marriage, but it will oblige us to settle strictly all of Gertrude's money, leaving her no power to deal with except by will. This settlement will be a certain loss of income to them, as the securities which satisfy trustees give very small interest, but that would not be our fault, as we are willing to deal as liberally as possible with Lord Colin, to whom we are much attached, and to whom we would wish to give every possible help in his career.'

The Duke of Argyll received Mrs Blood's letter at his London home, in Kensington not far from Thurloe Square. His reply was the only communication that ever passed from him to either of Gertrude's parents:

'Madam – I never supposed that you or Mr Blood had the smallest responsibility for my son's engagement. But it was impossible for me to approve that engagement, made on three days acquaintance, with no previous knowledge of each other's character and disposition. I have thought it my duty to withhold all approval and not to recognise it until it should be certain and irrevocable. As you now inform me that the engagement is irrevocable. I am disposed to make the best of what cannot be prevented and to make some arrangements on the subject you refer to. I cannot help thinking that as the total sum you can give to your daughter and I can give to Colin is only £16,000, the whole of it ought to be settled.'

The Duke was not alone in his lack of enthusiasm for the marriage. Lord Colin's attendant surgeon, John Propert, was questioned by Finlay:

'Before the marriage did you give Lord Colin certain advice?'

'I did.'

'What did you tell him?'

'I told him that if the marriage took place Miss Blood could only be his nurse and that no consummation could take place until I sanctioned it.'

After he had been thus advised, Lord Colin spoke to Gertrude. He was questioned on this conversation by the second man on his legal team, Frank Lockwood, QC.

A 40-year-old Yorkshireman, Lockwood was six feet two inches tall, with broad shoulders, a powerful frame, handsome face, and prematurely white hair. Extremely genial, with a fine sense of humour, he was one of the most attractive personalities at the English bar. He was a fine artist who often, during a trial, drew caricatures of lawyers, witnesses and even the judge.

'Where,' Lockwood asked, 'did your pre-marital conversation with Miss Blood take place?'

'At Thurloe Square, in June.'

'What passed between you on the subject?'

'I spoke to Gertrude after I had received a communication from Mr Propert. I said, "I have something to say which I feel some difficulty in telling. It is right you should know my doctors have said that in consequence of my operation it is unwise to fulfil my engagement with you to marry me. You must be prepared to nurse me for six months, or until the doctors have made some change in my state of health." Gertrude said she perfectly understood. She was affectionate and asked me to let her make a full communication to her mother. Afterwards I received a letter from Mrs Blood.'

'Have you got the letter?'

'I did not keep it, I am sorry to say.'

'Tell us what the letter contained.'

'Mrs Blood said that Gertrude would be only too willing to nurse me for such time as might be necessary.'

Numerous newspapers referred scathingly to this pre-nuptial agreement. In a typical comment, the London *Figaro* said, 'There were the strongest reasons why Lord Colin should have refrained from asking a young girl to become his wife, and there were the strongest reasons why she should have refused.'

But Gertrude did not refuse. She was asked about this by the man who conducted her direct examination, the second of her three advocates, Frederick Inderwick, QC.

Although a junior in this case, Inderwick, 50-years-old, was a veteran barrister with a fine reputation. The author of an authoritative book on divorce law, he had more knowledge of and experience in the Divorce

Court than any other advocate in the case. More genial than his leader, he belonged to five clubs, played golf, and was an enthusiastic first nighter.

'Was it communicated to you,' he asked, 'that Lord Colin suffered from an illness that would delay consummation of the marriage?'

'Yes.'

'What was said to you on the subject?'

'Lord Colin telegraphed me to go to him at Bryanston Square, saying he wanted to see me on pressing business. My mother and I drove over and were shown into the dining room. He seemed annoyed at seeing my mother, and said, "If you don't mind, I want to speak to Arab alone. [Because of her dark complexion, Gertrude was sometimes called "Arab."] My mother did not like this, but as he made a point of it she went out. He then said he had something to say of great importance. He said it would be necessary after we were married to occupy separate rooms. He asked, "Do you mind marrying me under those conditions?" I said, "Not in the least."'

'Did he communicate to you the nature of his complaint?'

'Not in the least.'

'Was that all he told you?'

'Yes, except that he pressed me to keep the matter secret. I said, "I will do so, with one exception. I must tell my mother." He objected very much and said, "If you tell your mother she will tell your father, and the matter will get out." I said, "I must tell her. I will pass my word that the matter will go no further."'

'Did you tell your mother?'

'Yes.'

'Did she mention it to anyone?'

'Never.'

In his opening statement, Finlay said that Mrs Blood pushed her daughter into the marriage. Russell questioned her on this:

'Did you in any shape or form coerce Lord Colin into this marriage?'

'Certainly not. I spoke to him strongly as to his family's discourtesy toward my daughter. I said, "If you presented your father with a butcher's daughter he would have welcomed her with effusion if she had plenty of money. [There was laughter in court.] He ought at least to treat my daughter with courtesy." He replied, "That is true, and it makes his conduct only the more disgusting."' [Renewed laughter]

Mrs Blood was cross examined by Finlay:

'Did you urge on the marriage?'

'No, I did not. I was very anxious to break it off. I remonstrated very strongly with Lord Colin about the discourtesy of his family.'

'Do you say you tried to break the marriage off?'

'Yes, I do. I said it must be either on or off.'

'When you heard that they could not live together as man and wife did you think it advisable to postpone the marriage?'

'No, I cannot say that I did.'

'Your view was that there was no reason for postponing the marriage?'

'You may take it that way.'

'Did you tell Lord Colin that your daughter would be perfectly satisfied to be his nurse?'

'No. That is an entire falsehood.'

'When you said it should be on or off, did you not mean to urge it on?'

'I did not. I should have preferred it to be off.'

'You wish me to believe that?'

'Yes, although I liked Lord Colin at that time.'

'Did you tell him your daughter's health was suffering from the long engagement?'

'I don't think I did.'

'Will you swear you did not?'

'I will swear I do not remember saying so.'

CHAPTER 5

A Wedding and a Lost Bracelet

On 21 July, 1881, Gertrude Elizabeth Blood became Lady Colin Campbell.

The wedding took place in a small grey stone building hidden below the Strand on Savoy Street, the ancient Royal Chapel of the Savoy. Guests included the Queen's daughter Princess Louise, who was the groom's sister-in-law, and a scattering of dukes, marquises, and earls.

The bride wore a dress of white *crêpe de Chine*, trimmed with old Brussels lace, and her jewels consisted of a necklace, pendant, and bracelets of diamonds, diamond solitaire earrings, and a diamond catseye and opal brooch. The six bridesmaids wore costumes after Sir Joshua Reynolds, pale blue *voile de vierge* overskirts of white lace, large fichus of Indian muslin, caps tripped with pale blue ribbon, and, gifts from the groom, 'merry thought' brooches with the initials 'G. C.'

Three clergymen officiated: the Rev. Henry White, chaplain in ordinary to the Queen; the Rev. Pellew Arthur, chaplain of Trinity College, Cambridge; and the Rev. William Loftie, chaplain of the Savoy.

There were hundreds of bridal presents, including diamond solitaire earrings, Oriental brass vases, a case of silver fish knives and forks, two black satin armchairs, two silver coffee-pots, a silver tea-pot, a silver hot-water jug, a pearl and gold scarf pin, silver ice spoons, a gold and enamel scent bottle, a gold bracelet, a diamond and black opal spider brooch, a silver-backed toilet set, silver candlesticks, a silver eagle ink-stand, a Dresden china lamp, a silver mounted paper cutter, a set of pearl and diamond necklace, pendant, earrings, and bracelet, a polar bear rug, Japanese folding screens, and an antique brass bell.

After a reception, the couple left on their honeymoon. High society's favourite newspaper, the *Morning Post*, reported that they were headed for the Continent. The socially-oriented weekly journal *Truth* said their destination was Switzerland.

Actually Lord and Lady Colin Campbell spent the first five days of their marriage in the town of Ventnor, on the Isle of Wight. And they were not alone. Their constant companion was Elizabeth Wright. Among Lady Colin's earliest recollections of married life were honeymoon breakfasts with her husband and her husband's surgical nurse.

From the Isle of Wight, the threesome returned to London and stopped briefly at the medium-priced Hotel Grosvenor, adjoining the Victoria Station and bordering on Pimlico, then a known district of prostitutes.

After a couple of days at the Grosvenor, they moved into a flat in Westbourne Place, just off Sloane Street.

At once the Campbells began to establish a pattern for their life-style. As one part of the pattern, Lord Colin lay in bed sick. For ten days he was an invalid, suffering from a chill contracted on his honeymoon. He was asked about it by the third member of his legal team, Richard Searle:

'When you were ill in Sloane Street, how often did you see your wife?'

'In the morning and the evening, but rarely in the daytime. She paid me mere visits.'

Although he sat in the second row, Searle was older than either of his two senior counsel. He had practised at the Bar for 28 years, and, except for Inderwick, had had more experience in the Divorce Court than anyone else in the case. Despite all of his divorce work, he was jolly and good-natured. Like Judge Butt, he wore bi-focal glasses.

Searle questioned Elizabeth Wright on life in Sloane Street:

[17]

'Were there a number of visitors?'
'Yes.'
'Were they mostly ladies or gentlemen?'
'Gentlemen.'
'Whom did they see?'
'Lady Colin.'
Russell had an explanation for these visitors:
'Try to realize Lady Colin's position. The Duke was opposed to the marriage and only finally yielded consent. Did he or the ladies of the family take her by the hands after the marriage? They did not. She was launched on her life under exceptional circumstances which ought to appeal to everybody of tender heart and just mind. She was left without that care and kindness which might have been rendered by the Campbell family.'

Sir Charles did not say why care and kindness were provided primarily by male visitors.

'Do you remember a bracelet of Lady Colin's?' Searle asked Wright.
'I do.'
'What pattern was it?'
'It was a snake pattern.'
'Do you remember when it was lost or mislaid?'
'Yes.'
'Did Lady Colin speak to you about it?'
'Yes. she told me not to mention it to Lord Colin.'
'Did a gentleman caller appear a few days later?'
'Yes.'
'Who let him in?'
'Lady Colin.'
'Did you hear what passed between them?'
'I heard him say, "The lost property has been found."'
'Did you on that day see the bracelet again?'
'I saw Lady Colin wear it in the evening.'

Lady Colin acknowledged the loss of the bracelet. 'It is a fact,' she said, 'that I told the servant [the nurse, Elizabeth Wright] not to tell Lord Colin about it. I had lost my keys, and he made a great many remarks about my carelessness. I said to Mrs Wright, "Don't tell his lordship about this or he will worry me about it as he did about the keys." The bracelet was found in the drapery of one of my evening dresses.'

'In Sloane Street,' Searle asked Wright, 'did you give a letter by mistake to Lord Colin one morning?'
'Yes, and her ladyship was very angry.'

'After that, what did she do about the letters?'
'Her ladyship went downstairs and waited for the postman.'

CHAPTER 6

The Marriage is Consummated

In the Sloane Street flat there was no sex. Lady Colin practiced what the Birmingham *Daily Mail* called 'compulsory virginity.'

After a couple of months, the couple went for a brief holiday to Bournemouth. On the second day, Lord Colin said, his wife suddenly left 'without giving any reason except that she was obligated to return to London.'

He could hardly have been ignorant of why she abruptly departed. Sir Charles Russell explained:

'Lord Colin cut out a portion of a letter from Mr Propert suggesting that intercourse would be beneficial to him. He handed this slip of paper to his wife. This is hardly the way in which a man with feelings of delicacy would put such a matter to a young, pure-minded wife. It caused in her a feeling of revulsion, and the marriage was not then consummated.'

Finlay defended his client's action:

'Before intercourse took place, Lord Colin received a letter from his surgeon, Mr Propert, written after consulting with Mr Allingham, in which he said he thought it advisable to relax the restriction imposed at the time of the marriage. My learned friend Sir Charles Russell denounced Lord Colin. For what? For not being wiser than two eminent surgeons? For acting on their advice?'

Actually at that time Lord Colin's conduct was not outrageous. The Victorian family was based on a wife's obedience to her husband's wishes, particularly his sexual wishes. In 1891 Parliament would pass a law that denied a husband 'conjugal rights' without his wife's consent, but until then consent was not necessary. Judged by standards of 1881 Lord Colin was not unreasonable. He may indeed have been more moderate than many husbands. After all, he did not prevent his wife from returning home alone.

[19]

After ten more sexless days, the Campbells went to the principal Argyll residence, the Castle of Inveraray.

The mid-eighteenth-century mansion is not architecturally distinguished. It is no more than a large, square Gothic style building, a quadrangle with turrets. Yet it has been lavishly praised. An English visitor called it 'the noblest place in Scotland,' and another referred to it as 'one of the grandest residences in the United Kingdom.' Samuel Johnson, no lover of Scottish things, saw it on his tour to the Hebrides and 'was much struck by [its] grandeur and elegance.' And the scene was the inspiration for a memorable water colour by Turner.

Turner and the others were really less impressed by the castle than by the picturesqueness of its site – the woodlands, the lake, the steep hills. It is a breathtaking vista.

The building's interior is celebrated for its furniture, paintings, and Flemish tapestry.

(One negative note was struck on 1 January 1880 by the London journal *Truth*, which noted that 'the tenants on Argyll's estate are wretchedly lodged.')

All in all, Argyll Castle would seem like a fine place in which to make love. And it was there in October 1881 that Lady Colin Campbell lost her virginity.

It was not a pleasant experience. 'The first intercourse,' Russell said, 'was accompanied by shameful injunctions from Lord Colin which could not but shock his young wife. He advised her to take precautions against an infection.'

The subject came up during Lockwood's cross-examination of Lady Colin:

'You said Lord Colin suggested a certain precaution?'

'Yes.'

'I need hardly say it is painful to ask these questions, but I am bound to do so. Did you follow the suggestion?'

'I did. He said also I had better ask my sister what to do.'

'Did Lord Colin know what precautions you were using?'

'No.'

Lockwood also questioned Lord Colin on this matter:

'Did you ever suggest to your wife that she should take precautions?'

'Never. Whenever questions regarding her health were raised, I told her she should consult her sister [the older of her two sisters, Mrs George Bolton, who was dead at the time of the Campbell trial].'

Lord Colin was cross-examined by Russell:

'Did you really never speak to your wife on the subject of taking

[20]

precautions?'

'I do not remember whether I ever used that word.'

'Well, did you ever speak on the subject?'

'I asked her in any question affecting her health to consult her sister.'

'I want to know specifically whether there ever was a conversation on the subject of taking precautions.'

'I cannot recollect it.'

If there had been such a conversation, it must have occurred after the act. The 'precautions,' then, would have been to prevent, not a pregnancy, but the catching of a disease, presumably a venereal disease.

CHAPTER 7

Lord Blandford

After a week in Scotland, without more sex, the Campbells returned to London.

They moved into the family town house in Kensington, near Holland Park on Camden Hill. A Regency villa built in 1815, it had been the Duke of Bedford's home from 1823 to 1852, when it was bought by Lord Colin's father and named Argyll Lodge. It was not as lavish as the Inveraray Castle – not quite. It had fourteen principal bedrooms, six secondary bedrooms, a billiard room, four reception rooms, and extensive offices. And, a great luxury at the time, there were two bathrooms. Twenty bedrooms and two bathrooms. The grounds covered four acres, with sweeping lawns, Dutch flower gardens, a rookery, numerous trees, a gardener's lodge, and two tennis courts. For rating purposes, Argyll Lodge was valued more highly than the famous nearby Holland House. And it was quiet and peaceful. Approached by a cul-de-sac, removed from all traffic, it was a large, secluded retreat within the metropolis. (The Lodge was demolished in 1955. Its site is now occupied by the Holland Park School.)

Not unexpectedly, Lord Colin began his Argyll Lodge residency in bed. Alone in bed. In Scotland he had caught a cold which would incapacitate him for a couple of weeks.

Lady Colin was questioned by Inderwick on her role during her husband's illness:

'At that time he had no nurse with him?'

'None.'

'Did you attend upon him?'

'Yes, certainly.'

'Did you dress his wounds?'

'I did everything.'

On the same subject, Lockwood examined Lord Colin:

'Who attended you at Argyll Lodge?'

'Mrs Wright.'

'Were you attended by Lady Colin?'

'No.'

'Do you remember her going out when you were ill?'

'Yes.'

Elizabeth Wright in fact was present uninterruptedly at Argyll Lodge during Lord Colin's illness.

Wright was asked by Lockwood about Lady Colin's conduct:

'At Argyll Lodge did Lady Colin go out much?'

'She went out every day.'

'Did she go out in the evening?'

'She went out every evening except one.'

'What time did she usually return?'

'Sometimes as late as one o'clock.'

'Did she say anything to you about a latchkey?'

'She requested me to ask the housemaid for a latchkey.'

'Did she get one?'

'The housemaid said, "The Duke of Argyll did not allow anyone to have a latchkey except himself."' (Laughter in court)

The housekeeper, Margaret Lowe, was questioned by Lockwood:

'When Lord Colin was confined to his bedroom, was Lady Colin in the habit of going out?'

'Yes.'

'What time did she generally come in?'

'I have let her in at twenty minutes to one.'

Robert Finlay made it clear what he thought, or professed to think, about Lady Colin's behaviour: 'They had been married for only two months, and one might have thought that she would have been assiduous in her attentions to her husband. I am sorry to say that she was nothing of the kind. She left Lord Colin in his bedroom; she was out all day, dined out in the evening, had her own visitors, and followed her own interests.'

Since her husband was not seriously ill and was watched over by a nurse, why shouldn't Lady Colin have followed her own interests? Because of the prevailing point of view, expressed by a contemporary newspaper editorialist: 'The ministry of women is one of help and sympathy. The essential principle, the key-note of her work in the world is *aid*; to sustain, succour, revive, and shelter man in the struggle and duty of life, is her great mission.' Lady Colin, then, should have been home with her husband.

In Argyll Lodge, as in Sloane Street, visitors called, mostly men. Margaret Lowe was asked about one visit:

'Do you remember, in October 1881, a gentleman calling?'

'Yes.'

'Who was that gentleman?'

'Lord Blandford.'

'Whom did Lord Blandford see?'

'Lady Colin.'

'Where was Lord Colin?'

'In bed.'

'What time did Lord Blandford call?'

'Between six and seven.'

'How long did he remain?'

'About an hour.'

'During the whole of that time was Lady Colin alone with Lord Blandford?'

'Yes.'

'Who let him out?'

'Lady Colin.'

Because a social visit might in itself be suspicious, both participants were asked about it.

Lady Colin gave her evidence when cross-examined by Lockwood:

'Did Lord Blandford call at about seven o'clock?'

'I do not remember what time he called.'

'Do you know that he stayed until dinner-time?'

'I know nothing of the kind. I believe his visit lasted about half-an-hour.'

'Did you tell Lord Colin who had called?'

'There was no necessity because Lord Blandford's card was brought up to where Lord Colin was.'

'Did he say anything about Lord Blandford having called?'

'He knew it.'

'That is not quite an answer. Did he not say, "I don't know Lord Blandford"?'

'I don't remember.'

'Do you suggest that he had ever met Lord Blandford?'

'I do not say—'

'Don't, Lady Colin, answer me so precipitately as to cause me to interrupt you.'

'I am *so sorry.*'

'Do you suggest that Lord Colin had ever met Lord Blandford before he called upon you at Argyll Lodge?'

'I cannot say. I don't know when they met.'

Lord Blandford was questioned by his principal advocate, Britain's Attorney-General, Sir Richard Webster, QC.

The Attorney-General was the nation's highest legal officer, and until 1892 he could represent private clients. Sir Richard Webster, 44, was the picture of ròbust health, befitting one of Cambridge's most illustrious former athletes. He had been an outstanding cricket player and a great runner. The highlight of his athletic career came when he won the mile and two mile races in a Cambridge-Oxford track meet. (His best time for the mile was four minutes and 36 seconds, quite good in the 1860s.) He was a vigorous, industrious man who rose at four or five o'clock and never came to court without being totally prepared. After Russell, he was probably the second highest-paid member of the Bar.

'When you called,' Webster asked, 'did you know whether Lord Colin was well enough to see visitors?'

'No.'

'About what time did you call?'

'It was five o'clock. I called in the ordinary way.'

'Do you remember what you talked about?'

'I have no recollection.'

Lord Colin was asked by Lockwood about the visit:

'When were you made aware that Lord Blandford had called?'

'After he had left the house, I asked my wife who her visitor was. She replied, "Lord Blandford." I said, "I wish you to understand that I do not know Lord Blandford."'

Nurse Wright was near by at the time. Searle questioned her:

'After the visit did Lord Colin say anything in Lady Colin's presence?'

'Yes. He said, "I do not know Lord Blandford." Lady Colin then said, "Oh, we have been only talking about Gladstone."' (William Gladstone was in the second year of the second of four terms as Prime Minister.)

Upon hearing this, most of the courtroom spectators roared with laughter. (The only women present were Lady Colin, her mother, her sister, and her cousin.) Because of the vacuousness of high society, any report of a serious discussion would have caused some chuckling. But for a woman, especially a beautiful woman, to converse on a topic of significance was beyond belief. Women were expected to be shallow and frivolous, to have no more than secondhand opinions on anything that was important. Femininity did not encompass intellectuality.

The Attorney-General did not find the visit to be humorous or questionable:

'Lady Colin was dressing for dinner, and Lord Blandford called. I ask you whether there is any evidence of guilt in his calling on a newly-married couple in the most open way.

'Lady Colin came down in a tea gown such as ladies wear for a five o'clock tea. I am told – though I know nothing about the customs of the rank of society in which Lord Colin moved – that the dress was what an honest married woman would wear to receive her friends. She came down and saw Lord Blandford, but there is no proof that anything happened that might not have happened between an honourable man and a modest woman.

'She then went upstairs and was asked by Lord Colin who her visitor was. She said at once, "It was Lord Blandford. We have been hauling Gladstone over the coals." Since Lord Colin, his distinguished father, and Lord Blandford were all politicians, was such a conversation improbable?'

Although not then personally acquainted with Lord Blandford, Lord Colin had an opinion on his wife's guest.

'Before you married,' Lockwood asked him, 'did you become aware that Miss Blood knew Lord Blandford?'

'I did.'

'Was he known to you except by reputation?'

'Only by reputation.'

'Did you have any conversation with Miss Blood with regard to her acquaintance with Lord Blandford?'

'Yes. She told me that she had been to the theatre with him. I said, "I don't think you were in very good company."'

Lord Colin could not but have known about the 37-year-old Lord Blandford's reputation, gained through his connection with several lurid divorce cases, most notoriously Aylesford v. Aylesford, in 1878. While Lord Aylesford was on a government mission to India, Lady Aylesford was having an affair with Blandford. Aylesford heard about it, hurried home, and came to a separation agreement with his wife. She promised not to see Blandford, but before long they were staying together at the Hotel Rivoli in Paris as Mr and Mrs Spencer. Aylesford obtained a divorce.

Blandford was cross-examined by Finlay on this matter:

'Proceedings were taken against you on account of adultery with Lady Aylesford?'

'I do not deny it.'

'Did you commit adultery with Lady Aylesford under her husband's roof?'

'Yes.'

'Lord Aylesford being an old friend of yours?'

'No.'

'A friend, then?'

'A friend.'

'You left your wife and lived with Lady Aylesford for two years as Mr and Mrs Spencer?'

'No. I once visited Paris for a few days with Lady Aylesford under the name of Mr and Mrs Spencer.'

'You deserted your wife?'

'A technical desertion.'

'Lady Blandford forgave you, and you lived together again?'

'Yes.'

'You then went off again with Lady Aylesford?'

'Never.'

'You again committed adultery with Lady Aylesford?'

'(In a very low voice) I did.'

At that time Lady Aylesford's name was stricken from guest lists, and she was 'cut' in public. Lord Blandford moved about pretty much as usual. No doors were closed to him.

Blandford hardly looked like a Don Juan. Short, moderately stout, with a pale complexion, curling moustache, and balding head, he seemed the antithesis of a playboy. Actually he was not just a rake. There was more to him than notoriety.

George Charles Spencer Churchill – Lord Blandford – was the eldest son of the seventh Duke of Marlborough, first in line to take over the title created in 1702. (In this book he will usually be referred to as Blandford, but occasionally he will be called Marlborough since he had succeeded to the Dukedom at the time of the trial.) Born in 1844, he had been educated at Eton and Oriel College, Oxford, and was an officer in the Horse Guards. His marriage to the daughter of the Duke of Aberdeen had taken place in Westminster Abbey.

'The Duke of Marlborough's eldest son was born clever,' *Vanity Fair* editorialized in June 1881. 'He is bright, vivacious, witty, and a ready and facile talker out of a copious vocabulary. He is a man of brilliant parts and acute intelligence, ready to receive audacious ideas and to adopt solemn paradoxes.'

He was a multifaceted man: chairman of the London Electric Lighting Company, then in its infancy; a director of the telephone company, also newly established; fluent in French; and, like his father, who had assembled a superb collection of paintings for Blenheim Palace, the principal Marlborough residence, a knowledgeable patron of the arts.

In his memoirs, the Victorian statesman Lord Redesdale called George Churchill 'a youth of great promise, shining in many branches of human endeavour, clever, capable of great industry, and within measurable distance of reaching conspicuous success in science, mathematics, and mechanics.' He never lived up to these expectations and spent most of his life in the shadow of his brother Randolph, who in 1881 was a leading figure in the House of Commons. Some people felt, however, that George was the abler and more clever brother and might have had a successful political career but for the scandals. (Randolph's son, seven years old when his uncle visited Lady Colin at Argyll Lodge, would become his nation's wartime prime minister.)

In her direct examination, Lady Colin said that she had met Lord Blandford in the spring of 1880 in the home of her sister, Mrs Bolton.

She was cross-examined by Lockwood on their relationship:

'Was Lord Blandford a friend of the family?'

'Of my sisters. I do not think he knew my mother.'

'Did you know anything about him?'

'Will you please say what you mean?'

'To put it plainly, did you know that he had seduced Lady Aylesford?'

'I knew there had been some talk about it.'

'Did it make any difference in your acquaintance with him?'

'Certainly not.'

Mrs Blood's attitude was brought out by Finlay:

'Did your daughter's association with Lord Blandford meet with your approval?'

'Yes. I saw no reason to prevent it.'

'Were you aware of Lord Blandford's antecedents in the Divorce Court?'

'Yes.'

'Do you consider him a proper associate for a beautiful young married woman?'

'I do.'

'Are you expressing your own views or those of society?'

'As you please. Many men, married and unmarried, are just as bad or

worse than Lord Blandford.' (Laughter)

In Finlay's mind, these opinions were quite singular:

'It is extraordinary to find Lady Colin and Mrs Blood coming forward to say that their knowledge of the antecedents of the Duke made no difference in the relations with a man who has appeared in the Divorce Court in every capacity except that of a petitioner. A woman with any knowledge of the world who associates with a man of such antecedents must know that her reputation is thereby imperilled.'

Russell responded to this:

'My learned friend indulged in highly moral observations on the impropriety of any acquaintance or association with Lord Blandford. Let us have no mock affectation. Who amongst us who lives in the world and keeps his eyes and ears open is not conscious that in every condition of public life – in politics, in social life, aye, even in the professions – men are received, not shunned and ostracized, whose lives more or less notorious do not make them the most beneficial companions to ladies young or old. Let us not have too much Pecksniffian morality about this.'

Probably the public, and certainly the press, sided with Finlay on this question. In a representative comment the afternoon daily newspaper the *Echo* castigated 'ambitious mothers who can see no harm in allowing their unmarried daughters to freely associate with a man whose life has been so notorious that every man in England knows the story.'

CHAPTER 8

Cadogan Place

While the Campbells were living in Argyll Lodge, their own home was being prepared for occupancy. The Blandfords would also soon move into a new house. The two dwellings were within a ten-minute walk of each other. Soon after Blandford's visit to the Lodge, he and Lady Colin took this walk. Webster asked him about it:

'Do you remember seeing Lady Colin's home when unfurnished?'

'Yes.'

'How did you go there?'

'I met Lady Colin in the street with Miss Gordon, and she said they were going to the new house. I asked her to let me see it, and she did. Both Lady Colin and Miss Gordon came.'

'Was it entirely unfurnished?'

'It was partly unfurnished. Miss Gordon was with us the whole time.'

'Had you at that time taken a house in Cadogan Square?'

'Yes, Number 46.'

'Was it furnished?'

'No, it was in the way of being furnished.'

'Do you remember whether on the day you went to Lady Colin's house that she inspected your house?'

'Yes, she inspected my house just as I inspected hers, and Miss Gordon was with us the whole time.'

Miss Gordon was only a casual friend of Lady Colin, but on this occasion she seems to have become an extremely important person.

Immediately west of Sloane Street, Cadogan Square had been developed in the 1870s by the noted architect Norman Shaw. The square is lined by huge five- and six-storey red-brick homes obviously intended for people with fat bank accounts. Since there is no greenery, the builders must have assumed that the super-rich residents would satisfy their thirst for gardens in country mansions. The Blandford home, number 46, on the south-east corner, was one of the most luxurious, with six windows facing the square on each of its five floors. (Some years later it would be bisected and renumbered 55 and 57.)

About two hundred yards directly east of the Blandford home, across Sloane Street, was where the Campbells would live, at 79 Cadogan Place.

To nineteenth-century English upper and middle classes, more than to most people, a home was not just a place in which to live. It was a sign of status, and also protection against the encroaching world of mercantilism. One's home had to be the right house in the right location. For the Campbells, the right house in the right location was 79 Cadogan Place.

Beginning four streets north of Sloane Square, Cadogan Place is 100 yards wide and 500 yards long. As London's first big square, it had become fully developed in 1877 with two gardens containing 49 trees. It was peaceful, almost like a woodland, for although two omnibus lines travelled in Sloane Street, there were as yet no tramways anywhere in the vicinity. Cadogan Place is not now what it once was. In the 1960s a 354-car underground garage was built there; its cost included the loss of fourteen trees (nine of which were later replanted), and traffic noises have destroyed some of the serenity.

The physical appearance of Cadogan Place, however, untouched by wartime bombing, hasn't changed much. The western boundary is Sloane Street. The other three borders are residential. The northern extremity contained the palace of Cadogan Place, Chelsea House. Completed in 1875 at the corner of Lowndes Street, it was the home of Chelsea's most illustrious personage, George Henry Sloane, fifth Earl of Cadogan. In the late 1950s it was demolished to make room for the Hotel Carlton Towers. Most of the other original houses on the northern fringe are also gone, but the eastern and southern boundaries are as they were the 1880s.

The eastern houses are five-storey mansions with white pillars, Tuscan porticos, and iron balconies. Everything about them suggests affluence. In 1881 the residents included Viscount Tarbat, DL, JP; the Marchioness of Queensberry; General Henry James Barre, CB; Rt. Hon. Lord Bramwell; Sir Spencer Wilson, Bart.; Lady Amelia Blackwood; the Lord Bishop of Derry; Admiral Sir A. L. Montgomery, Bart.; Lady Bowen; Admiral Sir George Willes, KCB; Lieutenant General Sir Edmund Whitmore, KCB; and nine people preceded by 'Hon.' All of them lived in one-family homes. (No single-family dwelling is there today.)

Very different is the south rim of Cadogan Place, closest to the unconventional, bohemian areas of Chelsea. Here the homes are conspicuously smaller and more modest. Rate books for 1881 show that the average value of a home on the northern or eastern side of Cadogan Place was more than three times that of the southern edge. Before the Campbells arrived, the southern residents were all just plain Mr and Mrs. Three of the dwellings, including number 79, were lodging houses.

For Lord and Lady Colin, their unpretentious new home had two big advantages, an affordable rent and a fashionable address. And although it wasn't a mansion, they weren't exactly moving into a shack. Number 79 has the usual servants' quarters below the stairs and five floors above ground with fourteen rooms. This would seem adequate to the needs of a young couple without children.

CHAPTER 9

The Fire Chief

Victorian 'ladies' did not customarily perform physical work. It would stigmatize them even more than it would their 'gentlemen.' Lady Colin ignored this precept. The transformation of 79 Cadogan Place from a lodging house to the home of a Duke's son and daughter-in-law was carried out under her direction. Inderwick asked her about it:

'Did you superintend the furnishing of the house?'

'Yes.'

'You were there every day?'

'Exactly.'

'You saw the tradespeople and attended to other matters?'

'Yes.'

'Because of your finances, you could not be extravagant in buying furniture?'

'No, I could not.'

'Did you go to sales to buy furniture at reasonable prices?'

'Yes.'

'Did you see to the whole arrangement of the house yourself?'

'Yes.'

'With your hands did you decorate the house, actually putting up and hanging curtains?'

'Yes.'

She worked hard, but she also had moments of relaxation. The caretaker, Elizabeth French, was questioned by Finlay:

'Before the house at 79 Cadogan Place was ready, was Lady Colin often there?'

'Yes.'

'And other people?'

'Yes.'

'Were they ladies or gentlemen?'

'Sometimes Mrs Bolton called, and there were a great many

gentlemen.'

'Whom did the gentlemen see?'

'Lady Colin.'

'Where did they see her?'

'In the drawing-room.'

'In what state was the drawing-room?'

'The furniture was all packed up.'

Elizabeth French was cross-examined by Russell:

'Did Lady Colin see gentlemen about the decorations, furnishing, and so forth?'

'Yes, she saw a number of gentlemen.' (Laughter)

'She saw cabinet-maker, upholsterers, painters, and so on?'

'Yes, of course she saw them.'

'You know that Lord Colin was too ill to take any part in arranging matters there?'

'He did not do so.'

'Did not ladies also call?'

'Sometimes.'

'You have only told us that Mrs Bolton called. Did anybody else call?'

'Yes, there was a Lady Someone who used to come in a carriage. I do not recollect her name.'

'You recollect that from time to time ladies and gentlemen came together?'

'Yes, but I don't recollect their names.'

One of Lady Colin's visitors was a man who arrived alone and had nothing to do with the work. He was Eyre Massey Shaw, usually called Captain Shaw. He was 51-years-old, and for twenty years he had been Chief Officer of the Metropolitan Fire Brigade. He was London's fire chief, with his headquarters and residence in Southwark Bridge Road, south of the river.

In many ways Shaw was unlike Lord Colin. He was tall, robust, ruggedly handsome. His clear, piercing eyes; his distinctive sideburns, combed upwards; his moustache extending over a goatee – these facial features suggested leadership. A former army officer, he walked with a military bearing and ran his department with an iron hand. Arrogant, independent, he might have paraphrased Louis XIV's assertion: 'I am the fire brigade.'

An Irishman, Shaw had been Belfast's fire chief before coming to London. He was now, in 1881, regarded as one of the world's great fire fighters. He placed fire alarm boxes throughout the metropolis, and he initiated a system of inspecting exits and fire appliances in theatres.

Thanks largely to him, London's fire department was probably the world's finest.

Like Blandford, Shaw was highly literate. He had earned two degrees from Trinity College, Dublin, and had written four good books on fire-fighting and fire-protection. One of them was the first to deal with fires in theatres.

Off the job, Shaw was a popular figure in society, noted for his pleasant smile and cheerful voice. His friends included the Prince of Wales, who more than once had ridden to a fire with him. In 1879 Shaw had been made a Knight of the Bath, and in 1891 he would become a Knight Commander of the Bath.

For a number of years Captain Shaw had been friendly with the Campbells and the Bloods. One of his daughters had been a bridesmaid at Gertrude's wedding.

At least once Shaw visited Lord Colin when he was sick in Sloane Street, but he preferred the company of Lord Colin's wife, as Elizabeth Wright suggested when questioned by Searle:

'While at Sloane Street did you ever know Captain Shaw and Lady Colin to drive out together?'

'Yes.'

'How long were they out?'

'As a rule, about half-an-hour.'

Lord Colin was asked by Lockwood about his wife and Shaw during these early days of the marriage:

'When you were living in Sloane Street, do you remember asking your wife where she was going?'

'Yes. she said she was going to the Bristol Hotel. The company was to include Captain Shaw, her sister, and others whose names I cannot recollect.'

'Can you tell me what passed?'

'We had some words about Captain Shaw that caused an estrangement between us. I objected to her driving with him.'

'Was that the only time in Sloane Street that you spoke to your wife about Captain Shaw?'

'No. On another occasion she said she had been on a visit to her mother. We had some words on the subject, and she confessed that, in spite of my request, she had been driving with Captain Shaw. I remonstrated with her, and she became very violent.'

Lady Colin was questioned on this by Inderwick:

'Your husband said he objected to your driving about with Captain Shaw. Had you driven about with him?'

'On one or two occasions I went with him, with a large party while he was making his visits to the fire stations.'

'After dark?'

'Yes, but I do not think I did so on more than one occasion after my marriage. I never drove with him in his phaeton or allowed him to drive me about London.'

Lady Colin seemed eager to offer unrequested information.

Sometimes when he was riding about town, Captain Shaw would stop at friends' homes. Caretaker Elizabeth French was asked by Finlay about one of these visits:

'Do you remember when a gentleman called at Cadogan Place and saw Lady Colin Campbell for some time?'

'Yes.'

'Who was the gentleman?'

'Captain Shaw.'

'When did this visit take place?'

'It was on a Sunday afternoon late in November, about three o'clock.'

'What room did he go to?'

'The drawing-room [on the first floor].'

'How long did he stay?'

'About two hours.'

'Who was with him during that time?'

'Lady Colin Campbell.'

'What was the state of the drawing-room?'

'Everything was covered except an easy chair.'

'Were there any tradesmen about?'

'None at all. It was Sunday.'

'Were Captain Shaw and Lady Colin alone during all of the time that they were together.'

'Yes.'

'While they were in the drawing-room, was the door open or closed?'

'Quite closed.'

'Was there any seat for people?'

'No.'

'How long had it been dark before these people went away?'

'Some little time. More than an hour.'

'Was there any light in the room?'

'None at all.'

Captain Shaw told his counsel that 'nothing took place except ordinary conversation.'

He was cross-examined by Lockwood:

'How long did you remain on the visit?'

'I should think about half-an-hour.'

'No longer than that?'

'No. I should think that was a long a visit as I ever made there.'

'Was there a chair to sit down upon?'

'I think there was an ottoman.'

'Was it big enough for two?'

'It was big enough for three or four.'

'Was there any gas in the house at the time?'

'I really can't say.'

'Then you sat in an unfurnished room for half-an-hour with Lady Colin without light?'

'No, there were lights. There was plenty of light.'

'Where did the light come from?'

'I think there were candles.'

'Do you remember candles being brought up?'

'No, I do not.'

Light was generally provided in residences by oil and gas lamps. There were none in the Campbell home because unattended lamps were a fire hazard.

This Sunday afternoon visit in November was not Captain Shaw's only pre-occupancy appearance at 79 Cadogan Place. Lord Colin was questioned on this by Lockwood:

'Before moving into Cadogan Place, do you remember taking a number of letters and papers there to sort?'

'I do. I had had a conversation with my wife as to whether I would go or not and told her I should not go.'

'Did Lady Colin then go out?'

'She did.'

'Did something occur to make you change your mind about going to Cadogan Place?'

'Yes. I went to Cadogan Place at about half-past three.'

'Did you go up to the drawing-room?'

'Yes, I did.'

'Whom did you find there?'

'Lady Colin and Captain Shaw.'

'Was the house in a position for receiving visitors?'

'No, it was unfurnished.'

CHAPTER 10

The Lady's Maid

Before moving into 79 Cadogan Place, the Campbells, more particularly Lady Colin Campbell, had to consider the question of a domestic staff.

One of the most visible aspects of Victorian life was the presence of servants. Houses were built to accommodate them. A winding staircase led from the pavement down to their living quarters below ground. The topmost floors contained their bedrooms. The family rooms were connected to a complex network of bells so that the pull of a cord would summon a servant instantaneously. According to government census reports, 'The English family is composed of husband, wife, children, and servants.' In that order.

Most servants were women. A greater proportion of British women were in service than in any other country. In the early eighties, one-third of all females between the ages of 15 and 20 were domestic servants. Throughout most of the century the preparation of girls for service was scarcely questioned.

This does not mean that they all liked their work. Far from it. Many loathed what they had to do. Well into the third quarter of the century, servants were expected to be unconditionally obedient. They lived in cramped quarters – a basement kitchen and an attic bedroom. They rose before seven and retired at their employer's convenience, perhaps after working for sixteen hours. They could be called at any time of the day or night.

They seldom had time off. They received low wages, as little as £16 a year. They could not receive letters addressed to them as 'Miss,' and they usually could not have gentleman callers. Domestic servitude was truly the last vestige of British feudalism. It existed as such because servants came mostly from poor families in small towns and rural areas, and well into the Victorian period they had to go into service or join the world's oldest profession. No other doors were open to them.

The doors, however, could not forever remain closed. The Victorian age was one of change, social progress, spreading democracy, affecting all aspects of life, including that of master and servant. After the Compulsory Elementary Education Act of 1870 most young women were literate. Literacy was a passport to better jobs. (Late in the century many teachers would in earlier years have been domestic servants.) Then there was the railroad, which meant cheap mobility and increased bargaining power. New factories needed workers, and there were job openings in Canada and Australia. Women could become dressmakers, milliners, shop assistants, telegraph clerks. Household service wasn't everything.

Of course there were still many domestic servants, but the relationship with their employers was becoming less personal than mercenary. Like other workers, servants began to be mostly concerned about pay and working conditions, and unlike earlier generations they moved about freely from one family to another.

Because of the changed conditions, one big problem in the seventies and eighties was that of getting and keeping good servants. In letters to magazines and newspapers, mistresses complained that the household help was disobedient, insolent, selfish, ungrateful, lazy, incompetent, inefficient, extravagant, and dishonest. But mistresses were not faultless. In 1881 a writer for a popular magazine said, 'Some ladies insist on maids trotting up and down the stairs to do the merest trifles. They will not shut a door or draw a window-blind but "ring the bell for Sarah." And some mistresses live in a region of ice and won't speak to servants except to give orders. All classes now live in a different style from past generations. For better or worse, mistresses must recognise that times have changed.'

Even with changed times servants were essential to upper and middle class life, and on 4 November 1881, three weeks before moving into her new home, Lady Colin Campbell hired the first member of her staff. She was Rose Baer, from Switzerland, a personal lady's maid.

A lady's maid carried up a cup of tea in the morning; she laid out her mistress's clothing and helped her to dress and undress; she cared for the jewellery; she was expected to be adept in hairdressing, needlework, and dressmaking. Ladies' maids, in short, did what most women did for themselves. They formed a tiny portion of the domestic work force, usually working in upper class homes or for women who were especially active socially. They were the ultimate status symbol.

Although few foreigners were employed in British homes, young women from France and Switzerland were greatly in demand as ladies' maids. They added a touch of exoticism to a household. They were a mark of distinction. Despite a modest income, a small home, and no family to care for, Lady Colin selected as her first domestic servant a Swiss lady's maid.

Rose Baer was not attractive. She had close-set eyes, a prominent nose, thin lips, and a sallow face. But she was not hired for her looks. She came well recommended as a dressmaker and was fluent in English, French, and German. (Lady Colin usually spoke to her in French.)

Soon after Rose Baer had been hired, Lady Colin was faced with a serious problem unrelated to her new employee. She told Inderwick about it:

'How long after consummating the marriage did you suffer from pain or illness?'

'I first felt it in November [of 1881].'

'Was your suffering the result of sexual intercourse with your husband?'

'Yes.'

'Was your suffering so unusual and so painful that it caused you alarm?'

'Yes.'

'Did you know from what you were suffering?'

'Not in the least.'

'From then until the beginning of 1885 were you free from that illness?'

'No.'

As Sir Richard Webster remarked, she suffered in silence: 'Lady Colin's loyalty to her husband made her keep this matter a secret. She was suffering from consequences of intercourse yet was obliged to go about as if there was no terrible skeleton in the household closet. The very nurses attending on Lady Colin were ignorant of the fact that it was necessary for her to take the most extraordinary precautions. The medical part of this story is perfectly horrible ...'

The Attorney-General did not spell out the precise nature of Lady Colin's ailment. Nor did anyone else speak in specific terms. Even Lady Colin herself, as we have seen, did not know what was the matter with her. And so I asked a prominent present-day gynaecologist for his views. His 'hundred-years-later' opinion was that there were two possible causes of Lady Colin's suffering. She may have contracted from her husband a pelvic inflammatory disease. Or he may have given her a dose of gonorrhea.

Whatever its cause, the situation didn't seem to bother Lord Colin.

'Did you speak to anyone of your pain?' Inderwick asked Lady Colin.

'Yes, I spoke to my sister, Mrs Bolton.'

'After speaking to her, did you tell your husband of your pain?'

'Yes.'

'What did he say?'

'He said, "Oh, that is of no consequence. All women have that sort of thing." '

Lord Colin was cross-examined on this by Russell:

'Did you tell Lady Colin that her illness was nothing, that it was an illness incidental to married ladies?'

'(Warmly) Sir Charles –'

'Answer the question, Lord Colin.'

'It is absolutely untrue.'

Perhaps so. But if Lady Colin did speak truthfully, Lord Colin's response was not extraordinary. Many husbands thought that nothing was more natural than a wife's suffering, that her duty was to suffer and be still.

CHAPTER 11

A Pretty Housemaid

Late in November, the Campbells moved into 79 Cadogan Place. Lady Colin hired two more servants, a cook and a housemaid.

A cook's job is obvious. A housemaid's duties were also clear: she swept, dusted, made beds, cleaned bathrooms, carried bath water, etc. If she doubled as parlourmaid, she answered the door, announced visitors, and laid the table for dinner.

The cook was Annie Morrell, who plays no role in the narrative. The housemaid was Amelia Watson, 22-years-old, tall, slim, with beautiful black hair, a gently curving profile, and pert lips. She was wide-eyed and innocent, prim and proper, strikingly attractive.

At Cadogan Place, Amelia Watson was called Mary. This was not a nickname. For the Campbells she was Mary. Servants were not usually allowed to have fancy names. On several pages, selected at random, from the 1881 census book for Kensington, 130 female servants are listed. Among the 130 there are only fifteen names: Mary (26 times), Annie (26), Elizabeth (24), Sarah (15), Emma (14), Jane (14), Eliza (7), Alice (6), Clara (4), Kate (3), Rose (2), Anna (1), Lizzie (1), Fanny (1). By way of contrast, these are some non-servant female names on the same pages: Ada, Alma, Antoinette, Augusta, Cecile, Coralie, Dorothea, Eleanora, Eulalie, Evelyn, Rosina, Sophia, Vivian.

Three servants would seem adequate for a childless couple living on a tight budget in a not overly large house. In the Kensington census book 40 of the first 67 families listed had three or fewer servants. But Cadogan Place was not in Kensington. There were 64 homes on the élite northern and eastern sides. One had one servant; three had two servants; eleven had three servants; fifteen had four servants; nine had five servants; twelve had six servants; six had seven servants; four had eight servants; two had nine servants; one had ten servants. (The last was a household with several children and three nursemaids.)

In Cadogan Place, a respectable minimum number of servants was four. Lady Colin hired a fourth servant, Albert De Roche.

Domestic service was primarily for women, in part because they could be paid less than men. In 1881 female servants outnumbered males by a ratio of 22 to one. The male indoor servant, the butler, regarded by some as a prerequisite to gentility, was present less for need than for show. Although hard-pressed financially, the Campbells were almost never without a male servant.

De Roche, an Irishman, and an estate agent at the time of the trial, was questioned by Searle:

'Did you sleep in the house, or did you go away nightly?'

'I did not sleep there.'

'What time did you go in the morning?'

'About eight o'clock.'

'When did you leave in the evening?'

'From nine to eleven.'

'What were your duties?'

'To wait on her ladyship and answer the front door.'

'Who engaged you when you entered their service?'

'Lady Colin.'

'Did you have anything to say to Lord Colin?'

'No.'

In the new home, the first big event, on 19 December, was William Allingham's second operation upon Lord Colin.

Actually it was the second noteworthy occurrence, as Lord Colin acknowledged under Russell's cross-examination:

'Did you have marital intercourse on the night before the operation?'

'Yes, but I did not know there was going to be an operation.'

'Lord Colin, do you say that?'

'I do. My medical man had told me that it would be necessary to put me under chloroform only to be examined.'

'Did you tell Lady Colin that the doctors said intercourse would be good for you?'

'She asked if it would be good for me, and I answered, I dare say, to that effect.'

And so, Russell told the jury, 'On the eve of that most serious operation, Lady Colin had to submit to the embraces of her husband because he informed her that it would be useful for her to do so.'

Except for Sir Henry Thompson's hospital – which resembled a small luxury hotel – all of Lord Colin's surgery occurred in private residences. Nineteenth-century hospitals were mainly for poor people, who were often admitted because there was no one to care for them at home.

On the day of the operation, a nurse, Sarah Ann Bristowe, was hired to attend Lord Colin and to live at Cadogan Place. (Elizabeth Wright had departed some time earlier.)

On the next day, 20 December, Lady Colin and her maid travelled to Leigh Court, her cousin's country mansion near Bristol, where she remained until 2 January.

Lady Colin was not needed at home. The nursing would be done by Sarah Ann Bristowe. Her departure nevertheless was an unconventional action. She was expected to stay by her husband's side. Even if he had been well, it would have been unusual for her to travel alone. An anonymous magazine writer said, 'A woman's proper sphere is her *home*. She is to be a participator in her husband's happiness, the consoler of his sorrows, the support of his weakness, his friend under all circumstances.' This was the traditional female role, one that Lady Colin Campbell did not choose to play. In many ways, the story of her life is that of a woman trying to elude the nets which had been put in place by society.

Although the trip to Bristol was, in a sense, a declaration of independence, Lady Colin did not forget her husband.

'Did Lady Colin write letters to you constantly from Leigh Court?' Russell asked Lord Colin.

'Yes.'

'I think she wrote to you every day?'

'I cannot say every day.'

'But very frequently?'

'Yes, very frequently.'

'Affectionate letters, giving you an account of her proceedings?'

'She did not write to me every day.'

'Well, were the days rare when she did not write to you?'

'I admit she wrote frequently when she was at Leigh Court.'
'Were her letters affectionate?'
'Yes.'

At Leigh Court, Lady Colin didn't spend all of her time writing letters. In a pre-trial statement, Rose Baer mentioned a Christmas Ball: 'On the night of the ball the billiard room was used as a cloakroom, and I was there with the maid of Lady Miles [Lady Colin's cousin]. Lady Colin passed several times into the smoking room, each time on the arm of a different man. I did not see any other ladies go into the smoking room.'

CHAPTER 12

Lady Colin's Social Life

Early in December, before Lady Colin went to Bristol, Elizabeth French was still on duty.

'After they came to live at Cadogan Place, was Lady Colin much at home?' Finlay asked her.

'She would go out in the morning and sometimes come home to luncheon. She would go out again to dinner and return at eleven or twelve at night.'

Nurse Bristowe spoke to Lockwood on the same subject:

'What were the room arrangements when Lord Colin was confined?'

'For the first six weeks his room was on the third floor in front of the house; mine was behind it. Lady Colin's was on the second floor, in front, and Rose Baer's was behind.'

'Did Lady Colin spend much time in her husband's room?'

'I do not think she saw him much.'

'Can you speak of Lady Colin's habits of going out?'

'She was out a good deal, but I took little notice of it. I was at the top of the house.'

One person who did notice was Rose Baer, examined by Searle:

'Was Lady Colin in the habit of going out during the evening?'

'Yes, she always went out.'

'About what time?'

'About eight o'clock.'

'What time did she return?'

'Sometimes very late, as late as two or three o'clock.'

During Lockwood's cross-examination, Lady Colin answered questions on her social life:

'Had you before your marriage been much in society?'

'Yes.'

'After your marriage you continued to be a good deal in society?'

'Yes.'

'Did you stay much in your own house?'

'Not much. It was very small.'

'Were most of your evenings taken up with the fulfilment of social duties?'

'A great many of them.'

'Did you go to your husband's room in the morning?'

'Yes.'

'How long did you stay?'

'I used to sit and write my letters in the room.'

'You generally went out before lunch?'

'I generally went out at about half-past twelve or so.'

Lady Colin elicited this comment from Robert Finlay: 'She led an independent life. She was out all day, returned late at night and behaved as if there was no tie between her and Lord Colin. The name of Lady Colin Campbell served as a warrant which an unmarried woman cannot have.'

On this aspect of the case, the press was unanimously unfriendly to her. The *Standard*, for example, observed, 'If Lady Colin had been less careless of conventionalities, had condescended to observe the old-fashioned notions of a wife's duty, she would have escaped the terrible breath of slander and suspicion. Lady Colin has not shown that her life was ordered on the lines which a woman in her position was bound to follow.'

Under the friendly questioning of Inderwick, she provided one reason for going out alone:

'We have heard that you went to dinners and entertainments without Lord Colin. Was that by his express desire?'

'By his express desire.'

'Did he give you any reason?'

'He did not wish his illness to be known, and he thought if I went into society his absence would not be noticed. If anyone asked, I was to say he was at the House [of Commons].'

Lord Colin, when cross-examined by Russell, gave his view of his wife's social life:

'Did you know what your wife's social engagements were?'

'Oh, no, no, it is not so.'

'Did you not think it right to ask?'

'I don't think she liked to be asked.' (Laughter)

'Did she ever refuse when you asked her to tell you?'

'Yes. When I had recovered from my illness, I would ask her to drive with me, and she would say she was going elsewhere. She would not tell me where.'

'Didn't you ever ask?'

'Sometimes I did.'

'What did she say?'

'She said she had other things to do than to go with me.'

A cab driver, Thomas Aldis, might have contributed to this part of the story. Before the trial, he had made a statement to Lord Colin's solicitor. In court he went mute and became a hostile witness whom Lockwood had to cross-examine:

'On January 29, 1885, did you say, "I am a cab driver. I know Lady Colin Campbell. Three years ago I was living close to Cadogan Place when her ladyship's butler used to come and call me round"?'

'Nothing of the kind.'

'Nor this: "I used to go very frequently, sometimes four or five times a week, generally in the morning, about ten or eleven, to drive her ladyship to various places, frequently to Lord Blandford's house in Cadogan Square." Did you say that?'

'Nothing of the kind.'

'Or this: "Sometimes she would request me to wait for her at the corner of Cadogan Square, where she would get in. At other times I took her up at the house. Her brother sometimes asked me to be in Pont Street or Sloane Street at a certain time." Did you say that?'

'No, sir.'

'Or this: "I drove her ladyship to Captain Shaw's, in Southwark, Bridge Road, three or four times." Did you say that?'

'No, sir.'

[44]

CHAPTER 13

Special Visitors

If Lady Colin's favourite visiting places were the homes of Lord Blandford and Captain Shaw, they didn't hesitate to return the calls. De Roche was questioned on this by Searle:

'Did her ladyship instruct you on what to do when certain visitors called?'

'She said I was not to announce Captain Shaw or Lord Blandford in his lordship's hearing.'

'What did you do when they called?'

'I made evasive excuses. Sometimes I put the name of the caller on a sheet of paper.'

Asked by Russell if he was ashamed of himself for doing this, De Roche replied, to the accompaniment of laughter, 'No, sir, it is a general thing I have done in service.'

Captain Shaw, De Roche said, generally came about twice a week to Cadogan Place, where he saw only Lady Colin, and was entertained in the drawing-room.

Always on the first floor, the drawing-room was controlled by the mistress of the household. Here she lived, talked, played, and entertained. At 79 Cadogan Place, as in many homes, there were two drawing-rooms, or two sections of one room, one facing the street and the other looking over the back of the house. At the first floor head of the stairs a door led into the rear drawing-room, and then, forward along a brief corridor, another door opened into the front room.

Lady Colin entertained in the front drawing-room, where the second most frequent guest was Captain Shaw. First place went to Lord Blandford.

Before De Roche was hired, Amelia Watson answered the door. She was questioned by Lockwood:

'Did you see Lord Blandford at the house?'

'Yes, I let him in four times.'

'Did he ring the bell, or did he knock?'
'He rang the bell.'
'Did visitors usually knock?'
'Yes.'
'Did Lord Blandford ever knock?'
'No.'
'When did he call?'
'Usually in the afternoon.'
'How long did he stay?'
'Generally about an hour.'
'What room did you show him into?'
'The drawing-room.'
'Who was there?'
'Lady Colin.'
'Anybody else?'
'Never.'

De Roche didn't stay long. His replacement, James O'Neill, came in February 1882. When asked by Lockwood if Blandford 'frequently called,' he replied, 'Yes, very often.'

Rose Baer agreed with O'Neill. She was cross-examined by Russell:
'How often did Lord Blandford visit the house?'
'Very often.'
'The question I put is, how often?'
'Twice a week.'
'Do you mean an average of twice a week?'
'Yes.'
'But sometimes Lady Colin was out of town?'
'Yes.'
'So that in some weeks he called oftener than twice a week'
'Yes.'
'Three times?'
'Yes.'
'Possibly four or five times?' (Laughter)
'Oh, no.'
'Always in the afternoon?'
'Yes.'
'During the ordinary visiting hours?'
'Yes, and sometimes in the evening.'
'Tell us the exact time.'
'Between two and seven.'
'These are within visiting hours?'

'Yes.'

'Other visitors occasionally calling?'

'Yes.'

Once a Blandford visit led Amelia Watson to be deceptive. It happened when Lord Colin was ill.

'On this occasion,' Lockwood asked her, 'was Lady Colin with her husband?'

'Yes.'

'What did you do?'

'I told her the cook wanted to see her. When she got down to the drawing-room I said, "Lord Blandford is here."'

'What did Lady Colin say?'

'She said, "Thank you, Mary."'

'She was not cross with you?'

'Oh, no.'

'Why did you tell her that the cook wanted to see her?'

'I was told that Lord Blandford had run away with somebody's wife. I thought he might be interfering with another young married couple.'

Blandford himself was questioned on his visits by the Attorney-General:

'Did you call in the afternoon on Lady Colin Campbell?'

'I did.'

'In the same way as you called at other houses?'

'Exactly.'

'Did you ever make any assignations or appointments to meet her or anything more than call in the ordinary way?'

'Never.'

The Attorney-General did not question his client on his manner of announcing his presence at 79 Cadogan Place, but his opponents did not overlook this point. Lockwood asked O'Neill about it:

'Did Lord Blandford knock or ring the bell?'

'He always rang the bell. He never knocked.'

'Was that usual for visitors?'

'No.'

'Did any other visitors ring the bell?'

'Captain Shaw did not knock. He was the only other one.'

'Did you attach any suspicion to the fact that Lord Blandford always rang?'

'I thought it rather funny that he did not knock.'

'Did you think he was up to no good?'

'That's about it.' (Laughter)

Robert Finlay made much of the bell ringing:

'When a gentleman calls upon a friend, he generally uses the knocker, and when that gentleman happens to be an aristocrat, he usually thunders. (Laughter) But we are told that Lord Blandford, with that peculiar humility which sits so gracefully upon him (renewed laughter), actually rang the bell. It certainly seems strange that where there was the ordinary means of announcement, by way of a knocker, Lord Blandford should prefer to use the humble mode of announcement.' (Laughter)

In point of fact, the knocker, which made a resounding sound heard throughout the house, was almost invariably used by social visitors. The brass bell, which was not pressed but was pulled out, could be heard, in these pre-electric days, only downstairs in the servants' quarters. It was used by tradesmen.

The servants agreed that Blandford and Shaw, uniquely among the visitors, used the bell. But on a related matter there was disagreement.

'Did you ever,' Inderwick asked Lady Colin, 'give a servant instructions on announcing visitors?'

'No, never.'

'No, directions to show in one and not another?'

'Never.'

On this question, Amelia Watson and De Roche's successor concurred with Lady Colin rather than Albert De Roche, denying that they had ever received special instructions concerning the announcement of visitors.

CHAPTER 14

A Disarranged Dress

At about the time of Amelia Watson's message that 'the cook wanted to see her,' Lady Colin was visited by a man who often accompanied her at recitals, Signor Francesco Tosti, a well-known singing teacher, pianist, and composer. Born in Italy, he had been singing-master to his Queen, and after settling in London in 1880 he acquired the same position with the British royal family. (In 1908 he would receive a knighthood.) Lady Colin and Tosti were close friends, and he did not charge for his services at her home or at recitals. She had a full contralto voice, and Tosti said that if she had dedicated herself totally to music she might have become a leading singer with a major opera company. For Lady Colin, however, singing was one of numerous fields of endeavour, and she never became more than a frequent performer at second-line concert halls.

Albert de Roche, wearing glasses, was questioned by Searle on Tosti's visit:

'Do you remember when the music master called?'

'I remember a gentleman who instructed her ladyship in singing.' (Laughter)

Judge Butt observed, 'The witness does not like the term "music master."' (Renewed laughter)

'Did you,' Searle asked, 'announce him to Lady Colin?'

'Yes.'

'Where was she.'

'In the drawing-room.'

'What happened?'

'Lord Blandford was with Lady Colin, and she got up in a flurried state. She said, "What is it, De Roche?"'

'Where had she been sitting?'

'In the settee.'

'Where was the marquis?'

'By her side.'

'Did you notice how they were sitting?'

'His lordship had his arm in this position (stretching his arm as if to encircle something). I could see that his arm was around her ladyship's waist.' (Laughter)

'Did you notice anything about her ladyship?'

'She was disarranged in her dress and in an excited state.'

'Do you know how long they had been there?'

'I cannot say.'

De Roche was cross-examined by Russell:

'When you were in Lady Colin's service did you wear spectacles?'

'No.'

'Was your eyesight dim?'

'Yes, there was a sort of quivering.'

'Your eyesight, in short, was bad?'

'Yes, one eye was affected.'

'Will you oblige me by taking off your spectacles?'

De Roche removed his glasses.

'Are your eyes good enough to see Lord Blandford in court?'

'If I have my glasses on, I can see any gentleman in court.'

'Without them see if you can find Lord Blandford.'

'It is so long ago I have forgotten his features.'

'Can you identify this lady?'

Russell pointed directly at Lady Miles.

'This is Lady Colin.'

'You see where I am putting my hand?'

'Yes, that is Lady Colin.'

'Did not Lady Colin press upon you to wear glasses?'

'Never.'

'She never spoke to you about your eyesight?'

'Never.'

'Now a singing master was in the habit of giving lessons to Lady Colin?'

'I saw him once or twice.'

'You do not suggest that he came without appointments?'

'I do not know about that.'

'But you would presume that Lady Colin was aware that the music master was coming at a particular time to give a lesson?'

'I cannot say.'

'What was the name of the music master?'

'I cannot remember.'

'You went upstairs to the drawing-room to announce him, believing that Lady Colin was there. Did you knock at the door?'

'I used to knock at the door.'

'Did you on that occasion?'

'I think so, sir.'

'Do you mean to say that having knocked at the door, when you opened it you saw Lord Blandford with his arm around Lady Colin's waist?'

'I opened the door, and I would impress that upon your mind if in any shape or form I can ...'

'Do not make speeches, Mr Estate Agent, answer the question. Did you have any order to knock?'

'Never. It is the custom for a servant to do so.'

'It is a practice you learned as a servant – to knock at a drawing-room door before announcing visitors?'

'I have always done so in the highest families.' (Laughter)

'I know something of the usages of society, though nothing of the highest families. (Laughter) Do you mean to suggest that it is usual for a servant announcing a visitor to knock at his mistress's drawing-room door?'

'No, sir.'

'What do you mean, then?'

'If a visitor is in the drawing-room, it is usual for a servant announcing another visitor to knock before opening a door.'

'Well, this is a revelation.'

Lady Colin said that it had never been the practice for servants to knock at her drawing-room door. The authoritative society journal *Truth* stated unequivocally, 'It is not the custom for a man servant to knock at a drawing-room door.' It was proper to knock at the door of a bedroom or dressing-room before entering, but it was considered vulgar to do so at a drawing-room, dining-room, or library.

'Now, Mr De Roche,' Russell said, 'be kind enough to attend me, please. Is the drawing-room at 79 Cadogan Place hung round by what is called a reed curtain?'

'Yes.'

'Is it a door you cannot open without considerable noice?'

'I can't say that.'

'Does it not make a considerable rustling noise?'

'I have never known it to do so.'

'Was there a screen beyond the curtain which you had to go around before you got into the drawing-room?'

'Yes.'

'Where was the sofa on which you say you saw Lady Colin and Lord Blandford?'

'It was just as you turn to the right in front of the wall.'

'You had to go around the screen to get into the drawing-room?'

'Yes.'

'Do you think after knocking with your knuckles and getting around that screen you could possibly have seen Lord Blandford with his arm round Lady Colin's waist?'

'I am sure of it.'

'Of what are you sure?'

'That he had his arm in a suspicious position.'

'Was it his left or right arm?'

'His right arm.'

'Lady Colin was flurried?'

'Yes.'

'And her dress was disarranged?'

'Yes.'

'How was it disarranged?'

'It was up like this (pulling up his overcoat).'

'Did you see her petticoat?'

'Yes.'

'Her underclothing?'

'I can't say underclothing.'

'How high was her dress?'

'I could not say.'

'Oh, but this was a shocking thing. You had never seen anything like it in the highest families before? (Laughter) Come, sir, tell us.'

'I can't say how high it was because I did not take notice. I only apologized for coming in.'

When Blandford was in the witness box, Webster asked about what De Roche claimed to have seen:

'Is it true that you were found with your arm round the waist of Lady Colin?'

'Certainly not.'

'Were you ever in that position ?'

'Never.'

'Is it true that on any occasion in your presence Lady Colin had her dress disarranged?'

'No.'

'Is there one word of truth in the story?'

'None whatever.'

Before finishing with De Roche, Russell turned to another matter:

'After you left Lady Colin's service, did you get into difficulties and write to her, beseeching her to help you?'

'I never wrote to her.'

'Did you go to her?'

'Yes.'

'Did she not visit your wife and pay your rent?'

'I never knew that she visited my wife.'

'As a matter of fact did she pay your rent?'

'Yes.'

CHAPTER 15

Lady Colin's Letters

With the telephone in its infancy and rarely found in a private residence, correspondence was important to virtually any story set in London in the 1880s.

Mailing letters was cheap – there was a nationwide penny postage rate – and it was fast. This was the collection schedule at the Pont Street letter box, the one nearest the Campbells' home: 1.00, 3.00, 8.45, 9.45, 11.45, 12.05, 12.45, 1.45, 3.45, 4.45, 5.30, 6.00, 7.00, 8.00, 9.00. A letter dropped in the morning or early afternoon would reach any London address on that day.

Rose Baer was asked by Searle about incoming mail at Cadogan Place, where there were four daily deliveries:

'Did Lady Colin give you directions about letters that came for her?'

'Yes. I was not to leave them in the hall but to take them upstairs to her bedroom.'

'Do you know what she did with the letters after she had read them?'

'Some she burned, and others she put away in a box.'

'Where?'

'She kept a box under the bed.'

'Was it locked?'

'Yes.'

As for Lady Colin's outgoing letters, they provided the household staff with some titillation.

'Who,' Lockwood asked Amelia Watson, 'posted Lady Colin's letters?'

'Rose Baer always did.'

'Did she ever show them to you?'

'Yes, repeatedly.'

'How often?'

'Every night.'

'Did she bring them to you?'

'Yes. She would bring them to me in the kitchen, or if she met me on the stairs she would show them to me.'

'Why?'

'Because there were so many gentlemen she was writing to.'

'Can you remember the names of any persons to whom they were addressed?'

'I recollect constantly Lord Blandford's name.'

'Any other?'

'Captain Shaw's.'

Sarah Ann Bristowe was also questioned by Lockwood:

'Do you know Rose Baer?'

'Oh, yes. I used to sit in her room nearly all day.'

She had been employed to care for Lord Colin!

'Did you know,' Lockwood asked, 'that she posted Lady Colin's letters?'

'Yes.'

'Did you ever see any of those letters?'

'Yes, every day.'

'Do you remember any names to whom the letters were addressed?'

'Yes, I saw a great many letters addressed to Lord Blandford and Captain Shaw.'

Shaw, cross-examined by Lockwood, provided an explanation for the correspondence directed to him:

'Did you receive letters from Lady Colin?'

'Occasionally.'

'And occasionally you wrote to her?'

'I have no doubt that I did.'

'Do you have any of the letters she wrote to you?'

'No.'

'What happened to them?'

'They were all handed to my wife because they referred to matters with which she was concerned.'

'On matters in which your wife was interested, Lady Colin wrote to you?'

'Yes.'

'Why did she not write to your wife direct?'

'I don't know.'

On letters to Blandford, Rose Baer was questioned by Searle:

'Have you ever posted letters from Lady Colin to Lord Blandford?'

'Yes.'

'How often?'

'Every day.'

'How long did this go on?'

'The whole time that I was there.'

'Did you take notes personally to Lord Blandford's?'

'Yes.'

More details came out during Russell's cross-examination:

'You say Lady Colin wrote to Lord Blandford every day?'

'Yes.'

'Including Sunday?'

'Yes, always on Sunday.'

'Sometimes twice a day?'

'Yes.'

'Occasionally three times a day?'

'Yes.'

'On rare occasions, four times a day?'

'No.' (Laughter)

'Were these sent by the post?'

'No, only one a day was sent by the post. The others I took to his home.'

'Did Lady Colin have a large correspondence?'

'Yes.'

'And the rest of the letters you took also?'

'Yes.'

'Were you ever told to conceal the fact of letters being sent to Lord Blandford?'

'No.'

'Was there any secrecy about the matter?'

'No.'

'Was any direction given to you when you took those letters?'

'Yes, I was to ring the bell and run away.'

'Run away?'

'Yes, put the letter in the box and run away.'

'Why were you to run away?'

'I don't know.'

'Did you always do that?'

'Yes, always.'

'On the memorable occasions when there were three letters in one day, did you run away three times?'

'Yes.'

Occasionally the butler was given letters to post or to deliver personally to Lord Blandford. De Roche and O'Neill both denied ever receiving any special instructions on this.

At least once O'Neill did more than just deliver a letter. He told Lockwood about it:

[55]

'Do you remember seeing a letter upon a desk in the drawing-room?'
'Yes.'
'Did you read it?'
'How did it begin?'
'It commenced, "My dear George,"'
'Did you read anything else in the letter?'
'Yes. As far as I can remember, it was "meet me" somewhere. I think it was "Kilburn."'
'When you read it, was Lady Colin in the room?'
'*No sir.*' (Laughter)

The implication was that 'George' was George Churchill, Lord Blandford. In his opening statement Finlay said, 'Lady Colin perpetually corresponded with Lord Blandford and began her letter, "My dear George."'

Asked by his counsel if he had ever been addressed as 'George,' Blandford said, 'Never in my life.'

The letter in fact was written to Lady Colin's brother-in-law, George Bolton.

Lady Colin denied writing daily letters to Blandford or instructing Baer to ring and run. Questions about her correspondence came up during Lockwood's cross-examination;

'Were you in constant correspondence with Lord Blandford?'
'Constantly, no. On various occasions.'
'Have you any of his letters?'
'No, I never keep letters.'
'How did Lord Blandford sign himself?'
'"Blandford," I think, or "N" with a small "d" over it.'
'How did you sign your letters?'
'"Sincerely yours, G. E. C."'
'Nothing else?'
'No.'
'How did he address you?'
'"Dear Lady Colin"'
'How did you address him?'
'"Dear Lord Blandford"'
'Do you mean to say that that was the mode and manner in which you and Lord Blandford habitually addressed each other?'
'Certainly.'
'What have you done with those letters?'
'I told you. I do not keep letters.'
'You destroyed them?'

'Certainly. The house was not big enough to keep the letters we received.'

During his direct examination, Blandford said that he also had destroyed the letters from Lady Colin. In his cross-examination, Finlay returned to this point:

'When did you first correspond with Lady Colin?'

'Probably a few weeks after her marriage.'

'Have you exchanged letters more or less regularly since 1881?' (The question was asked late in 1886.)

'As much as any gentleman would be justified in corresponding with any lady.'

'Have you any letter that you received from Lady Colin?'

'Not a line.'

'You have not saved one letter from Lady Colin?'

'Not a line.'

'This is most extraordinary. Not a single letter on either side has been kept.'

Victorians in fact usually retained their correspondence, no matter how trivial or potentially embarrassing it might have been.

The alleged reason for letters passing between two close neighbours was foreshadowed in two apparently irrelevant questions Russell asked De Roche:

'There were not many books at Lord Colin's house?'

'I did not see many.'

'Not many book shelves?'

'No, it was a small house.'

The pertinence of this exchange came out when Inderwick examined Lady Colin:

'Did any notes pass between you and Lord Blandford?'

'Yes.'

'With reference to what?'

'Books. He used to lend me books.'

'What sort of books were they? Name some of them.'

'Carlyle's works, Bacon's Essays, Bain's *Philosophical Treatises*, Draper's *Intellectual History of Europe*, and books by Mr [William] Lecky.'

'While you were reading these books you communicated with Lord Blandford as to fresh ones, and in this way notes passed between you?'

'In this way.'

None of the servants mentioned books coming to or going from the house. Lockwood was undisguisedly sceptical:

When Lord Blandford was sending you books, was he also studying them?'

'They were books in his library.'

'When he called, did you discourse on these subjects?'

'Probably. I cannot recollect.'

'Would an afternoon be devoted to a discussion of an essay by Bacon?'

'I don't know.'

Sir Richard Webster was not amused:

'Lady Colin is a woman of very great literary attainments and ability. In those years when she was studying Lord Blandford's books, she was educating her mind. This is borne out by the fact that when she became separated from her husband she immediately began to maintain herself by contributing articles to the *Saturday Review* [a highly prestigious literary weekly]. I venture to say that there are not many men in this court who would have been able to do this.'

Had there been any female spectators, one might have heard someone shout 'Bravo!'

CHAPTER 16

A Shocked Nurse

If Lord Blandford's books went undetected at Cadogan Place, other objects did not go unnoticed. Lockwood asked Lord Colin about one of them.

'Do you remember whether your wife had any photographs of Lord Blandford?'

'Yes, she had a framed photograph of Lord Blandford always on her writing table.'

Lockwood also queried Lady Colin,

'How many photographs of Lord Blandford have you had at one time?'

'One, I think.'

'How many of yours has he had?'

'One, I think. I have some remembrance of giving him one once.'

'Was his photograph in a frame on your writing desk?'

'My writing desk was covered with photographs.'

'Had Lord Blandford the honour of a position there?'

'Quite possibly.'

Then there was a ring, which a nurse, Annie Duffy, who joined the staff in September 1882, mentioned in her direct examination. In cross-examination, Russell asked about it'

'What is the story about the ring?'

'Her ladyship had got an emerald ring. I constantly saw her wearing it with the stones outside, but each time she came to Lord Colin's bedroom, the stones were in the palm of her hand.'

'Do you suggest that this was done to conceal the ring from Lord Colin?'

'I believe so.'

'Do you suggest that the ring was a present from somebody whom she was afraid to acknowledge?'

'I believe so.'

Lady Colin gave her explanation of the ring to Inderwick:

'Have you ever received an emerald ring from a gentleman?'

'No. I had one of Lady Miles's for some time, but I found it too big for me.'

Judge Butt recalled the earlier testimony that 'whenever she went into Lord Colin's room she turned the emeralds.'

'What do you say to that?' Inderwick asked.

'It was a very large ring, and it slipped round my fingers sometimes.'

'Is it a fact that you were in the habit of hiding it whenever you went into your husband's presence?'

'Good gracious, no. There was nothing to hide. If there had been anything to hide, I should not have worn it.'

The ring was not the only small object that provoked suspicion.

'Did you ever notice a particular key which Lady Colin had?' Searle asked Rose Baer.

'Yes.'

'What sort of key was it?'

'It had a key at each end.'

'What did you understand this key with two ends to be?'

'I thought it was a key to 46 Cadogan Square.'

Lady Colin denied ever owning or even seeing such a key. 'Have you ever seen anything that will answer to it?' Inderwick asked.

'I have this that I have always used (holding up an object). It is a key at one end and a pencil case at the other.'

Lockwood asked Annie Duffy about something less ambiguous:

'Did you ever see a book about?'

'Yes, the housemaid called my attention to a book of a very disgusting nature. It was of a sort I had never seen before in my life.'

'What sort of book was it?'

'It was a book touching on the diseases of men – and women.'

'Where did you see it?'

'It was in her ladyship's bedroom and was covered with white notepaper.'

'At this point Lady Colin turned to Russell, sitting just behind her and in a stage whisper said, 'The liar!'

Lady Colin's ownership of such a book would have startled many respectable citizens, who believed in a pure woman's ignorance of certain subjects. One paper reported, 'A young man declared that he would not allow his own mother to read such a book under discussion.' It is surprising, however, that a nurse, even a Victorian nurse, was shocked to learn of its existence.

It was not just the book that staggered Annie Duffy. She also saw 'several articles which Lady Colin said a doctor ordered her to use. But as she was not sleeping with his lordship she would not want these things.' Duffy's conclusion: 'Lady Colin must have been unfaithful to his lordship.'

The articles were not identified, but from Duffy's answer to a question by Lockwood we might make an educated guess:

'Do you remember a conversation about your sister-in-law?'

'Yes. It was in Lady Colin's bedroom. I told her of my sister-in-law, who was very near confinement. She said, 'My poor little sister-in-law is in the same state. It is so silly for women to have children when there are ways and means to prevent it.' I replied, 'Indeed?' This was the first time I had heard of such a thing. I did not know what she meant.'

Inderwick asked Lady Colin, 'Did you hear Mrs Duffy's evidence on a conversation she alleges took place as to your sister-in-law?'

'Yes.'

'Is that true?'

'Quite untrue? I never mentioned the subject to her. I never discussed these matters with my servants.'

Lady Colin, of course, knew about contraceptive literature, which had been sold underground since the 1820s. One book on the subject, Annie Besant's *The Law of the Population*, published in 1877, was a best seller, with 175,000 copies sold in three years. Nurse Annie Duffy's professed ignorance of birth control seems incredible.

CHAPTER 17

Dining with Lord Blandford

In mid-February 1882, Lord Colin left his bed, and, in a limited sense, resumed his normal way of life. A few days later there may have been a melodramatic scene in the drawing-room of 79 Cadogan Place. Russell asked him about it:

'In February 1882, do you recollect coming into your house and sitting down with your wife and weeping?'

'Weeping?'

'Yes, weeping, in February 1882?'

'(Smiling) No, I do not.'

'It was not discreditable to you, Lord Colin. Did you say how cruel people were, and how even some of your own friends had been saying that you ought never to have married?'

'No, I do not recollect that.'

'Will you swear that the conversation never took place?'

'No, I accept the part that says "Some of my friends."'

'Did you not complain of a cruel suggestion that you should not have married?'

'No, I cannot remember it.'

'Did you say how cruel people were?'

'I have no memorandum of the conversation.'

'Did your wife say, "Oh, what is it, dear?" And did you say, "It is nothing. I really cannot talk about it." Did she not say in an excited way, "Good heavens, you are torturing me," and then did you not say that people had said you ought not to have married?'

'No, I do not recollect.'

'Did Lady Colin say, "What business have these people to interfere with our private affairs?"'

'I do not recollect.'

For Inderwick, Lady Colin displayed a better memory:

'In February 1882 you had a conversation with Lord Colin in which he

[61]

made observations on some cruel reports?'

'Yes.'

'Tell us what took place.'

'I was sitting up for him when he returned from some visits he had made. He sat down on the sofa beside me and began to cry. He said, "People are very, very cruel." I said, "What on earth do you mean?" He said, "They are spreading the most cruel reports about me." I said, "For God's sake what have they said?" He said, "People say I ought never to have married." Then he said, "I should not have married on account of my health." I was very angry and said, "How wicked of people to interfere in our concerns." '

A few days later, Lord Colin accompanied his wife on his first social function of the year. They dined at, of all places, 46 Cadogan Square.

'Did you,' Lockwood asked Lord Colin, 'notice anything in the conduct of Lord Blandford and your wife on that occasion?'

'My wife was very irritable that night. It got to be very late, and she was very angry with me several times when I reminded her of it. Afterwards, when we came downstairs Lord Blandford said, "Colin, your coat is there," and pointed in a peremptory manner into the front hall. He and my wife went into a small vestibule at the bottom of the staircase, where they remained in close conversation for several minutes. Afterwards I complained to my wife of the way in which she treated me, keeping me standing in the front hall when it was particularly cold and I was not very strong.'

Russell asked him, 'Did you know Lord Blandford well?'

'I did not know him at all.'

'How is that he addressed you as "Colin"?'

'You had better ask Lord Blandford for an explanation.'

Lady Colin gave Inderwick her version of the incident:

'Do you recollect going into a vestibule with Lord Blandford?'

'Certainly not. There is no such room as Lord Colin described. Nothing whatever occurred on that visit to which I attached any importance.'

'Did your husband complain of your keeping him waiting?'

'No, there was no conversation about that whatever.'

Blandford was questioned by Webster:

'Do you remember seeing Lord and Lady Colin downstairs when they dined with you?'

'There was nothing special to mark the circumstances on my recollection.'

'Did she stay behind to talk to you in a place where Lord Colin could not see you?'

'Oh, dear, no. It would have been impossible owing to the construction of the hall.'

To illustrate the point, he drew a sketch of the hall and stairs leading to it from the dining-room.

On the day after the dinner, 23 February 1882, Albert De Roche quit. This early departure signifies little about his relationship with the Campbells. The tenure of male servants had become notoriously short. As with the women, they had other job opportunities. De Roche was replaced by a man in his mid-twenties, self-assured, self-assertive, with a neatly cropped moustache, James O'Neill, who would remain for six months.

O'Neill was important to this case. Indeed, because of him, the trial was postponed for a week. He had been in America, and everyone waited for his return to England. The hundreds of thousands who followed the proceedings in the popular press were happy for the delay because some of the most amazing testimony came from O'Neill. For this reason it would be instructive to examine his background and to speculate on his possible motives for giving evidence.

O'Neill had gone to the States early in 1884, a few months after leaving Cadogan Place. In May of that year he heard from Messrs. Humphreys, solicitors, whereupon he wrote to Lady Colin:

'My Lady – I received a letter from Messrs. C. O. Humphreys and Sons, requiring my services as a witness in a divorce case in Lord Colin Campbell's favour. I need not tell your ladyship how sorry I should be to appear against you, but if I go to London they could oblige me to appear. If I do not come over they want me to make a sworn statement here. I shall do nothing until I hear from you, as I do not wish to have anything to do with the case if possible. I hope you will be able to advise me.'

George Lewis replied, 'Neither Messrs. Humphreys nor ourselves can compel you to answer questions. If, however, you will kindly make a statement to our agent he will call upon you, and we shall be happy to pay any expenses you may incur.'

O'Neill appeared as a witness for Lord Colin. He was cross-examined by Russell:

'Why did you go to America?'

'To better myself.'

'When you started, did you have a fixed destination?'

'No.'

'What was your first employment in America?'

'I was engaged on board Mr Jay Gould's yacht, the *Atlanta*.'

'How long did you remain in his service?'

'About twelve months.'

'Your next employment?'

'It was with Mr Pulitzer, editor of the New York *Herald*.'

'How long did you stay with him?'

'Only about a week.'

'After this?'

'I entered the service of Mr J. R. Bennett, the patent lawyer.'

'How long did you stop with him?'

'I guess it was a little over six months.' (Laughter)

'Then where did you go?'

'I went to a situation in Chicago.'

'What kind of situation?'

'It was a large place, carried on in a highly respectable scale, not on a low scale.' (Laughter)

'Was it a restaurant?'

'Not exactly a restaurant.'

'A billiard room?'

'Not exactly a billiard room, but it had billiard rooms. It was a large place, like Delmonico's, in New York.'

'How do you describe it?'

'Not a hotel. You may say a restaurant on a very large and most respectable scale.' (Laughter)

'How long did you stay at this most respectable establishment?'

'I was there until it was closed up.' (Laughter)

'What did you do next?'

'I went back to New York. I went to a hotel by the seaside.'

'Were you a waiter?'

'Yes.'

'How long did you remain?'

'Till the house closed in September.'

'What next?'

'I came back to New York, and got employment as a butler and valet.'

'How long?'

'Until this summer.'

'Where did you go next?'

'To the Everett House Hotel, in Union Square, New York City.'

'How long did you remain there?'

'I left to come here.'

'You have been a good deal of a rolling stone?'

'Well, I like travelling.' (Laughter)

'Where are you stopping?'

'At Russell Road, opposite Addison Road Station, West Kensington.'

'Who took lodgings for you?'

'Mr Humphreys's clerk.'

'Now as to your letter to Lady Colin. You expected Lady Colin, who is not an English lawyer, let alone an American lawyer, to advise you on whether you would be compelled to appear?'

'Yes.'

'If she had written and said you were not compelled to appear, you were willing not to do so?'

'Yes.'

'How is it, then, that you made a statement to Judge Troy?'

'Some of my friends advised me to go.'

(Judge Troy, in Brooklyn, was Charles Humphreys's American agent. O'Neill gave him a statement late in the summer of 1884.)

'Did you object to making a statement before Judge Troy?'

'I did.'

'Were you taken by the scruff of the neck?'

'I guess I should have resisted if I had been taken by the scruff of the neck.' (Laughter)

'Then you went willingly?'

'I said I would go and see Judge Troy.'

'Did you get any money for going to him?'

'Yes.'

'How much?'

'Sixty dollars.'

'That is about £12.'

'You are the best judge of that.'

'What was the money for?'

'For the expense of going back and forth between Manhattan and Brooklyn.'

'The fare by the elevated railway is five cents?'

'It was then ten cents.'

'Did they volunteer the payment, or did you ask for it?'

'I told them I could not be losing my time.'

'What did you mean to suggest?'

'That I had something else to do besides going to Judge Troy.'

'Were you recently paid more money?'

'Yes.'

'How much?'

'Two hundred and seventy-five dollars.'

'Who paid you that?'

'Judge Troy.'
'When?'
'Two weeks ago.'
'Did you pay your fare to England out of that?'
'Yes.'
'How much was your fare?'
'Twenty dollars.'
'Did you take a return ticket?'
'No, I took a single ticket.'
'But you could go more economically by taking a return?'
'I did not think about that.'

James O'Neill did not need a return ticket. He remained in England.

At the trial, O'Neill told of one of his first experiences at Cadogan Place. It involved that once most popular of English institutions, afternoon tea. He said that while Lord Colin rested in bed, he served tea to Lady Colin and Lord Blandford. With a tray holding a silver teapot, cream jug, sugar basin, tea cups, spoons, thin slices of bread and butter, and small cakes, he walked up two flights of stairs to the drawing-room. He expected to enter and place the tray in front of his mistress, but, he told Lockwood, he could not do so:

'Had you any special order as to when the tea was to be taken up?'
'No, to take up tea, that is all.'
'How long did it generally take to make tea?'
'About fifteen minutes.'
'On this occasion how long did it take?'
'About five minutes.'
'When you reached the drawing-room, did you find anything about the door?'
'Yes, the door was locked.'
'What did you do?'
'I went downstairs to the pantry.'
'How long did you wait?'
'About ten minutes.'
'Did you then go up again?'
'Yes.'
'Did you again try the door?'
'Yes.'
'Was it locked?'
'No.'
'Did you notice the condition of the furniture?'
'Yes, the cushions on the sofa were disarranged.'

'Was anybody doing anything on the sofa?'

'Lord Blandford and Lady Colin were sitting on it.'

'Were they together?'

'Yes.'

'Did you notice Lady Colin's appearance?'

'I noticed that her dress was disordered and her face was flushed.'

For Finlay the explanation was clear: the tea arrived ten minutes earlier than expected.

O'Neill was cross-examined by Russell:

'Was the tray one which you had to carry with two hands?'

'Yes.'

'You would have to put it down before opening the door?'

'No, I could rest the tray on my knee and open the door with my hand.'

'Standing on one leg?' (Laughter)

'Yes, so.' (Much laughter as he showed how he did it.)

'Did you knock at the door?'

'No, I never knocked when entering the drawing-room.'

'And Lady Colin knew that was your practice?'

'Of course.'

'You were momentarily expected?'

'Well, I don't know about that.'

The involved parties were asked about this alleged incident. Both categorically denied O'Neill's story.

For the Attorney-General, this narrative was too much to swallow: 'Lady Colin is a lady of delicacy and refinement. Yet we are asked to believe she is so abandoned that she rang for tea, and while waiting locked the door, committed a gross act, and then admitted the servant to see her with her dress disordered and the furniture in a condition as to leave no doubt as to what had occurred. Really, is this likely?'

CHAPTER 18

Lady Colin's Hat and Dress

On 4 March 1882, *Vanity Fair* reported, 'On Sunday night Mr and Mrs Langtry gave a small, select party at their rooms in Victoria Street. Mrs Langtry was surrounded by friends and members of her family. Among the guests were His Royal Highness the Prince of Wales, Lord and Lady Walter Campbell, Lord and Lady Colin Campbell...' Further down on the list were the names of Henry Irving, James Whistler, and Mrs and Mrs George Lewis. The hostess was the actress Lily Langtry, one of the few woman who might have defeated Lady Colin in a beauty contest.

For Lady Colin, the Langtry party was exceptional. She did not share much of a social life with her husband. On 15 March she wrote to her mother, 'It is really most trying that in all these dinner invitations, as they come in, he says "accept," and when the date arrives he says, "these engagements will be the death of me." These last few days I have refused all invitations without asking him. Tonight is especially aggravating, as the Duchess of Marlborough [Lord Blandford's mother] sent me a ticket for a small dance.'

'Does that,' Inderwick asked Lady Colin, 'correctly represent the state between you and your husband at that time?'

'Precisely.'

'Did you in fact accept invitations for both of you, and when the time came he was not able to go?'

'Yes, and he desired me to go alone.'

'Was the result that you went a great deal into society without your husband?'

'Yes.'

Lord Colin did not deny this.

'Is it not a fact,' Russell asked him, 'that the invitations came for you as well as Lady Colin?'

'Probably some of them.'

'Did you not tell her to accept the invitations, and when the time came for them to be fulfilled excuse yourself on the ground that you were not well enough to go?'

'That would frequently happen. The doctors told me I was not strong enough to go out to dinners and evening parties, and, acting, on their advice, I have asked my wife to go without me, but she never made the least complaint.'

When she went out at night, Lady Colin usually walked about 240 yards to a point midway between the northern and southern extremities of Cadogan Place. This was Pont Street, built in the Victorian period, dominated by red brick buildings, and, in 1882, possessed of the closest cab stand to Number 79.

'When Lady Colin went to the Pont Street cab stand,' Searle asked Rose Baer, 'did you accompany her?'

'Yes, her ladyship used to tell me to come to the corner of the street with her.'

'What then?'

'She told me to go back.'

'And you left her?'

'Yes.'

'When you went with her to Pont Street, how was she dressed?'

'She wore her dinner dress and a fur cloak and a thick veil over her face. Under the cloak she carried a hat.'

'What sort of hat?'

'A man's hat.'

'What do you mean by that?' Judge Butt asked. 'A man wears more than one kind of hat.' (Laughter)

'I don't know what hat you call it.'

'What was its shape?'

'It was a low, round hat.'

'Do you mean it was what is called a "crush " hat?'

'I don't know. I don't know its English name.'

'What was it made of?' Searle asked.

'A sort of felt.'

'How did she carry it?'

'She took it, as I tell you, in her arm under a cloak.'

During his cross-examination, Russell asked Baer about this hat:

'Why do you understand she carried it?'

'I do not know.'

'Did you form any reason in your own mind?'

'No.'

'Was it in your own mind suspicious?'

'It was.'

'Why?'

'Because why should her ladyship take a hat and not put it on?'

'What did you think was suspicious about it?'

'I thought she would put it on in order to disguise her.'

'Oh, you thought she carried it for a disguise when she would do something improper?'

'Yes.'

'But she made no concealment to you on this matter?'

'Oh, yes, she did. She took it out of the wardrobe when she did not think I saw her.'

'How often did this "suspicious thing" happen?'

'Two or three times.'

'In what year?'

'1882.'

'Did she ever come back in the hat?'

'No, it was under her cloak again.'

'You sat up for her?'

'Yes.'

'Then she took off the cloak and the mystery was revealed?'

'No, she would put the hat in the wardrobe herself.'

'You went into her room after she came home?'

'Yes.'

'Just as she was surreptitiously putting the hat into the wardrobe, concealing it from you?'

'Yes.'

'You saw it when she put it under her cloak and when she put it in her wardrobe again?'

'Yes, but she thought I did not see her.'

Asked by Inderwick if she had ever gone out with a hat under her cloak, Lady Colin said, 'on one occasion I believe I did. I was going to my mother's and meant to walk home with my father or brother. I did not put it on because I thought I should get a cab directly I had left the house. I only took it because I might walk home.'

When Lady Colin returned home at night, Rose Baer was waiting for her. It was the duty of a lady's maid to help her mistress undress and put away the jewels.

'What time did Lady Colin return?' Searle asked Baer.

'Sometimes very late.'

'How late?'

'Sometimes between two and three in the morning.'

[70]

'Can you tell us whether she drove home or walked?'

'She would drive to the corner of the street [Sloane Street at Cadogan Place] and then walk the rest of the way.'

'How could you tell that the cab stopped at the corner?'

'Because I heard it.'

'And she would come in shortly afterwards?'

'Yes.'

'And you had to undress her?'

'Did you notice anything when you undressed her?'

'I noticed that she had had her dress off.'

'How did you know that?'

'Her dress was half off when she came back. It was not done up altogether.'

Judge Butt asked, 'Do you mean that it was laced at the back and not entirely laced up when she returned?'

'Sometimes it would be laced and sometimes not. The skirt was open.'

Searle asked, 'What did you notice about the skirt?'

'Sometimes it was open and the petticoat was hanging down.'

'How often did you notice this disarrangement?'

'Three or four times.'

'Have you any doubt that her dress had been off between your fastening it and her coming back?'

'No.'

'You believe that still?'

'Yes.'

CHAPTER 19

The Police Officer's Report

Lord Blandford and Captain Shaw were not exactly Lord Colin's favourite persons. One day late in March 1882 after coming home and finding them in the house, he spoke to his wife about them.

'Do you remember a conversation with Lord Colin about Lord Blandford and Captain Shaw?' Inderwick asked Lady Colin.

'Yes. Lord Colin said he did not like the evident admiration which Lord Blandford and Captain Shaw had for me. I laughed. He said he did not like these afternoon visits when he was out. I said, "Well, I will tell them not to come again. Do you want me to cut them when I meet them in society?"

He said, "Oh, no, I do not mean that. I only object to their calling here." I said, "Very well, but I am going to the launch of the *Invicta* at Blackwall on Captain Shaw's launch. It is possible that Lord Blandford will be there. Do you have an objection to my going?"

He said, "No, I just object to their calling here in the afternoon."'

Lord Colin gave his version of the exchange to Lockwood:

'We had a long conversation about Captain Shaw and Lord Blandford. I told her that I had been informed that there was scandalous gossip about her and Lord Blandford. I complained of his visits to Cadogan Place, and also about Captain Shaw. She promised me that they should not continue to be visitors. She asked me not to be suspicious because it hurt her so. She was particularly affectionate and implored me not to suspect her.'

Lady Colin spoke to the men on 5 April at the facilities of the Thames Iron Works and Shipbuilding Company, four miles east of London Bridge, at Blackwall. The occasion was the launching of the *Invicta*, a paddle steamer that would cross the Channel between Dover and Calais in the record-breaking time of one hour. Lady Colin and Lord Blandford went on one of Captain Shaw's launches. About sixty people attended the affair.

'What did you say to Lord Blandford and Captain Shaw?' Inderwick asked

'I said, "I hope you will not think me rude, but Lord Colin does not like afternoon callers, and I hope you will not come back."'

'You spoke to them separately?'

'I did.'

'What did they say?'

'Captain Shaw said, "How ridiculous these Campbells are." (Laughter) Lord Blandford used pretty much the same words.'

'Was Lord Blandford ever in the house after that?'

'Never.'

'Or Captain Shaw?'

'Never.'

During his cross-examination of Lady Colin, Lockwood asked, 'When Captain Shaw said, "How ridiculous these Campbells are," did you think that was disrespectful to your husband's family?'

'I thought it a very natural answer under the circumstances.'

'And Lord Blandford?'

'He treated it in the same way.'

'Did he laugh at the family in the same way?'

'He laughed at the ridiculous character of the idea.'

Blandford was asked by Finlay, during cross-examination, 'Did Lady Colin say that her husband objected to your evident admiration of her?'

'She never said anything about evident admiration. She mentioned the subject of visitors.'

'Did not Lady Colin convey to you that Lord Colin objected especially to you?'

'No. If she had, I should have entirely discontinued Lady Colin's acquaintance.'

'May I take it that you understood from Lady Colin that her husband objected to gentleman visitors in general?'

'I understood from Lady Colin that there was no distinction between myself and anybody else. Otherwise I should have felt the remark to be personal.'

Captain Shaw also said that he had understood that Lord Colin had objected to gentleman callers generally. He was cross-examined by Lockwood:

'How long have you known the family of the Duke of Argyll?'

'For about 25 years.'

'When you were ill, were you nursed at Argyll Lodge?'

'Yes, I was.'

'And did you once recuperate from an illness at the castle at Inveraray?'

'Yes, I did.'

'You have received very great kindness from the Campbells?'

'Yes, very great.'

'Then what did you mean by saying, "How ridiculous these Campbells are."?'

'I don't know what I meant. I spoke in the heat of the moment.'

Each of the men swore that he never again set foot at 79 Cadogan Place.

Neither of them, however, stopped seeing Lady Colin. Lord Blandford may have seen a great deal of her. On this question the star witness was Police Constable Edward Dalby.

London's police force in 1882 included about 11,000 constables, foot patrolmen who walked a beat, the most visible police officers. According to the *General Regulations, Instructions, and Orders*, a police constable was 'expected to possess such a knowledge of the inhabitants of each house [on his beat] as to enable him to recognise their persons.' Each constable visited every street, lane, road, court, and alley in his beat every day he was on duty. The constables were polite and efficient, but they were not noted for their intelligence and were frequent subjects of jokes in *Punch* and elsewhere.

One of the police beats in 1882 was in Chelsea-Knightsbridge. Its daytime officer was Edward Dalby. He was examined by Lockwood:

'Was part of your beat Cadogan Square?'

'Yes.'

'Did you know Lady Colin Campbell by sight?'

'I did not know her till I made inquiries.'

'When did you first ascertain?'

'After I first saw the lady with Lord Blandford.'

'When did you first see her accompanied by Lord Blandford?'

'About two o'clock on a day in the spring of 1882.'

'Where were they?'

'In Cadogan Square.'

'What were they doing?'

'Walking beside each other.'

'Did you see them again shortly afterwards?'

'Yes, the following day.'

'In the same place?'

'Yes.'

'At the same time?'

'Yes.'

'Did this happen frequently?'

'Yes, about a dozen times.'

'Did you see them always in Cadogan Square?'

'Yes.'

'Always in the afternoon?'

'Yes.'

'Did the lady sometimes have a collie dog with her?'

'Yes.'

'Have you ever seen them at any other time and place?'

'Yes. Sometimes I saw them in Lennox Gardens at about seven o'clock in the evening when coming off my beat.'

Dalby was cross-examined by Russell:

'Did you know Lord Blandford well?'

'Yes.'

'Did you know Lady Campbell?'

'I did not until I made inquires.'

'When did you inquire?'

'On the second day that I saw them.'

'What made you inquire?'

'Well, I was given to understand that Lord Blandford's wife was away from him.' (Laughter)

'Who gave you to understand that?'

'People talk, and I asked a coachman who was sitting there on his box.'

'I want to see how the police obtain their information. You asked a coachman sitting on his box whether Lord Blandford's wife was away from him?'

'Yes, I said something like that to him.'

'What did you ask him?'

'I asked him who that tall lady was along with Lord Blandford, and he said, "That is Lady Colin Campbell."'

'Was there anything to attract your attention to this lady and gentleman?'

'No, there was nothing.'

'Why did you inquire about them?'

'Because Lord Blandford was a short man and Lady Colin was a tall woman. That was my reason.' (Laughter)

Lord Cadogan's caretaker, Solomon Giddings, confirmed Dalby's testimony, and added that he had also seen the couple walking elsewhere, including Pont Street, 'a great many times.'

Lockwood asked Lady Colin, 'After Lord Colin objected to Lord Blandford, did you think it right to walk with him?'

'Yes. I did not think it was wrong if I met him.'

'Did you walk with him in Cadogan Square?'

'No, not in the square.'

'Did you walk round and round the square?'

'Round and round is not correct. I may have walked across the square when going to see my mother.'

'Were these meetings with Lord Blandford accidental or by appointment?'

'Accidental.'

'On every occasion you accidentally met Lord Blandford?'

'Yes, I met him while on the way to my mother's house, in Thurloe Square.'

Lord Colin, asked by Lockwood if he had known about his wife's walks with Blandford, replied, 'Certainly not.'

The Attorney-General asked incredulously, 'Are two people who have known one another for a considerable time not to speak to one another in the street or walk together in a square?'

The predominant view, however, was that of a writer for the *Standard*: 'Lady Colin was not very careful to guard against the appearances of evil.'

A married woman could create an appearance of guilt just by walking in public with a man who was not her husband.

CHAPTER 20

Leigh Court

In the spring of 1882, Lady Colin and Lord Blandford saw each other beyond Cadogan Square. In April they were contemporaneous house guests in the luxurious mansion Leigh Court, near Bristol, principal home of Sir Philip and Frances Miles.

Sir Philip, 57, the second baronet in his title, educated at Eton and Trinity College, Cambridge, was the Conservative MP for East Somerset and a partner in a Bristol banking firm. He was very rich.

Frances Elizabeth Miles, Sir Philip's wife of 34 years, daughter of an Irish baronet, was a first cousin of Mr Blood. As a girl, after returning with her family to England, Gertrude Blood became attached to the Miles's three daughters. Now she and Lady Miles were extremely close. Along with George Lewis, Lady Miles sat beside Lady Colin every day of the trial. Once known as 'the Venus of Miles,' she showed why she had gained this name. She was past fifty, but some reporters judged her to be on the sunny side of forty.

'On your visit to Leigh Court in the spring of 1882,' Lockwood asked Lady Colin, 'were you and Lord Colin invited?'

'Yes. Lord Colin was invited with me, but he had gone to Edinburgh, and when he came back he said the journey had tired him, and he decided not to go. He remained in town.'

While cross-examining Rose Baer, Russell asked her about this:

'Do you recollect that Lord Colin was to have gone down with Lady Colin?'

'I do not know anything about it.'

'As a matter of fact he was indisposed?'

'Yes.'

'Did he for that reason remain in town?'

'Yes.'

In his re-examination, Finlay returned to this point:

'Did you before today know that Lord Colin had intended to come down to Leigh Court with Lady Colin?'

'No.'

'Had preparations been made for this, and was Lord Colin at the last moment prevented by illness from going?'

'I never heard of it before.'

In any event, in April of 1882 Lord Colin stayed in London when his wife and her maid went to Leigh Court.

In no phase of life was the Victorian age more revolutionary than in transportation. At the beginning of the century, going from London to Bristol took three days – for the few who could afford it. In 1882, the Great Western Railway sent six trains every weekday over the 118 miles from Paddington Station to Temple Meads'. One of them, the *Flying Dutchman*, was advertised as the world's fastest. It was a luxury train without third class carriages (in which 90 per cent of the nation's passengers rode). On their trip to Bristol, Lady Colin and Rose Baer went on the *Flying Dutchman*. Baer was in a second class compartment while her mistress rode forward in first class. At 11.45 the train left Paddington, and for nearly an hour travelled at a mile a minute. There was a ten-minute stop at the town of Swindon to pick up refreshments (not even luxury trains had restaurant cars). At 1.58 there was another pause for passengers to get off at Bath. Finally at 2.21 there was the familiar 'Tickets ready, please,' and the arrival at Temple Meads Station. (Nowadays an express train does the trip in one hour and 27 minutes.)

From the station the two women rode in a hackney carriage for six-and-a-half miles along the Bristol-Portishead road, then through the impressive Ionic gateway at the entrance of the estate known as Leigh Court.

In the midst of farms, orchards, gardens, and stables was the home built by Sir Philip's grandfather, creator of the family banking fortune. Frequently compared to a palace, Leigh Court was built in the Greek Revival style. The front entrance is dominated by four giant Ionic pillars and leads into a domed vestibule with six white marble columns. From there a visitor in 1882 stepped into an enormous central hall surrounded by a suite of eight rooms: drawing-room, dining-room, morning-room, library, study, billiards room, saloon, and art gallery.

Two spectacular parallel flights of stairs lead up to the first floor, where an Ionic, brass balustraded gallery surrounds the interior. From any part of the gallery, one many look down upon, and be seen from, the main hall. During the Miles's tenure, fourteen guest rooms, along with dressing rooms and nurseries, opened onto the first floor balcony. On the second floor there were fourteen rooms for maids and eight for male servants. (Today Leigh Court is a home for mental patients.)

In 1882, the Miles's had one of the world's great private art collections, with pictures by Andrea del Sarto, Fra Bartolomeo, Giovanni Bellini, Canaletto, Annibale and Lodovico Carracci, Claude, Correggio, Carlo Dolci, Domenichino, Holbein, Leonardo da Vinci, Michelangelo, Murillo, Poussin, Raphael, Rembrandt, Salvator Rosa, Rubens, Titian, Van Dyke, Velasquez, and Veronese. (Most of them would be sold at Christie's in 1884.)

One might have studied art history in these works, but this wasn't the main reason that people enjoyed being invited to Leigh Court. And there were always plenty of guests. Sir Philip's butler said, 'they were coming and going all the time.' The domestic arrangements indeed had to be carefully structured. As in a hotel, each person signed a register, which in 1882 was kept by the Miles's daughter, Violet.

According to the register, Lady Colin occupied Room 29 during the spring visit, and Lord Blandford was in Room 37. Finlay noticed that most of the entries in the register were in the handwriting of one person, presumably Violet Miles, but a small group of insertions had been written by another person.

'Are these figures referring to the Easter party,' he asked Lady Miles, 'in your handwriting?'

'Yes.'

'Can you account for the thick appearance of the figures in the book for the Easter party?'

'I can only account for it by believing that the ink was not very good.'

'I must ask you, have not these figures been put in by you long afterwards?'

'Certainly not.'

'Do you swear it?'

'I swear it.'

The longtime Miles's family butler, Stephen Ansell, was questioned by Russell on the room assignments:

'Do you recall what room Lady Colin occupied on her visit at Easter 1882?'

'Room 29.'

'Is that next to the room occupied by Sir Philip Miles?'

'Yes.'

'Did you always attend upon Sir Philip?'

'Yes.'

'Do you know who occupied the room on the other side of Lady Colin?'

'It was a small dressing-room, but I cannot recollect if anyone occupied it.'

'What room did Lord Blandford occupy?'

'It was 37 or 38. There were so many people, I can't remember which.'

Two witnesses contradicted Lady Miles and Stephen Ansell. First, Rose Baer was questioned by Searle:

'What bedroom did Lady Colin occupy at Leigh Court?'

'Number 37.'

'Are you sure?'

'Well, it was 37 or 38.'

'What room did Lord Blandford occupy?'

'The room next to Lady Colin's.'

Leigh Court's housekeeping staff included a housekeeper, a head housemaid, and three housemaids. The head housemaid, Elizabeth Evans, was examined by Finlay:

'Did you attend to the preparation of the room for Lady Colin Campbell at the Easter visit in 1882?'

'Yes.'

'What was that room?'

'Number 38.'

'Are you perfectly certain of that?'

'Yes.'

'Did you ever hear it suggested that Lord Colin Campbell was to come over at Easter 1882?'

'No.'

'What room did Lord Blandford occupy?'

'The room next to Lady Colin's.'

'Are you sure of that?'

'Yes.'

This witness would receive an unsolicited character reference when Judge Butt, in summing up the case, said, 'Elizabeth Evans appeared to be a good, honest, straightforward person.'

'I appeal to you,' Finlay said in his summation, 'if the evidence of Miss Evans, the head housemaid, who prepared the rooms for the reception of visitors, is not absolutely conclusive of the fact that Lord Blandford and Lady Colin occupied rooms which adjoined each other.'

While continuing to insist that Lady Colin and Lord Blandford had not had adjoining rooms, Russell said that this really wasn't important: 'If

[79]

Lady Colin was degraded enough to receive Lord Blandford in her bedroom, I should have thought they would have had no difficulty if he had been placed two doors or even three doors away, and that the stillness of the night would have made access easy.'

Sir Charles had never visited Leigh Court. (Nor had any of the other barristers in the case.) If he had been there, he would have seen in each bedroom an inner connecting door permitting intramural passage without penetrating the outer gallery. With adjoining rooms, a couple desiring to get together would face no risk of detection.

Another disputed point concerned exactly when Blandford and Lady Colin had stayed at Leigh Court.

The two parties insisted that they had arrived and departed at different times and were together at Leigh Court for only two days. They were supported by Lady Miles, and by the family butler, questioned by Russell:

'How long did Lord Blandford stay?'

'He came on Saturday [15 April] and remained till Wednesday, the day after the ball [a fancy dress ball in a Bristol hotel].'

'Do you remember when Lady Colin came?'

'On the Monday, I believe, the day before the ball.'

'How long did she stay?'

'Till the end of the week, as I recollect.'

'So then, Lord Blandford and Lady Colin were together in the house two nights?'

'Yes.'

Rose Baer was asked by Searle for her recollection:

'How long did Lady Colin's visit last?'

'About a week.'

'Was Lord Blandford there when you arrived?'

'Yes.'

'Did he remain all the time Lady Colin was there?'

'Yes.'

Elizabeth Evans answered Finlay's questions:

'Do you recollect how long Lord Blandford and Lady Colin were there?'

'Yes, a few days.'

'Can you tell us whether Lord Blandford came down at the same time as Lady Colin?'

'Yes, at the same date, to the best of my recollection.'

'And when did they leave?'

'The same day, I believe.'

CHAPTER 21

Having Fun at Leigh Court

According to witnesses under oath, there were curious goings-on at Leigh Court. Rose Baer told Searle about one incident:

'Do you remember one night when you were washing Lady Colin's feet?'

'Yes.'

'What time was it?'

'After midnight.'

'When you were washing her feet, what happened?'

'Someone came up the staircase toward her bedroom.'

'What did Lady Colin do?'

'Directly she heard somebody coming she coughed.'

'Anything else?'

'No.'

'Where did that person go?'

'Into the next room.'

'Was that Lord Blandford's room?'

'Yes.'

'What happened next?'

'Directly after I heard the door shut in the next room, Lady Colin dismissed me.'

'Was it usual for her to dismiss you?'

'She usually dismissed me when I had finished her.'

Baer also reported on another similar occurrence:

'Do you remember one night when you were brushing Lady Colin's hair?'

'Yes.'

'What time was it?'

'It was after midnight.'

'Did you hear anything?'

'Yes, I heard someone try the door.'

'Did Lady Colin do or say anything?'

'Yes, she coughed.'

'Did she cough loudly?'

'Yes.'

'What happened next?'

'The person who was trying the door went away directly.'

'During his cross-examination, Russell asked, 'Was Lady Colin constantly coughing?'

'It happened only twice.'

Baer admitted that the gallery and stairs were covered with thick carpeting, leading the Attorney-General to conclude that it would have been impossible to hear footsteps.

Lady Colin's answer to Rose Baer's charges was that she had lied. She did not, however, question the veracity of Elizabeth Evans's report to Finlay on something she had observed:

'Do you remember anything happening one day when Lady Colin was standing by the organ in the hall?'

'Yes. I was going along the passage, and I saw Lady Colin take off her slipper and throw it at Lord Blandford.'

'I cannot help referring to this scene,' Finlay said, 'as a contrast to the view that their private intercourse had regard only to the works of Draper, Lecky, Green, rationalism, and science.'

The incident illustrates the frequently-observed frivolity of Victorian country-house parties. Other evidence against Lady Colin was rather more serious. This is from Searle's examination of Rose Baer:

'During the visit did anything attract your attention to Lady Colin's towels?'

'Yes, I noticed the towels were disarranged.'

'How were they disarranged?'

'They were thrown about on the floor.'

'Where were they on the floor?'

'Near the bed.'

'Had they been used for washing purposes?'

'Not all of them.'

'Did you notice anything on the towels that struck you?'

'Yes, I noticed that the towels were creased.'

'Did you notice any marks or creases on the bed?'

'I noticed creases on the bed.'

'Was it a single or double bed?'

'It was a double bed.'

'Could you judge whether more than one person had occupied it?'

'Yes, I saw that two persons had been in the bed.'

On the same topic, Finlay questioned Elizabeth Evans:

'Was it part of your duty to go into Lady Colin's bedroom every morning?'

'Yes.'

'Was there anything there that attracted your attention?'

'One morning I saw that the towels were strewn about the floor.'

'What do you mean "strewn"?'

'They were lying about the floor.'

'Had they been used for washing?'

'No.'

'Was there anything about their appearance that led you to form an opinion as to what they had been used for?'

'No, I cannot say for certain.'

One question not part of any advocate's examination was asked by Judge Butt at the end of Rose Baer's testimony:

'Do you believe that Lady Colin Campbell and Lord Blandford slept together every night during their visit to Leigh Court?'

'Yes, I do.'

If the sleeping ended at Leigh Court, the memories may have lingered on. Although both parties insisted that they had left on different days, Elizabeth Evans, as we have seen, the housemaid responsible for their rooms, was certain that they had departed together. And Rose Baer said they were on the same train, probably the 12.05 express, which reached Paddington at 2.40.

London's railway stations in the Victorian period were notorious as meeting places for lovers. Especially famed for this were Charing Cross and Victoria. But for a Lord and Lady the station that would provide the best backdrop for a tryst was that noblest of London's terminals, Paddington. (Because of the generous tips received there, it was the only London railway station that always had a full staff of platform employees.) With its great triple-arched room, the architecturally magnificent Paddington Station is well suited for aristocratic leavetakings.

If Rose Baer is to be believed, her Lady's farewell scene with Lord Blandford was not hurried. This is from her pre-trial statement to Lord Colin's solicitor: 'On the arrival of the train at Paddington, Lord Blandford and Lady Colin sat on a seat on the platform quite close together and seemed very unhappy at having to part from each other. They looked like two lovers, and Lady Colin kept looking to see if I was watching. While the luggage was got from the train and placed in cabs,

Lord Blandford taking one cab and Lady Colin the other, he remained with her until the luggage was ready.'

Baer was questioned on this by Russell:

'You say they seemed very unhappy at parting from each other and were like two lovers?'

'Yes.'

'What would two lovers do under such circumstances, seated on a bench at Paddington?'

Baer hesitated.

'You are recently married yourself,' Russell said to the witness who at the time of the trial was Rose Baer Fisher. 'You ought to know something.' (Laughter)

'I suppose everybody knows.' (Renewed laughter)

'You had your suspicions?'

'I had.'

'And you allowed your imagination to run away with you?'

'I had my suspicions.'

'It was a bench they were sitting on?'

'Yes.'

'Was it opposite to where the carriage drew up?'

'Yes.'

'You are sure it was a bench?'

'It was a seat, yes.'

'Do you swear there was a seat on the arrival platform at Paddington Station?'

'(Hesitating) There is a seat.'

'And they were sitting on it?'

'Yes.'

Benches at London's railway stations are always in waiting rooms but rarely on platforms. Contemporary photographs do not show benches or seats of any kind on the arrival platforms at Paddington Station.

CHAPTER 22

Domestic Gossip

In her pre-trial statement Rose Baer said, 'When the party was leaving Leigh Court, the ladies and gentlemen were outside the omnibus, except for me and Mr Fitzhenry, a painter. He had a great bunch of violets which he told me he had plucked for Lady Colin, but she would have nothing to do with him because she had so many others. But he would make up for lost time as they were going to Paris together.'

'This gentleman,' Russell asked Baer, 'told you he was going to Paris with Lady Colin?'

'Yes.'

'He took you into his confidence over a bunch of violets?'

'Yes.'

Fitzhenry was never again mentioned.

Another cameo appearance was made by a man named Wright. He was Lord Blandford's valet, who had accompanied his master to Leigh Court.

Baer reported that Wright had also told her that Lady Colin would be going to Paris and that her travelling companion would be Blandford. In her direct examination, Baer said that the couple had been in Paris together. Russell asked her about this:

'You say that after Easter 1882 Lady Colin and Lord Blandford were in Paris together?'

'Yes.'

'And your only reason for saying this is Wright's statement?'

'Yes.'

Lady Colin, in fact, after arriving in London on 30 April, went to Paris on 4 May. She stayed for ten days.

'Her chaperone,' Finlay said, 'was Lady Miles, and you, gentlemen of the jury, will decide whether the austere control of that estimable lady could prevent mischief at Paris any more than at Leigh Court.'

On this topic, Lord Colin had no doubts.

'When Lady Colin visited Paris in May 1882,' Lockwood asked him, 'do you think Lord Blandford was also there?'

'Yes. Lady Miles told me that Lord Blandford was in Paris. On this occasion I believe that she told the truth.' (Laughter)

'Do you think that your wife and Lord Blandford were together in Paris?'

'Yes, I do.'

Lady Colin was asked about this by Inderwick:

'In May 1882 were you in Paris with Lord Blandford?'

'Never. I went over with Lady Miles to see my mother, who had caught rheumatic fever while on her way up from Italy.'

'Did you see Lord Blandford at all in Paris?'

'No.'

'Is it true that he was there?'

'Not that I am aware of.'

Mrs Blood was questioned by Russell:

'Do you recollect your daughter visiting you in Paris in the year after the marriage?

'Yes, in May. She came up to my room and stood for a few seconds on the threshold. I did not know her at first. She was ghastly and stood gasping for breath. I saw that she had been suffering in health.'

'So far as your knowledge goes, did she go to Paris to meet Lord Blandford?'

'Certainly not.'

'Did she see him?'

'No.'

While Lady Colin was in Paris, the household staff at Cadogan Place was thoroughly enjoying itself. British servants have long been noted for gossip. This is especially true of ladies' maids, whose aimless talkativeness was a source of comedy for eighteenth- and nineteenth-century dramatists and novelists. Rose Baer fitted the stereotype. Her name came up during Russell's examination of James O'Neill:

'Was there scandalous talk among the servants about her ladyship?'

'Yes.'

'Where was the scandalous talk?'

'In the kitchen, generally at meal times.'

'Was Rose Baer one of the contributors?'

'She was the principal one.' (Laughter)

Russell called Rose Baer 'the principal gossip in the servants' hall, the *fous et arigo undi* – the one who set the ball of suspicion rolling.' Then he delivered a *tour de force*:

'Who does not believe that Rose Baer was a foreign maid servant with a gossiping, scandalous tongue? She set this slander and calumny into existence, and anyone who knows anything of the readiness with which men and women accept stories of evil about others knows that if you give calumny a short start it will enjoy a long, healthy life.

'I do not know if you remember a passage which has always struck me as one of the most remarkable in any language. It is from *The Barber of Seville*, and it brings to mind how easy it is to predispose people to believe a slander.

'The writer says, "Calumny, sir! I have seen the most respectable people overwhelmed by it. Believe me, there is no wickedness, no horror, no absurd talk that you cannot make the idlers of a village believe. First, a little humming sound, skimming the ground like a swallow before the storm, *pianissimo*, *pianissimo*, murmuring and buzzing, and spreading the poison as it goes. A breath catches it up, *piano*, *piano*, it glides into your ear adroitly. The harm is done, it takes root, it climbs, it travels like the devil. Then, all at once you see it raising its head, swelling itself out, growing monstrous under your very eyes. It rises, takes flight, whirls round you, clutches you, drags you along, bursts forth, and becomes, Heaven help us! a general shriek, *crescendo*, a universal chorus of hatred and proscription. Who can withstand it?"

'In the case before you, Rose Baer began all the calumny.'

In her pre-trial statement, Baer provided support for Sir Charles's eloquence: 'On my return from Leigh Court, I told O'Neill that Lord Blandford had slept with Lady Colin every night at Leigh Court. This was my surmise from what I had seen. The conduct of Lady Colin and Lord Blandford was the constant topic of conversation amongst the servants.'

For nearly two weeks, Lady Colin's servants had a field day, and then on 14 May she was back in Cadogan Place. If she had deceived her husband at Leigh Court and in Paris, the deception may have continued in London. This exchange is from Russell's cross-examination of Lord Colin:

'Did you at any time detect Lady Colin telling a lie in reference to any of her engagements?'

'A lie?'

'Yes, that is my question.'

'I am bound to say she practised deception.'

'My point was in reference to her engagements. Did you ever detect her telling an untruth?'

'That is my impression.

'Mention a case.'

'One day she told me she was going to dine with Mrs Roche.'

'When was that?'

'It was in May or June 1882.'

'Yes?'

'On the next day Mrs Roche called at my house and asked whether Lady Colin was in town or not.'

'Did you see Mrs Roche?'

'I did not.'

'Oh! Then you are telling what somebody else told you?'

'I cannot help that.'

Lord Colin's knowledge of Mrs Roche's visit came from the servant who had answered the door. He could not remember who it was. He also could not cite another instance in which his wife had lied.

Lady Colin was asked by Inderwick, 'Did you ever tell your husband that you had dined with a Mrs Roche?'

'Certainly not. I have no recollection of ever dining with Mrs Roche in London.'

'Did Lord Colin speak to you about that?'

'No, he never spoke to me on the subject.'

'Was this the first time you have heard anything about this matter?'

'Yes.'

Mrs Roche was not called as a witness.

CHAPTER 23

Lord Colin and Amelia Watson

In eighteenth and nineteenth century England, pursuing servant girls was an upper and upper-middle class sport. Samuel Richardson's famous novel *Pamela*, deals entirely with this subject. As with Pamela and Lord B., social barriers vanished when sex was the objective. If they were caught in the act, the consequences fell upon the servant. Unless, that is, a wife was seeking evidence for a separation or divorce.

Among the servants who worked at 79 Cadogan Place during the Campbells' tenure, the prettiest was Amelia Watson. If Lord Colin were going to have his intramural extramarital diversion, she would seem the most likely partner.

Rose Baer, who apparently knew everything that was going on, was asked by Searle, 'Did you ever see any impropriety between Amelia Watson and Lord Colin?'

She answered with one word: 'Never.'

But according to Lady Colin's divorce petition, in June of 1882 Lord Colin had a fling with the housemaid. The only witness was Lady Miles, who was often in London staying at her town house at 75 Cornwall Gardens. She told her story to Inderwick:

'What happened at Cadogan Place on June 17, 1882?'

'I dined at the house in Cadogan Place. Lady Colin had begged me to keep company with Lord Colin as she had an engagement. He was not very well, and she did not like to leave him alone. After dinner we went into the drawing room for coffee, and Lord Colin complained of a pain in his stomach. I advised him to lie down and have a linseed poultice put on. He consented and went upstairs.'

Lady Miles paused. She was asked, 'Were directions given to anyone to make the poultice?'

'Mr Inderwick,' she said irritably, 'I am coming to that. Be patient.'

After the loud laughter had subsided, Lady Miles said, 'I went upstairs when I thought he had had time to get to bed. I rang for the housemaid and told her to make a poultice.'

'Was this Mary Watson?'

(Although Robert Finlay regularly called Amelia Watson by her real name the opposing legal counsel habitually referred to her as Mary)

'Yes.'

'What did she say?'

'She was very insolent. She said, "If you want a poultice for my Lord, make it yourself. I am not going to do it." I asked Lord Colin if he would permit a housemaid to speak to me in this manner.'

A surprised Judge Butt asked, 'Was this said in Lord Colin's presence?'

'Yes, my Lord.'

'Where?'

'In his bedroom.'

Resuming, Inderwick asked, 'What did Lord Colin say?'

'He said, "Poor little thing! She is jealous of you, Muzzie."' ['Muzzie' was Lord Colin's nickname for Lady Miles.]

'Then what happened?'

'I was much surprised and said, "A housemaid jealous of me! What has she to be jealous of?" The girl would not go downstairs by my orders, and so Lord Colin told her to make the poultice. She went down and brought up a very badly-made, quite dry poultice. I told her she had better go and fetch another. Once again she checked me. (Laughter) Lord Colin again took her part and accepted the poultice.'

'How long after that did you remain with Lord Colin?'

'Till about a quarter past eleven – a little more than an hour.'

'Did Lord Colin speak to you at this time about Mary Watson?'

'Yes. He said that she was a kind, good little thing. He said she was a very pretty girl and was very fond of him. He said she had very pretty hair which he used to take down and play with. (Laughter) This remark confirmed my suspicions.'

'What happened afterwards?'

'I went downstairs and pretended to go out. I slammed the door without going out.'

'Then what occurred?'

'I went into the dining-room and remained for a short time. I then went back upstairs, expecting to find the girl with Lord Colin. She *was* with Lord Colin. (Laughter) She was sitting on the side of the bed embracing him. His arms were round her neck, and she was leaning against his knee.'

'How was Lord Colin dressed?'

'In his night-shirt.'

'What did you do?'

'I came away directly.'

'Did they see you?'

'Oh, no. They were much too well occupied to see *me*.' (Much laughter)

'Did you ever speak to Lord Colin about sending her away?'

'Yes. I said he had better send her away because she was much too pretty to be a housemaid. (Laughter) I told him she was a very awkward person to have in the house.'

'Did you ever tell Lord Colin of what you had seen?'

'Yes, I told him about a week later.'

'What did he say?'

'That a man should not have to account for every little thing he did.' (Laughter)

'Did you charge him with maintaining Mary Watson as a mistress?'

'Yes, and I told him he could not deny it. He did not deny it.'

Finlay's lengthy cross-examination of Lady Miles included these questions and answers:

'When this happened, where was Lady Colin?'

'I think she was at a concert.'

[90]

'Were there other servants in the house?'

'Yes, the cook.'

'Weren't there other servants there besides Amelia Watson and the cook?'

'I didn't see others, and I didn't hear anyone.'

'Wouldn't you expect Lady Colin's maid to be waiting for her when she came back from the concert?'

'I don't know anything about Lady Colin's maid.'

'Was there also a man-servant in the house?'

'I did not see one. He did not wait on us at dinner.'

'When you went into the room and saw Lord Colin with Amelia Watson's arms round his neck, were you very much shocked?'

'I never went into the bedroom.'

'How did you see?'

'I saw from the staircase.'

'Was the door open?'

'Yes.'

'So that anyone passing up the staircase could see?'

'Yes, if they cared to do so.'

'Were you very much shocked?'

'Yes, very much shocked indeed.'

'You had never seen anything like it before?'

'No, never, and I hope I never shall again.'

'Did it alter after your feelings toward Lord Colin?'

'Yes, very much.'

'You felt like a mother toward him?'

'Yes, and I still do.'

'As a mother toward an erring child?'

'Yes.'

'Now, Lady Miles, can you explain why in all of your correspondence with Lord Colin [which had been subpoenaed for the trial] there is not the slightest allusion to his having been found in adultery by a person who had been as much as a mother to him?'

'I do not put these things in writing. Letters often get mislaid.'

'Lady Miles, what enables you to fix on the seventeenth of June as the date of the occurrence?'

'I put it down in my Prayer Book.'

'Will you allow me to see that valuable document?'

'I can send for it if you like.'

'Where is it?'

'At Leigh Court.'

[91]

'Is it there in church.'

'No, it happens to be in my bedroom.' (Laughter)

'Can you send for it?'

'Yes, it could be sent for.'

'Pending its arrival, would you please tell us in what part of the Prayer Book you entered the date of Lord Colin's adultery with Amelia Watson?'

'I always read the Psalms in the morning. (Laughter) It was on the 17th day of the month, and so I put a line under "17" and another under the "M" in Morning Prayer.'

'What does that mean?'

'It means "the 17th, Mary W." I remembered that it was in the month of June. It was the day I was afraid of forgetting.'

'Your entry in the Prayer Book consists simply of a line under "17" and a line under "M"?'

'Yes, that is sufficient for me.'

The Prayer Book arrived on the day after Lady Miles's cross-examination. It produced this outburst from Finlay:

'Gentlemen of the jury,' he said holding the book in his hands, 'this appears, from its inscription to be a gift from Lady Miles to her daughter Violet, who died in April 1883. Lady Miles says she was in the habit of reading the Psalms in the morning, a very good thing for neighbours in the West Country, and she had no book for making a memorandum of an act of adultery so convenient as her Prayer Book. But it was her daughter's Prayer Book. It bears the inscription, 'To my daughter from her loving mother, June 1876.' Her daughter was still alive, and she made a memorandum of an act of adultery in her daughter's Prayer Book. Did you ever hear such a thing! Was she in the habit of illustrating her Prayer Book with breaches of the commandments? All we have here are two crosses, which I do not hesitate to say were made for the purposes of this case. Just fancy the state of mind of a woman who could read the Psalms every morning and make a memorandum which would call to her mind every time she read the 107th Psalm an act of adultery. Can you conceive a more revolting compound of virtue and depravity than that?'

The principal party to the alleged act, Amelia Watson, gave Lockwood her recollections of the evening of 17 June, 1882:

'Is it true that you brought up a linseed poultice to Lord Colin's room when Lady Miles was there?'

'No, it is not true.'

'Were you insolent to Lady Miles?'

'Lady Miles spoke most pleasantly to me, so why should I be insolent to her?'

[92]

'Well,' Judge Butt asked, '*were* you insolent to her?'

'Never.'

'Did you prepare any poultices for Lord Colin?' Lockwood asked.

'Yes, I prepared three that evening.'

'Was Lady Miles there when the poultices were taken up?'

'No.'

'Are you sure?'

'Perfectly certain.'

'And you took up three poultices?'

'Yes.'

'Why did you take them up?'

'The butler [James O'Neill] was out. Had he been in, he would have taken them.'

'Had Lord Colin complained of pain?'

'Lady Miles said so, but he looked well to me. She said, "Lord Colin must have a linseed poultice."'

'What did you do?'

'I went to make the poultice as fast as I could.'

'What did you do with the poultice?'

'I put it on the bed.'

'Then you took up another?'

'Yes, the first was too large.'

'And then you took up a third?'

'Yes, the second was hard.'

'Was this done before dinner?'

'Yes.'

'Did you ever sit on Lord Colin's knee?'

'It is absolutely untrue.'

'Did any familiar intercourse ever take place between you and him?'

'Never in the least.'

'Did Lord Colin ever take your hair down and play with it?'

'Never.'

'Did he ever ask you to take it down?'

'No.'

Judge Butt asked, 'Nothing of the sort?'

'Nothing of the sort. He was most distant in his manner to his servants.'

Lord Colin denied that there had been any familiarity between him and his housemaid, and Watson received a character reference in Rose Baer's pre-trial declaration: 'Mary Watson attended to the nurse's orders and took up into Lord Colin's room what she was ordered to take. I do not believe she ever saw or spoke to Lord Colin or went to his bedroom except in the course of these duties. I consider Mary Watson quite a respectable girl who would hardly look at a man.'

Watson's most important testimonial came from two medical men. First, Clement Godson, consulting physician to the City of London Lying-in Hospital and assistant physician-accoucheur at St Bartholomew's Hospital, unloosed a thunderbolt.

'This morning,' Lockwood asked him, 'did you examine Amelia Watson?'

'I did.'

'Did you examine her along with Dr Gibbons?'

'Yes.'

'Did you examine her in order to come to an opinion on whether or not she is *virgo intacta* [a pure virgin]?'

'I did.'

'Are you of the opinion that she is *virgo intacta?*'

'Yes.'

'Do you have any doubt about this?'

'None whatever.'

Dr Gibbons confirmed Dr Godson's testimony.

The woman upon whom Lady Colin's case depended was declared by two examining physicians to be unquestionably a virgin!

'Was this charge brought against Lord Colin by conspiracy with Lady Colin?' Finlay thundered. 'Was it concocted by these cousins and intimate friends? I do not know what idea of female virtue prevails in the circles in which they move, but I do know that to a respectable servant girl her character is the breath of life. Without an unspotted character, she could have no chance of employment out of a brothel. And yet these women, to injure Lord Colin, entered into a conspiracy to ruin her fair name. Is not that scandalous and outrageous?

'The charge against Lord Colin has been pulverized. Nothing is left of it but the ruined reputations of Lady Miles and Lady Colin.'

CHAPTER 24

Rose Baer's Departure

If not sexual misconduct, perhaps Amelia Watson might be charged with impertinence. She denied it, but if she had been insolent to Lady Miles, hardly anyone in London society would have been surprised. In the seventies and eighties, magazines and newspapers constantly published complaints about the insubordination of servants. Typical was this letter to *The Times*: 'Servants as a class have become almost intolerable.... From my own servants I have consistently received insolence, ingratitude, and indifferent service.' Not everyone placed all blame on the servants. In 1880, *Tinsley's Magazine* editorialized, 'Bohemian households of the present day are the ruin of good servants. Impromptu suppers at midnight, cabs to fetch in the small hours, and late breakfasts soon demoralise the best of servants, and they lose all sense of order and discipline.'

One result of the state of affairs was that servants were often dismissed. Lady Colin's first sacking came in mid-1882.

Servants discharged for incompetence, inefficiency, laziness, or for no valid reason, were entitled to a month's wages. Anyone terminated for more serious causes had no claim on compensation. Among grounds for dismissal without severance pay were insulting the master or mistress, insobriety, dishonesty, and disobedience.

It was Rose Baer who had to leave Cadogan Place without an extra month's wages. She was questioned by Searle:

'Did Lady Colin once come home unexpectedly from Leigh Court?'

'Yes.'

'When?'

'On the 4th of June, 1882.'

'On the next morning did Lady Miles come?'

'Yes.'

'Were you then called up into the drawing-room?'

'Yes.'

'Who was there?'

'Lady Colin and Lady Miles.'

'Tell me what passed.'

'Lady Miles said I had blackened her ladyship's character and I must leave at once. She said if I did not go she would send for a policeman.'

'Did Lady Miles tell you where to go?'

'No. She said she did not care what became of me.'

'Did you ask for any further reason for your dismissal?'

'No, I did not.'

'Was anything given to you for expenses or wages?'

'Yes, Lady Colin gave me £10.'

The Judge asked, 'Was that for wages due you?'

'Some of it was.'

'How much?'

'About three or four pounds.'

'Were you,' Searle asked, 'to tell the other servants anything as to your leaving?'

'Yes. I was to say my father was sick and I was to go to him.'

Judge Butt asked, 'Who told you to say that?'

'Lady Colin.'

'Where were you to go?'

'To Switzerland.'

'Was your father living in Switzerland?'

'Yes.'

Resuming, Searle asked, 'Did Lady Colin say anything further before you left?'

'Yes, she said she had always regarded me as a sister, not as a servant, and she kissed me twice.'

'Did she say anything about Lord Colin?'

'Yes, she said it was his lordship who was sending me away.'

'Did you go to Switzerland?'

'Yes, I left at six o'clock that evening.'

Cross-examining, Russell suggested that the dismissal had occurred on 17 July, and that Lady Colin had said the sacking was due to Baer's gossiping about Lord Colin's illness. Baer insisted that she had gone in June, and she denied that Lord Colin's illness had been mentioned.

James O'Neill, examined by Lockwood, provided more details:

'Do you remember Lady Colin going away for a visit and leaving Rose Baer in Cadogan Place?'

'Yes.'

'How long was Lady Colin away?'

'I should say less than a week.'

'When she returned had you a conversation with her about Rose Baer?'

'Yes.'

'What did you say?'

'I told her that Rose Baer had said that Lady Colin had slept with Lord Blandford in Leigh Court.'

'What did Lady Colin say?'

'Do you want to know her ladyship's answer?'

'Yes.'

'Her ladyship said it was a "d - - - lie." ' (Laughter, with Lady Colin smiling)

All reports of the trial gave O'Neill's response as 'd - - - lie.' No one filled in the blanks.

Lady Colin gave Inderwick her version of Baer's departure:

'What day did you send Rose Baer away?'

'July 17, 1882.'

'You have not the smallest doubt about that?'

'Not the least.'

'It has been stated that you came up from Leigh Court and on the same day sent away Rose Baer. Is that true?'

'It is absolutely false.'

'In July of 1882 had you gone to Leigh Court with your mother.'

'Yes, my mother had been ill, and with the permission of Lady Miles I took her there for a few days.'

'Did you come up from Leigh Court on July 10?'

'Yes. We were there from the 5th to the 10th.'

'Did your mother come up with you?'

'Yes. She was worse in Leigh Court than in London, and on that account we returned.'

Lady Colin looked into her diary and verified the dates she had given.

'While you were at Leigh Court,' Inderwick asked, 'had you received any communication from your husband in reference to Rose Baer?'

'Yes.'

'Have you the letter?'

'No.'

'What was its substance?'

'He said that he would insist on my sending away Rose Baer as she had been gossiping in the most unpleasant fashion about him.'

'Did you answer the letter?'

'No. As I was coming to London, I waited to talk it over with him.'

'Did he mention the matter in London?'

[97]

'Yes, he said the same thing, that the girl had been gossiping. He was extremely angry and said I must send her away.'

'What did you say?'

'I said that Rose Baer was a good maid, and I thought he made too much of this thing, but I would send her away.'

'You gave her notice?'

'A month's notice.'

'Did you put an advertisement in the *Morning Post* on her behalf?'

'I did.'

'That was on July 15?'

'Yes.'

The following advertisement was read in court: 'A Lady wishes to recommend her maid; Swiss Protestant; first-rate dressmaker and hair dresser; speaks English, French, and German; no objection to travel. G. C., Bolton's Library, Knightsbridge.'

Lady Colin said, 'I gave the advertisement to Bolton's Library and told them to insert it.'

Bolton's was not a library in the usual sense of the term. It was an agency which performed a variety of services, including the booking of theatrical and concert tickets.

London's *Morning Post*, like its competitors, covered local, national, and international news, but it was best known as *the* fashionable journal of the *Beau Monde*, read by everybody in high society. Thus it was only natural for Lady Colin to place her advertisement in the *Post*.

Inderwick asked, 'Did the girl know of your inserting the advertisement on her behalf?'

'Certainly, and she was very grateful for it.'

'Did Lord Colin see the advertisement?'

'No, but I mentioned it to him.'

'What did he say?'

'He was very angry and said I had no right to put a girl like that in anybody's home.'

'Did he say anything further?'

'He said that I did not seem to consider about her gossip concerning him, but he believed I should consider it very much that the girl had been gossiping about my last visit to Leigh Court. I said, "What did she say?" He replied, "Ask the servants." '

'What did you then do?'

'I asked Mrs Bristowe, the housemaid, and the cook.'

'What did you learn from them?'

'Nothing except that Rose Baer was an ill-tongued woman. They did not go into details.'

'On the following day did you speak to O'Neill?'

'Yes.'

'Tell us about it.'

'I saw him in the dining room after breakfast and said, "I hear that Rose Baer has been gossiping in the kitchen. I insist upon knowing what she has been saying." He said, "Oh, my lady, she has said the most horrible things about his lordship's illness – things I could not possibly repeat." I said, "I do not ask you to repeat anything about his lordship's illness. I want to know what she has said about me." He made a great many excuses and said she was a most evil-tongued girl. I said, "I am not going to be put off like that. I want to know distinctly what she said about me." He replied, "Since your ladyship presses me so hard, I must tell you that she said that during your visit to Leigh Court, Lord Blandford used to go to your room."'

'What did you say in reply to this?'

'I said, "Are you quite sure that she said this?" He said, 'I am quite sure." Then I said, "Tell the girl to come to me."'

The Judge asked, 'Did you say, "It's a d--- lie"?'

'(Smiling) Certainly not, my Lord.'

'You sent for the girl?' Inderwick asked.

'Yes, into the drawing room.'

'Was Lady Miles there?'

'Yes.'

'Tell us what took place.'

'I taxed the girl with what she had said. She denied it, and I said I did not believe her.'

'What did you say further?'

'I said, "Have you been saying that Lord Blandford used to come to my room?" She denied it, and I said, "I do not believe you." She then began to cry and said she was very wicked. I said, "You know what a lie it is."'

The Judge asked, 'Was this in English or French?'

'In French.'

Inderwick asked, 'Did she say anything else?'

'She begged to be forgiven.'

'What did you say?'

'I said, "So far from forgiving you I shall withdraw the advertisement. I will not give you a character, and you shall leave the house this very day." But, as she had acknowledged telling the falsehood I said I would send her back to her friends. She was not fixed to go to another place, and I did not want her to go out on the streets of London.'

'Did you send her away that day?'
'Yes.'
'What did you pay her?'
A book was produced, which Lady Colin consulted.
'I paid her on July 17, £3 7s. 6d. and £2 5s. 0d.'
'Did you also pay her passage to Switzerland?'
'Yes.'
'Did you pay it yourself?'
'Yes. I told James O'Neill to take the girl to the station [Liverpool Street] and to see her off. I gave him money for that purpose.'

As we have seen, the date on which Baer went to Liverpool Street Station was a matter of dispute. She said it was June 4; Lady Colin said it was July 17. O'Neill said, "I think it was in June, but I can't fix the day." Baer and O'Neill, moreover, agreed that the dismissal had occurred on the day of Lady Colin's return from Leigh Court. Lady Colin, however, said that Baer left a week after she had come from Bristol. During that week, she said, to help Baer, she inserted an advertisement in the *Morning Post*, and, she added, Rose Baer and Lord Colin knew about it.

Russell questioned Baer on the advertisement:
'Did you not know that Lady Colin had advertised in the *Morning Post* for a place for you a few days before you were dismissed?'
'No.'
'Did she ever tell you that?'
'No.'
'I believe you are a Swiss Protestant?'
'Yes.'
'And you speak English, French, and German, and have no objection to travelling?'
'Yes.'
'Lady Colin never told you that she had tried to set a situation for you?'
'No.'

Russell also questioned Lord Colin on this matter:
'Did your wife say that she had given Rose Baer her notice and had advertised for a situation for her?'
'No. The subject was never discussed between us. I never heard of any advertisement.'

The Morning Post for 15 July, 1882, the issue in question, contained the usual assortment of advertisements pertaining to domestic servants. Here is a sampling of them:
'Can any lady recommend a really good French or Swiss maid? Must be a first-rate dressmaker and thoroughly understand all her duties.'

'Can any Lady recommend a thoroughly respectable young French girl, speaking good French as Lady's Maid to one Lady? She must be a good dressmaker and needlewoman, and willing to make herself useful.'

'Lady's Maid wanted by a Lady; must be young and willing to make herself useful; good plain needlewoman; a dressmaker indispensable.'

'Lady's Maid wanted for one Lady. Very good hairdresser, dressmaker, and unexceptional character required.'

Then came this notice:

'A Lady wishes to recommend her maid; Swiss Protestant; first-rate dressmaker and hairdresser; speaks English, French, and German; no objection to travel. G. C., Bolton's Library, Knightsbridge.'

CHAPTER 25

A Late Night Guest

In the same month that Rose Baer left Cadogan Place, Lady Blandford filed a petition for divorce. She charged her husband with adultery, desertion, and cruelty, and alleged, among other things, that he had struck her during pregnancy. Lord Blandford did not answer the petition, and Lady Blandford moved out of their home.

A few days after Lady Blandford's departure, Lady Colin may have visited her husband in Cadogan Square. Evidence on this was given by James Wilson, for nine years the coachman for Argyll's third son, Lord Walter Campbell, a stockbroker. Wilson was questioned by Searle:

'Do you remember driving Lord and Lady Colin to the House of Commons?'

'Yes, it was in July 1882.'

'When you got there, did Lord Colin get out?'

'Yes.'

'Did he say anything to Lady Colin?'

'He asked her to drive to Farlow's in the Strand [a fishing equipment shop], to fetch some fishing tackle, and to return for him.'

'You drove through Parliament Street?'

'Yes.'

'As you were driving, did Lady Colin speak to you?'
'Yes.'
'What did she say?'
'She said, "I want you to drive me to 46 Cadogan Square."'
'Did you drive her there?'
'Yes.'
'Did she go in?'
'Yes.'
'How long did she remain?'
'Half-an-hour or three-quarters.'
'Did you then take her back to the House of Commons?'
'Yes.'
'Where you picked up Lord Colin?'
'Yes.'

Inderwick asked Lady Colin about this coach ride:
'Lord Walter's coachman said that he drove you to Cadogan Square, where you remained for some time with Lord Blandford. Is that true?'
'No.'
'Did you ever have Lord Walter's carriage?'
'Yes, I think in the middle of May, 1882.'
'Do you recollect where you went on that occasion?'
'Yes. We went from Cadogan Place to call on the Blandfords.'
'You and Lord Colin?'
'Yes, we were together.'
'Was this the only time that you used Lord Walter's carriage?'
'Yes.'

After Lady Blandford had moved out, Lady Colin could easily see Lord Blandford at his home, but he may have continued to visit 79 Cadogan Place.

Rose Baer was asked by Searle about an event which, she said, took place after the launching of the *Invicta*:
'When Lady Colin came home at night did anybody ever come home with her?'
'Yes.'
'How often?'
'I remember two occasions.'
'On the first occasion who came?'
'Lord Blandford.'
'What time did they come home?'
'Between two and three o'clock in the morning.'
'Where did they go?'

'The dining room.'

'Was there supper?'

'Yes, supper was laid for them.'

'How long did Lord Blandford remain?'

'I don't remember exactly.'

'Who came with Lady Colin on the other occasion?'

'I do not know who it was.'

'What time was it?'

'It was earlier, directly after twelve.'

'Was it a gentleman?'

'Oh, yes, it was a gentleman.'

'But,' the Judge interjected, 'you could not see him, so how did you know?'

'I could hear his voice.'

Searle asked, 'Had they come up when you heard his voice?'

'Yes, they were in the dining room.'

'Was supper laid?'

'It was.'

'Can you tell me how long the man stayed?'

'No.'

Webster's cross-examination of Rose Baer helps to fill out her portrait:

'When you say Lord Blandford came home one night to supper, was supper laid before they came?'

'Yes.'

'Did Lady Colin open the door with a latch-key and let herself in?'

'Yes.'

From the well of the court came a distinct 'Never!'

'Did you,' Webster asked, 'look over the banisters on that occasion?'

'Yes.'

'Why?'

'Because I wished to know who was coming in.'

'Where did you see from?'

'From the stairs.'

'Could you see to the drawing-room floor?'

'You could if you went further down.'

'And you went further down?'

'Yes.'

'What was your object in spying?'

'I wanted to know who had come in.'

One other witness reported on Lady Colin's nocturnal entertaining, James O'Neill, questioned by Lockwood:

'Do you remember going to a servants' ball?'

'Yes, at a dancing academy in College Street, Brompton Road.'

These affairs had become quite common. On 15 January 1880 *Truth* reported, 'Of tenants' and servants' balls there are no end.'

'What time did you get back?' Lockwood asked.

'About half-past two in the morning.'

'You slept on the premises?'

'Yes.'

'Where was your bedroom?'

'At the end of the front hall.'

'After you had come in, do you remember anything happening at the front door?'

'Yes.'

'What happened?'

'I came in at the back door, and just as I entered my room I heard a key in the front door. I could see from my room to the hall door. My room door was ajar, and I just looked.'

'What did you see?'

'I saw her ladyship come in with a gentleman, shut the door quietly and walk up the stairs.'

'Did you see who the gentleman was?'

'To the best of my knowledge it was Lord Blandford, so far as I could see of his stature.'

'Where did they go?'

'Upstairs.'

'How did they go up?'

'Lady Colin first and the gentleman afterwards.'

'Did they make any noise as they went up?'

'No.'

'Could you tell which way they went, or did they go in such a manner as to prevent your hearing?'

'They made no noise. My impression was that they went to the drawing-room, but I could not swear to that.'

'How long did they remain?'

'About thirty minutes.'

'Did they then come down?'

'Yes.'

'What happened next?'

'Her ladyship let the gentleman out.'

'Did you notice how she shut the door?'

'She shut it easily so as to make no noise.'

'Do you remember whether Lord Colin was at home?'

'Yes, he was upstairs, sleeping on the floor just over the drawing-room.'

'When did this incident take place?'

'In June or July 1882.'

Russell asked O'Neill about the illumination in the house:

'Was the gas lighted in the hall?'

'No.'

'Was there any light in the hall,?'

'No.'

'Was there any light on the stairs?'

'No.'

'Was there a light on the drawing-room landing?'

'As far as I could see, there was not.'

'Then how can you undertake to say that you could see anything?'

'There was a gas-lamp in the street near the hall door.'

At this time, when the streets were not yet wired for electricity, lamp lighters still kindled the street lanterns every evening at dusk. One of the lanterns was directly opposite the front door at 79 Cadogan Place.

Lady Colin emphatically denied that she had ever brought Lord Blandford home for supper.

'Do you remember,' Inderwick asked her, 'any occasion on which a gentleman came in for supper?'

'Once an uncle of Lord Colin's drove back with me from a small dinner party at which we had both been.'

'When did this happen?'

'In the early part of 1882.'

'Who was it?'

'Lord Ronald Gower.'

'Did your husband know he was in the house?'

'I left him in the drawing-room and went up and told Lord Colin that his uncle was there.'

The advocates for Lady Colin and Lord Blandford insisted that O'Neill's testimony was preposterous. The Attorney-General said, 'If they had been out together for an improper purpose, is it not extraordinary that they should come home to a small house, with Lord Colin and his nurse at home? If this wicked and horrible affair had taken place, would they not have found a less risky means of satisfying their lust?' Russell said that, 'in this small, circumscribed house it would have been impossible for a single act of wickedness to have gone on without almost everyone under the roof being aware of it.'

[105]

Finlay, however, said, 'It is perfectly manifest that O'Neill is speaking the truth. He says the hall lamp was not burning, so he could not see clearly, but light came in at the open door from a street lamp. Now, depend on it, if that lamp was not in the position he describes, we should have heard of it from the other side. If O'Neill was a villain and invented this story, would he have said the hall lamp was out? If he was a miscreant, why did he not say that the gas in the hall was burning brightly, and that he could see distinctly and had not the slightest doubt it was Lord Blandford?'

CHAPTER 26

Peeping Through a Keyhole

Lady Colin's supposed night-time tryst with Lord Blandford was alleged to have been followed by an event which, Russell said, 'has not, in the experience of my Lord or my learned friends ever been rivalled.' The details came out during Lockwood's examination of O'Neill:

'Do you remember Captain Shaw coming to the house in July 1882?'

'Yes.'

'What time of the day was it?'

'About five o'clock.'

'What happened?'

'The bell was rung, and I answered the door.'

'Who was it?'

'Captain Shaw.'

In a few days he would leave for a lengthy visit to the United States.

'What did Captain Shaw say?' Lockwood asked.

'He asked if her ladyship was in. I said her ladyship was not in, but that his lordship was in. He said, "I will call again." '

'Then what happened?'

'He was about to go away when her ladyship came up in a cab. She brought Captain Shaw back and pushed him into the dining-room.'

'What do you mean by that?'

'She put her hand on his shoulder and put him in before her.'

'What did you do?'

'I shut the front door.'

'Then what did you do?'

'I went to the end of the hall and was about to go downstairs when the dining-room door opened. Her ladyship beckoned with her finger. She said if his lordship asked for her I was to say she had gone out.'

'What did you do after that?'

'I shut the door and went downstairs.'

'Did you hear anything?'

'Yes, a noise in the dining-room.'

'Were there other servants downstairs?'

'Yes, the cook was in the kitchen.'

'Was there a conversation between you and the cook?'

'Yes.'

'Did you then go upstairs?'

'Yes.'

'What did you do?'

'I went to the dining-room and looked through the keyhole.'

'What did you see?'

'I saw Lady Colin lying down with Captain Shaw on the carpet.'

'How long were you at the keyhole?'

'A few moments.'

'Did you see Lady Colin's face and head?'

'Yes.'

'And her feet?'

'No, I could not see them. They were towards the door.'

'Did you see her bust?'

'I certainly saw more than that.'

O'Neill then provided graphic details of Lady Colin's position, but no newspaper quoted his testimony. Even sensationalist papers like the *Evening News* and the *Evening Standard* said that the material was 'unfit for publication.'

'What did you see of Captain Shaw?' O'Neill was asked.

'He was over her, and I saw his head and body.'

'How low down?'

'To the waist.'

'After you had watched for a few moments, did you then go downstairs?'

'Yes.'

'Did you subsequently hear anyone go out?'

'Yes, Captain Shaw.'

'How long after your return downstairs was it?'

'Five or ten minutes.'

'Where were you when he went out?'

'I was looking from the kitchen window.'

'You saw him?'

'Yes, I could see him as he came down the bottom of the doorsteps.'

Captain Shaw, unsurprisingly, said that there was 'not a particle of truth' in O'Neill's story, that it was 'absolutely untrue from beginning to end.'

Lady Colin was equally categorical in her denial of what had been alleged by O'Neill.

Then there was Russell's cross-examination of O'Neill:

'Was your keyhole performance the first time you had ever gone through something of that kind?'

'Yes.'

'And the last?'

'Yes.'

'You are sure you are not drawing upon some recollection of an American brothel?'

'No, sir.'

'Would you mind going through that story again? (A pause) Just once more, please?'

'What story is that?'

'You know which. Tell the story again.'

'Ask me any question, and I will answer.'

'(Sternly) Go on, sir.'

O'Neill repeated the story of what he said he had seen at the keyhole.

'Lord Colin was upstairs in the drawing-room?' Russell asked.

'To the best of my knowledge he was.'

'Was your attention called by the cook to a noise in the room over the kitchen?'

'Yes.'

'A noise that could be heard very easily?'

'Yes, through the low ceiling. It is easier to hear a noise in an old house like that than in a new house.' (In 1882, the house was nearly sixty years old.)

'What was the noise like?'

'It was a sort of dull noise like somebody falling or something falling.'

'Thereupon your suspicions were aroused, and, after speaking with the cook, you went upstairs?'

'Yes.'

'Were you very much disgusted with Lady Colin's behaviour?'

'I was not exactly disgusted, but I knew his lordship had been "done wrong by."'

'Did you think she was acting in a shocking way towards her husband?'

'Yes.'

'Did you think it right to give him no information about it?'

'I was not in a position to give him any information.'

'Why?'

'As far as my living was concerned, I could not do it.'

'Why not?'

'If I had said anything, I might never have got another place in this city.'

'How did it come that you did not tell the cook anything when you went back down?'

'She had made a coarse remark, and as she was a peculiar sort of girl, I did not wish her to know about it. I told her when I went up that I was going up about some furniture.'

At this time the cook was Annie Brown, who had succeeded Annie Morrell on 17 July 1882, a few days before Shaw left for America. Annie Brown was questioned by Russell:

'Did James O'Neill at any time call your attention to a suspicious noise occurring overhead in the dining-room?'

'No.'

'Did you ever call his attention to anything of the kind?'

'No.'

'Did you ever hear any kind of noise upstairs that excited your suspicions about your mistress?'

'No, sir.'

A crucial question in this incident was that of whether or not it was actually possible to see through the dining-room keyhole. Russell asked O'Neill about this:

'Is it not a fact that if there is no key in the keyhole, on each side of the door a brass covering falls down?'

'I guess you know. I don't.'

'I am asking you, sir. Don't answer me in that way. Is there not a brass covering.'

'I don't remember.'

'Do you not know that if there is no key in the door the coverings fall down on both sides of the door?'

'In all probability they would.'

'And don't you know that it is the pressure of the key that keeps the covering up?'

'Certainly, I am alive to that fact.'

'And if the key is in one side of the door, the covering will fall down on the other side?'

'Yes.'

'Do you persist in swearing that you could see through the keyhole?'

'Not that I could, but that I did.'

Now Lady Colin's brother became a participant. His name was Neptune Blood. Slightly older than Gertrude, he was dark haired, black eyed, thin faced, thick browed, and bushy moustached. He looked a little ferocious, even intimidating. He was questioned by Russell:

'Since the question arose about O'Neill's evidence, did you go to look at the door of the dining-room at 79 Cadogan Place?'

'Yes.'

To do this, Blood had to get permission from the residents, who, obviously, were no longer the Campbells.

'When did you go?'

'Right after O'Neill gave his evidence.'

'How is the door fastened?'

'There is a brass fingerplate and brass handles and heavy brass drops over the keyhole.'

'On one side of the door or both?'

'Both.'

'Was there a key in the door?'

'Yes.'

'Was it on the inside or outside of the door?'

'To the best of my recollection, it was on the inside.'

'Assuming the key to be on the inside of the door, does the drop on the other side fall down over the keyhole?'

'Yes.'

'And if on the outside, the drop on the inside falls down?'

'Yes.'

'When the brass drops fall down, it is impossible to see through the keyhole?'

'That is correct. It is impossible to see through the keyhole.'

O'Neill's evidence would seem to have been destroyed. But this was not the last word on the subject. Members of the jury asked to see for themselves. After gaining permission from Judge Butt and the residents of 79 Cadogan Place, they took the unprecedented step of visiting the house and looking through the now-celebrated keyhole.

Judge Butt, who lived at 29 Cadogan Place, on the exclusive eastern side, was convinced of what the jurors would find.

After the jury had returned to the courtroom, the foreman said, 'We have been to the house at Cadogan Place, and what we have seen throws a good deal of discredit on the evidence of one of the witnesses.'

'Of course,' Judge Butt said, 'you mean O'Neill.'

The foreman said, 'No.'

The Judge was dumbfounded. After a few seconds of stunned silence, he asked the foreman to deliver his report.

The foreman rose and said, 'We find the escutcheons of the keyhole are very stiff and will stay up at right angles, and we found it impossible to put the outside escutcheons in a perpendicular position at all. One of our members is an architect, and if your Lordship considers it well, you can put him in the box.' (Loud laughter)

Judge Butt said, 'Oh, no, that would be entirely out of the question.'

The foreman's remarks ended in merriment, but he had made his point. As is often true of older houses, the escutcheons were upright. In the words of the *Morning News*, 'the aperture in question was not that absolute bar to curiosity that Sir Charles would have had the court believe.'

CHAPTER 27

A Weekend to Remember

The most distinctive British bird is the red grouse, found in Yorkshire and on the Scottish moors. In the 1880s, more than 500,000 grouse reached the London markets during the season, from 12 August to 10 December. The start of the season for grouse hunting, then as now, was welcomed by all sportsmen on the 'The Glorious Twelfth'. In 1882, the 'Southrons,' those who went up to hunt, included Lord Colin Campbell, on the only grouse-hunting trip of his married life.

Coastal steamers travelled from London to English, Scottish, and Irish ports, and on Thursday, 10 August, Lord Colin left by steamer for Scotland. Asked what his wife had planned to do while he was away, he said, 'She told me that she would stay at home in order to draw. She was making a little painting for the drawing-room.'

Lady Colin said, 'I did not go with him because my health was not good enough for the journey.'

'Do you remember,' Lockwood asked James O'Neill, 'Lord Colin going away to hunt grouse?'

'Yes.'

'While he was gone, do you remember Lady Colin going away for a short time?'

'Yes.'

'What day of the week did she go?'

'Saturday.'

'On what day did she return?'

'On the following Monday.'

'Do you remember any grouse being sent to Cadogan Place?'

'When did they arrive?'

'On a Monday morning.'

'Was that the same Monday that Lady Colin came back after leaving on Saturday?'

'Yes.'

O'Neill was strongly cross-examined by Russell on one aspect of his evidence:

'Do you remember Lady Colin coming down in the kitchen when the grouse arrived and taking some sprigs of heather?'

'I did not see her do so.'

'Do you know if she was there when the grouse arrived?'

'I don't know.'

'Was not the grouse delivered on Sunday, August 13?'

'To the best of my knowledge it arrived on a Monday.'

'I put it to you, did it not arrive on a Sunday, which was rather exceptional?'

'To the best of my knowledge it was a Monday.'

Amelia Watson agreed that the grouse had arrived on Monday, and on other points her testimony tallied with O'Neill's.

If, as they said, Lady Colin left London on Saturday, 12 August 1882, where might she have gone? Perhaps to a railway terminal? Possibly to Fenchurch Street Station?

In the City, immediately north of Tower Hill, is London's third oldest station and until the end of the century one of the busiest, Fenchurch Street. Several lines used it as the starting point for trips to places on the Thames below London and to other localities in the eastern rail district. Fenchurch Street was and is London's smallest station. This plain rectangular building with a flat, arched roof has one entrance hall and one small waiting room. Anyone in the room can see any other person who is there.

Among those in this waiting room on the afternoon of Saturday, 12 August 1882 were the Hon. Mark Bouverie and the Hon. Robert Villiers. ('Hon.' then referred to younger sons of earls, children of viscounts and baronets, certain public officer holders, and members of some legislative bodies. It is not clear why Bouverie and Villiers were addressed as 'Hon.') They were going to the ancient town of Gray's Thurrock, commonly called Gray's.

Bouverie was questioned by Finlay:

'At what time did you leave Fenchurch Street Station?'

'About a quarter to five.'

'Did you see anyone there you thought you knew?'

'Yes, a lady.'

'Who did you think she was?'

'Lady Colin Campbell.'

'What was she doing?'

'Sitting in the waiting room reading.'

'That was when you were going to your train?'

'Yes.'

Since Bouverie was a man of unquestionable integrity who had to be subpoenaed to appear at the trial, Russell, cross-examining, could only suggest mistaken identity:

'Could you tell me how she was dressed?'

'No, I could not.'

'Was she in black, brown, or gray?'

'I think it was a dark dress. I can't say more. It is four-and-a-half years ago.'

'Had she a bonnet, or hat, and a veil?'

'I could not say.'

'You did not pay any marked attention to her?'

'No, I tried to get out of her way.' (Laughter)

Because she was presumably on an assignation, Bouverie did not want to cause any embarrassment.

'How long have you known Lady Colin Campbell?' Russell asked.

'We were introduced ten years ago [six years before he allegedly saw her in the station].'

'Where?'

'At Cheltenham, at a ball.'

'Did you dance with her.'

'I don't think so.'

'I should not think you would forget such an incident as that. (Laughter) Have you seen her since?'

'Infrequently at race meetings.'

'How often have you talked to her?'

'Only once, when we first met.'

Since he scarcely knew her, might Bouverie have mistaken another woman for Lady Colin Campbell? Perhaps. But Lady Colin was tall, strikingly beautiful and dark-complexioned. How many tall, strikingly beautiful, dark-complexioned women could Bouverie have met?

The train carrying Bouverie and his friend was one of eleven covering one route of the London, Tilbury, and Southend Railway every weekday. This one left Fenchurch Street at 5.08 and reached Gray's at six o'clock. Gray's was the ninth stop, coming just after Purfleet, where the train arrived at 5.52.

Purfleet is sixteen miles southeast of Fenchurch Street. It is a picturesque hamlet with a small harbour and surrounded by rocky chalk hills with deep caverns. In the nineteenth century it was the site of a government powder magazine, with five storehouses and a barracks for an artillery company, but since 1854, when the railway arrived, it was better known as a resort. Its permanent population was only a few hundred, among whom was William Henry Whitbread, a member of the brewing family which, in the eighties, owned most of the town.

Purfleet has had a history going back to 1066. It was a stopping-place for pilgrims going to Canterbury, and from time to time something newsworthy happened there. In 1874 there was a highly-publicized murder trial. The victim was the five-year-old daughter of an army officer, and the man convicted of the crime and executed was the village schoolmaster. A ballad on the event became well known in London.

Purfleet had, and still has, one hotel, built early in the nineteenth century on a site overlooking the river. It is a white, late Georgian style brick building with a first floor balcony, and in the 1880s it had a garden terrace and a private sandy beach. Originally it was the Bricklayers' Arms Hotel, but after 1872, when the Prince of Wales was a guest, it became the Royal Purfleet Hotel.

In the eighties, the hotel was managed by John F. Wingrove, whose full-time staff included two waiters, a barmaid, a house-keeper, and a chambermaid. There were six guest rooms, all on the second floor. Other facilities attracted numerous non-residents. Its restaurant was noted for whitebait dinners and was often used for banquets, one of which was held on 12 August 1882. This was the menu:

Stewed Eels   Fried fillet
Turbot, and Shrimp Sauce
Whitebait, Plain, Devilled, and Curried

Kromesky's à la Russe
Stewed Kidneys and Mushrooms

Roast Ducklings   Peas
Roast Saddle of Mutton   French Beans

Sweets   Dessert

On weekends, when special dinners were held, a part-time waiter worked at the hotel. He was the only staff member to testify at the trial. His name was Cornelius Callingham, and he was examined by Finlay:

'During the past six years have you waited at tables from Saturday to Monday at the Royal Hotel, Purfleet?'

'Yes.'

'Is there anything that makes you remember the Saturday to Monday, August 12 and 14, 1882?'

'Yes, I remember the 12th of August very well indeed as the head waiter left the hotel on that day.' (Laughter)

'Was there an entertainment at the hotel on August 12?'

'Yes, sir.'

'What was its nature?'

'A Volunteer dinner.' (Laughter)

'Was there a large party of Volunteers?'

'No, only thirty.' (Laughter)

'Did you help wait on the Volunteers?'

'Yes.'

'After the Volunteers had finished, did you attend a lady and a gentleman in a private room?'

'Yes.'

'In what sort of room did you wait on them?'

'A private sitting room.'

The dining room was on the ground floor, and the sitting room was on the first floor.

'How long,' Finlay asked, 'did this lady and gentleman remain in the hotel?'

'From Saturday to Monday.'

'What did you serve them?'

'Some lemon squash.'

'On Saturday?'

'Yes.'

'On Sunday did you attend them at any meal?'

'Yes, at dinner.'

'Did you wait on them with anything after dinner?'

'I remember bringing them more lemons for lemon squash.'

'Do you see the lady in court?'

'Yes, sir.'

'Will you point her out?'

Callingham pointed to Lady Colin.

'Lady Colin Campbell?' Finlay asked.

'Yes.'

'Do you see the gentleman in court?'

Callingham looked over the press gallery. To the accompaniment of laughter, the Judge said, 'You need not look amongst those gentlemen.'

Callingham then gazed at the jury box.

Finlay said, 'You won't find him there.' The jurors joined in the laughter.

The witness looked toward the barristers and beyond. Seeing the Duke of Marlborough, Blandford's title at the time of the trial, he exclaimed, 'That's the gentleman, ain't it?' (Laughter)

Finlay asked Marlborough, 'Do you mind standing up?'

The Duke rose, smiling.

Finlay asked, 'Is that the gentleman you saw with the lady?'

'Yes.'

Since Callingham had no discernible motive for lying, Russell had to show that he might have been mistaken about events in the past:

'This happened four years ago?'

'Yes.'

'Did anything attract your attention to this lady and gentleman?'

'Well, they seemed very high class people.' (Loud laughter)

Judge Butt asked, 'How could you form that opinion?'

'They looked it.' (Laughter)

He might have said, 'They spoke it.' Nothing then established an English person's social class more readily than the manner in which s(he) spoke.

'Can you tell us at what time the lady and gentleman arrived?' Russell asked.

'They were in the hotel when I came, about ten minutes past five.'

As already noted, the train carrying Bouverie, Villiers, and the woman that Bouverie had seen in Fenchurch Street stopped at Purfleet at 5.52.

Russell asked, 'How many people slept in the hotel on that Saturday night?'

'Only two.'

'How do you know that?'

'Only two pairs of boots came down – a lady's and a gentleman's.'

At that time when a hotel guest retired for the night he left his shoes outside his door to be polished.

'Had you ever seen the lady or gentleman before?' Russell asked.

'Not that I know of.'

'Where did you see either of them next?'

'At Thurloe Square on January 8 last.'

'That would be three years and three months after you were supposed to have seen them at Purfleet?'

'Yes.'

'What did you see in Thurloe Square?'

'I saw a lady get out of a cab.'

'Who was with you?'

'Mr Gibbs.'

'Who is Mr Gibbs?'

'He is employed by Mr Humphreys.'

'Is he a detective or a clerk?'

'I could not say.'

Russell asked Finlay, 'Is he a detective or a clerk, Mr Finlay?'

Finlay said, 'He is an inquiry agent.'

Turning back to Callingham, Russell asked, 'Where did you meet Mr Gibbs?'

'At Mr Humphreys's office.'

'Did you go to Mr Humpheys's office to see if you could recognize these people you had seen more than three years earlier?'

'Yes.'

'Were some photographs shown to you?'

'Yes.'

'From the photographs did you recognize the people?'

'I said I believed it was them.'

'But you weren't sure?'

'Not till I saw them.'

'Was it shortly thereafter that you met Mr Gibbs?'

'Yes.'

'What did he tell you?

'He told me to come to Thurloe Square with him.'

'Did you go there with him?'

'Yes.'

'Did you take your stand outside a house in Thurloe Square?'

'Yes.'

'How long did you stay?'

'From eleven in the morning until five minutes past two.'

'Was that when a cab drove up and a lady got out?'

'Yes.'

'Was she fair or dark?'

Callingham started to look toward the solicitors' table.

'Don't look at her, please,' Russell said. 'Was she fair or dark?'

'(After some hesitation) Fair, as near as I could say.'

(Laughter)

'Was the lady you saw at Purfleet fair?'

'Yes, as near as I can say, but I can't be certain.'

'Upon seeing this lady get out of the cab, you think she was fair?'

'Yes.'

'And you thought it was the lady you had seen at Purfleet?'

'Yes.'

In this small hotel, everyone on the staff, including the manager, took an active part in everyday affairs. But none of them appeared as witnesses. Perhaps they could not identify the couple who had been guests on the pertinent weekend. Or perhaps these permanent hotel employees had been trained not to see or remember that which they were not supposed to see or remember.

The couple on whom Callingham had waited departed on the morning of 14 August. At about the same time, four miles up the river, Messrs. Bouverie and Villiers were leaving their hotel. Bouverie was questioned by Finlay:

'When you got to Purfleet Station, did you notice any people on the platform whom you knew?'

'Yes, I saw two people I thought I knew.'

'Who did you think they were.'

'One was Lord Blandford.'

'And the other?'

'Lady Colin Campbell, but I was not sure.'

'But you believed it to be her?'

'Yes.'

In cross-examination, Russell asked, 'When the train came to Purfleet, were a number of people awaiting its arrival?'

'Yes.'

'From the carriage window you saw people when the train ran into the station?'

'Yes.'

'Was that the only opportunity you had of observing the woman on the Monday?'

'Yes.'

'Did you stop at the platform at Fenchurch Street upon arriving?'

'No, I went straight to my office.'

'You did not see her at Fenchurch Street?'

'No.'

'Then you only saw her with a number of other people at Purfleet?'

'Yes.'

Examined by Finlay, Villiers, who did not know Lady Colin, said that he saw Lord Blandford in the Fenchurch Street Station and spoke to him.

Because of Bouverie and Villiers, Blandford could not deny that he had boarded a train in Purfleet, accompanied by a woman. It was his bad luck to select a train that carried two men who knew him. And if the woman in the Fenchurch Street waiting room on the preceding Friday was Lady Colin, it was bad luck doubled.

CHAPTER 28

Lady Colin's Alibi

Bouverie and Villiers made it necessary for Lady Colin to have an alibi for that weekend. It unfolded during Inderwick's examination:

'Lady Colin, what did you do on that Saturday night?'

'I went to the theatre with my friend the Baroness Estellfried. I think it was to see *Patience*.'

Gilbert and Sullivan's *Patience* was first produced at London's Opera Comique Theatre on 23 April 1881. In October of 1881 it was transferred to the newly-constructed Savoy Theatre, built for Gilbert and Sullivan operas. *Patience* satirizes, among others, Oscar Wilde and James

Whistler, both of whom were friends of Lady Colin. Arthur Sullivan was also her friend, and for part of one day during the trial he sat by her side. If Lady Colin saw *Patience* on that evening, it was probably not her first appearance at a performance of this light opera which had opened sixteen months earlier.

'On Sunday morning,' Inderwick asked, 'did you go to church?'

'Yes, to the Carmelite Church with the Baroness Estellfried.'

This was St Mary's Church, built in the late 1870s in Cadogan Terrace, just off Sloane Street. It was an élite church. On 24 June, 1882, Prince Alphonse, Duc d'Avigliano, and Lady Emily Pelham-Clinton, daughter of the Duchess of Newcastle, were married there in a ceremony performed by Cardinal Manning.

'Do you recollect,' Inderwick asked, 'whether you had luncheon at home on that Sunday?'

'I rather think I went round to the house of the Baroness Estellfried.'

'When you returned home, what did you find?'

'I found that some grouse had arrived from Lord Colin.'

'Where did you go in the afternoon?'

'I went to tea with Lady Miles. I took a brace of grouse with me.'

'Where did you go in the evening?'

'I went to my mother's in Thurloe Square. I took some grouse there.'

'Where did you sleep that night?'

'In Cadogan Place.'

'Have you endeavoured to get the Baroness Estellfried to come and give evidence?'

'I have made every endeavour to obtain her for this trial. She is a lady-in-waiting at the Austrian court and cannot get away from her court duties.'

Then, as now, evidence could be taken by deposition from witnesses who could not appear in court. In the Campbell case, depositions were taken from three witnesses.

'Have you ever been to Purfleet?' Inderwick asked.

'Never.'

'Do you know where it is?'

'I have looked it out on a map since the evidence was given about it.'

Really? She had never heard of Purfleet?

During his cross-examination, Lockwood asked a number of questions on that August weekend:

'Were you in the habit of making up a weekly account of your household expenses?'

'Yes.'

LADY COLIN CAMPBELL

The front door of
79 Cadogan Place,
the home of Lord and
Lady Campbell

Cadogan Place today

George Lewis, Lady Colin's
celebrated solicitor

Sir Charles Russell,
leading barrister for
Lady Colin

Robert Finlay, leading
barrister for Lord Colin

Sir Richard Webster,
the Attorney General

The Illustrated Police News, 4 December 1886

POLICE *THE ILLUSTRATED* NEWS
LAW COURTS AND WEEKLY RECORD.
No. 1,191.   SATURDAY, DECEMBER 11, 1886.   Price One Penny.

THE GREAT CAMPBELL DIVORCE CASE.

MARY WATSON GIVING EVIDENCE

THE JURY

IT IS UTTERLY UNTRUE

LADY MILES AND LADY COLIN IN COURT

Dr BIRD

LADY MILES

THE ... CAMPBELL AGAINST LORD COLIN

CAPTAIN SHAW

Mr BLOOD LADY COLIN'S FATHER

Mrs BLOOD LADY COLIN'S MOTHER

Mr FINLAY SPEAKING FOR LORD COLIN

BURNING A MOTHER ALIVE.

SHOCKING EXHIBITION IN FRANCE.

The Illustrated Police News, 11 December 1886

The Penny Illustrated Paper, 4 December 1886

The Illustrated Police News, 18 December 1886

POLICE THE ILLUSTRATED NEWS

LAW COURTS AND WEEKLY RECORD.

No. 1,193.   SATURDAY, DECEMBER 25, 1886.   Price One Penny.

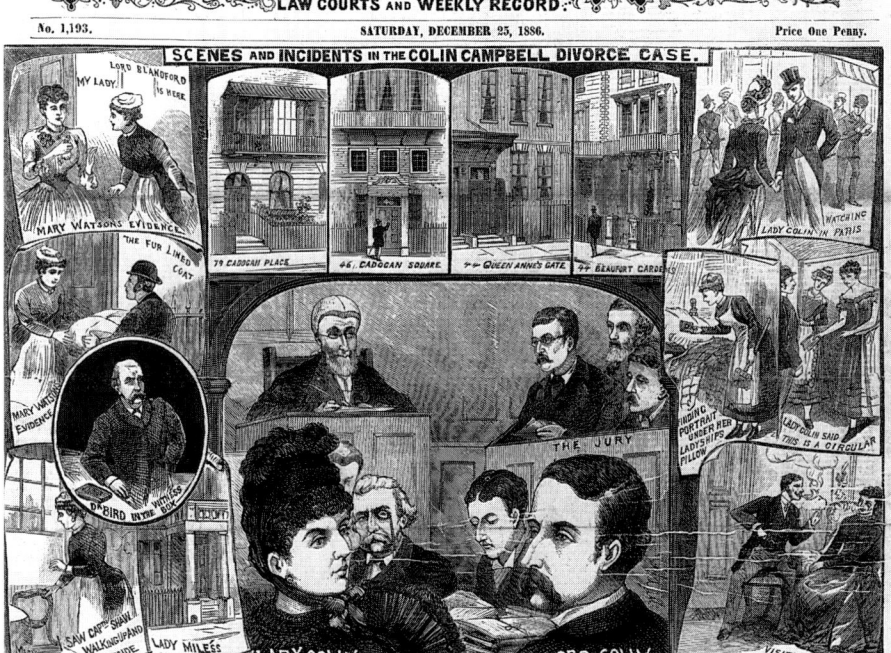

The Illustrated Police News, 25 December 1886

'Were these accounts usually made up on Saturday?'

'I could not tell you.'

'Will you look at these accounts?'

He handed her some papers.

'Yes, I see they were made up on Saturday.'

'I will show you one that was not. There is one for Saturday, August 12, 1882.'

Pointing to the account, Lockwood asked, 'That one was made up on Monday?'

'Yes.'

'You have your diary relating to the Saturday?'

'Yes.'

'What do you see in it?'

'There is one entry relating to my mother's health and another to a theatre.'

'Is there any entry that would suggest an engagement which would prevent your making up your accounts as usual on that day?'

'There is nothing in the book but those two entries.'

'Your entry of August 13, 'Coco's first grouse arrived – Mother slightly better – Dined at T. Square,' exactly fills the space allotted for the day. Did you first write it out on a piece of paper?'

'Certainly not. I knew what I had to write, and I wrote so as to get it in.'

If there was doubt about Lady Colin's whereabouts on that weekend, there were no questions concerning where Lord Colin had been. And indisputably he sent home some grouse.

Two Midland Railway employees, a clerk and a delivery man, said their records showed that a parcel of grouse had arrived on the morning of Sunday, August 13, and was delivered at 79 Cadogan Place later in the morning.

The Campbells's second cook, the recently hired Annie Brown, was questioned by Russell:

'Do you recollect a parcel arriving from Lord Colin in Scotland?'

'Yes.'

'On what day did that parcel come?'

'On a Sunday morning.'

'Was your mistress in the house when it arrived?'

'I don't remember.'

'Did she sleep in the house the night before?'

'Oh, yes.'

'Did she sleep in the house on the Sunday night?'

'Yes.'

'When the parcel arrived, was it brought down to the kitchen?'
'I went up and fetched it myself.'
'What did it contain?'
'Grouse.'
'Do you recollect your mistress coming to the kitchen later?'
'Yes.'
'Do you recollect her expressing surprise at the grouse having arrived?'
'Yes.'

Annie Brown was cross-examined by Finlay, who contended that the grouse had arrived on a Monday:

'I suppose the arrival of grouse is not an uncommon thing in your experience as a cook?'
'No, not very uncommon.'
'There was nothing remarkable about it at the time?'
'No.'
'You did not keep a diary or a notebook and enter this occurrence?'
'No, and I never asked a question nor knew anything.' (Laughter)
'Now this happened more than four years ago. Are you quite sure the grouse did not come on a Monday?'
'I am quite sure it did not.'
'What makes you recollect that it was a Sunday, and not a Monday?'
'I can swear it was a Sunday.'
'That is a lady's reason, Miss Brown. I ask you to give me one circumstance which enables you to fix the date as a Sunday and not a Monday?'
'I am certain it was Sunday.'

In re-examining Annie Brown, Russell pursued this point:

'Do you know that grouse are first legally shot on August 12?'
'Yes.'
'When it was received on Sunday, did it strike you that that was the first day it could be received?'
'Yes.'
'Do you recollect that Lady Colin expressed her surprise at receiving it so early?'
'Yes.'

Another new member of the Campbells' domestic staff was Lady Colin's personal maid Valerie Kautzmann, an Alsatian, who, speaking French, answered Russell through an interpreter:

'Do you recollect a parcel arriving on Sunday, August 13, 1882, and signing the sheet?'
'Yes.'

'Do you remember where Lady Colin was on the day – a Sunday – on which the parcel arrived?'

'I think she was at church, because I recollect that I lent her my Prayer Book.'

'Are you a Catholic?'

'Yes.'

'Did you lend it to Lady Colin because she had no Roman Catholic Prayer Book?'

'Yes.'

In addition to the two servants' testimony, there was much 'family evidence' offered to support Lady Colin's alibi.

The Miles family, who had been in London on that weekend, said that Lady Colin called on them with grouse. Lady Miles recalled her husband's cousin, Frank Miles, remarking that to reach London so early it must have been poached.

Frank Miles, 36, a well-known painter who specialized in female portraits, was questioned by Inderwick:

'How do you know that the Sunday was the thirteenth?'

'Because I made a remark about it. I thought it was curious that grouse should come on a Sunday.'

'I believe you suggested something about a poacher?'

'I believe I did.'

'Why do you recollect this particular day?'

'Because I am seldom in London in August. That was the only Sunday I ever spent in London in August.'

'Are you perfectly certain that you were at Lady Miles's on that Sunday and saw Lady Colin Campbell?'

'I have not the slightest doubt about it.'

Neptune Blood also said that he had 'not the smallest doubt' that on the relevant Sunday he had been with his sister. On that weekend he had been staying with his mother while his wife was out of town. Three letters which he had written to his wife on August 13, 14, and 15 were produced. Each referred to Lady Colin and the grouse. Victorians customarily retained letters with the envelopes in which they had been sent, but Neptune Blood said that he had not kept the envelopes because they would have taken up too much space.

CHAPTER 29

The Duke's Confession

Evidence on the second weekend in August of 1882 was also offered by the other party to the alleged tryst.

In his opening statement, the Attorney-General said, 'The Duke of Marlborough has been in the Regiment of the Blues. Some officers were in the habit of dining at Purfleet, and on this weekend the Duke was there with other officers. He spent Sunday there and came up on Monday morning, but he was never there with a lady.'

These words were delivered before the jury had heard Callingham, Villiers, and Bouverie.

The Duke himself testified after this trio had appeared. He was cross-examined by Finlay:

'Do you remember the Attorney-General saying, "The Duke of Marlborough was never there with a lady"?'

'He did say that. He made that statement on the strength of instructions he had received from my solicitors, confirmed by an interview with myself.'

'Is that true?'

'No.'

'He made the statement upon your instructions?'

'I accept the responsibility.'

'Under what name were you at Purfleet?'

'Mr Perry.'

'Was there a Mrs Perry with you?'

'There was.'

'Who was she?'

'She was a woman about London.'

'A woman of the town?'

'She was a woman whom I had known in town.'

'Do you mean a woman on the town?'

'I mean a woman who has been kept.'

[124]

'To put it in plain language, do you mean a prostitute?'
'No, I don't. I confine myself to what I say.'
'Where does this woman live?'
'Pimlico.' (Laughter, at once suppressed by ushers)
'Can you give me her address?'
'I only know it was Winchester Street.'
'Have you made any endeavour to find out where she is now?'
'No, I have not.'
'When did you last see her?'
'I have not seen her since that summer.'

It was natural for the Duke's revelation of his lady friend's residence in Pimlico to be greeted with laughter. Pimlico was then teeming with prostitutes, most of whom plied their trade on the Vauxhall Bridge Road and lived nearby, some of them on Winchester Street. Prostitution was not legal in London or anywhere else in Britain, but public opinion was lax on the question, and police officers rarely interfered.

As for one particular resident of Pimlico, 'Mrs Perry,' was she a tall, dark, beautiful woman whom Mark Bouverie could twice mistake for Lady Colin Campbell? Were her speech and manners such that Cornelius Callingham would consider her a 'high class' person. These questions cannot be answered because, like the Baroness Estellfried, she remained forever among the missing.

The Duke of Marlborough's turnabout in the witness box was thus explained by his counsel: 'Not until after that the alibi had been satisfactorily proved did the Duke make a confession. He did it because he was not going to perjure himself.'

A somewhat different view of the Duke's behaviour was offered by Finlay:

'Of all the extraordinary scenes which ever happened in a court of justice, I think that which happened here was the most extraordinary. The Duke of Marlborough told the Attorney-General that he had gone down to Purfleet alone. What a melancholy Sunday for the Duke. Spending a lonely day, perhaps with Bacon's essays or Lecky's *History of Rationalism*. (Laughter) When it appeared in print, it was too ridiculous, and so he invented another story.

'The Duke's second story is equally open to objections which are insuperable. He knew it was alleged that he was there with Lady Colin Campbell. If he was there with another woman, why were not efforts made to bring forward her evidence or that of other persons who could prove that she was with him? If she had been a married woman, we could understand that delicacy for her feelings might have prevented him from revealing her name, but with a woman of the kind he suggests such delicacy cannot be imagined.

'Does anyone believe that the Duke of Marlborough is so depraved and lost to every sense of honour that if his story were true he would not have made an effort to prove it? Bad as he is, I do not think him capable of such infamy as not to have made exertions to prove conclusively that the woman was not Lady Colin Campbell. I don't think you will believe him guilty of the incredible baseness of not vindicating the character of an innocent woman if he could.'

CHAPTER 30

Nurse Annie Duffy

On 6 September 1882 the rectal specialist William Allingham again performed an operation on Lord Colin. It took place at Leigh Court.

Lord Colin's nurse reported for duty on the day of the surgery. She was a sallow, forlorn, woe-begone woman with sagging eyes, prominent nose, and an almost total lack of feminity. She had had thirteen years of professional experience. Her name was Annie Duffy.

For a month Lord Colin could not leave his bed. Annie Duffy attended him day and night. During Russell's cross-examination she said, 'I seem to have spent years of my life with Lord and Lady Colin.'

'The mental anxiety, you mean?' Russell asked.

'Yes.'

'Why, when you were in a state of mental torture, did you not go?'

'Mr Allingham asked me to stay until Lord Colin was well. As a nurse I was anxious to see the end of a difficult case.'

One of her difficulties was revealed in Russell's examination of the Miles's housekeeper, Mrs Howe:

'Was Lord Colin always on good terms with his nurse?'

'Not always.'

'What have you seen?'

'I have seen the nurse coming down crying, and I heard her say that Lord Colin had slapped her face.'

Russell asked him about this:

'You quarrelled with Mrs Duffy?'

'No, I cannot say that.'

'Did she not complain of your personal violence?'

'I don't know. I was very irritable at the time.'

'You did use your hands once or twice?'

'I recollect it now.'

Although slapping nurses wasn't common, they weren't usually treated with much respect.

For a long time they had no status at all. Florence Nightingale once said that her vocation involved little more than administering medicines and applying poultices. Not until 1859, when St Thomas's Hospital began to accept probationers, were nurses given any institutional instruction. Almost any woman could call herself a nurse. And some pretty dreadful ones did just that. Dickensians will recall ignorant, drunken, brutal Sairey Gamp, in *Martin Chuzzlewit*, who, her creator said, had been 'drawn from life,' As late as 1867 Nightingale complained that nursing was generally done by those 'too old, too weak, too drunken, too dirty, too stolid, or too bad to do anything else.' They were paid scarcely more than some servants, and in some households they were regarded as just another pair of hands for household duties.

In the late seventies and eighties, thanks largely to Nightingale, conditions began to change, and, along with teaching, nursing came to be recognized as a respectable profession for women. Hospital conditions, however, continued to be unsatisfactory, and in the eighties two-thirds of all nurses worked as Annie Duffy did, in private homes.

Professionally-oriented nurses usually came from what was called 'the governess class' of females, noted for conscientiousness, punctuality, endurance, and love of discipline. They tended to be narrow-minded, humourless, and dull. All of the above applied to Annie Duffy.

Duffy was questioned by Lockwood on Lord Colin's relationship with his wife during his convalescence at Leigh Court:

'Did Lady Colin take much notice of and interest in Lord Colin?'

'(Warmly) None whatever.'

'Did she come into his room in the morning generally?'

'Generally.'

'For how long did she remain?'

'Sometimes five minutes, sometimes ten, sometimes a little longer.'

'Then generally when would she come back to see him?'

'Just before and just after luncheon.'

'Did Lady Colin pass evenings with her husband, reading or conversing with him?'

'No.'

Duffy was cross-examined by Russell:

'You have said very plainly that Lady Colin was not very attentive to Lord Colin?'

'In my idea she was not as attentive as a wife should be. She never relieved me once. It was Lady Miles who did that.'

'She came generally to his room in the morning, again before dinner, before she went out, and after dinner?'

'Yes.'

'You mentioned her not reading to Lord Colin. Did he wish her to read to him?'

'Not that I am aware of.'

'Nothing prevented Lord Colin from reading himself?'

'He used to read himself.'

'Did Lord Colin ever say one word of reproach to Lady Colin?'

'Never. He was always most kind to her.'

'As far as your observation went, did Lord Colin seem to feel that he was neglected?'

'No.'

During her husband's recuperation, Lady Colin had to deal with Rose Baer.

When Baer was discharged, Lady Colin refused to give her a character, without which it was almost impossible for a servant to get another position. A character was an indispensable passport for admission into a good household. For someone like Rose Baer, unsuited for other work, the denial of a character could be disastrous.

In the autumn of 1882, Baer wrote to her former mistress five times about this matter, three times from Switzerland, and after she had returned in October, twice from London.

This is a translation of the third letter, dated 26 September: 'My dear Lady, it appears that my Lady has not received my two letters as I have not received an answer. Since I left you, I have had nothing but misfortune. It has been impossible for me to obtain a place. I have written to Italy, France, Germany, everywhere, but no place. Times are very hard, for strangers have not come to this country as in former years. The only thing that remains for me is to go to Paris directly, where I have friends who will look after me. As my Lady has promised to be useful, and I know her good heart, I hope she will not refuse to send me the necessary money to make the voyage.'

The letter was unanswered.

Baer next wrote from Fulham Road, Chelsea: 'My dear Lady, I was in Paris for eight days looking for a place but was not able to find one. I decided to return to London, where I have a place in view, and I write to pray you, if you would be so indulgent, to help me. My Lady knows I did my duty when I was with her. If evil tongues have driven me out of her house I cannot help it. I would pray you to give me a certificate. I count, my Lady, upon your good heart to further a poor girl's interest.'

A couple of weeks later, Baer wrote again: 'My dear Lady, I have had no answer to my last letter. I hope you will not refuse me a reference. For three-and-a-half months I have been out of a place, and I venture to hope you will have pity upon a poor girl and not cause me to lose a place I have in view. Mrs Powell is coming to take my character. I have pleased her much, and it only depends on you whether I go to her.'

For the fifth time, Lady Colin ignored Rose Baer's plea. And yet less than two weeks later Baer became the personal lady's maid of Mrs Powell, 11 Chesterfield Street, Mayfair, where she remained until early 1885.

Mrs Powell had asked for 'a personal character from a lady,' and she received one. But it wasn't from Lady Colin Campbell. This is from Rose Baer's pre-trial statement: 'I wrote to her Ladyship again, threatening that unless she gave me a character I would expose her. After that, Mrs Bolton, Lady Colin's sister, wrote to me, stating that I was to call on her at Beaufort Gardens, which I did.'

Rose Baer was given a character, and she got the job.

'When you were hired,' Russell asked her, 'what did Mrs Powell tell you?'

'She told me that Mrs Bolton said I had left because I wanted to go home. She also told me that Mrs Bolton gave me a character because Lady Colin was out of town.'

Rose Baer finally obtained a position, but only after undergoing what must have seemed an ordeal of fire. It would appear as if she had excellent reasons for hating her former mistress and for desiring revenge.

CHAPTER 31

Tom Bird

While Rose Baer was begging for a character, another eventual co-respondent in Lord Colin's divorce suit entered the narrative. He was a surgeon who assisted Allingham and then remained at Leigh Court. His name was Tom Bird.

Bird's principal advocate was Britain's second highest legal officer, the Solicitor-General, Sir Edward Clarke, considered by many to be also the nation's second ablest barrister. He was extremely serious, devoid of lightheartedness, and was perhaps the neatest member of the bar, always wearing a carefully-set wig and a gown that fitted closely around the collar. In the next decade he would become renowned for his representation, in all three trials, of Oscar Wilde.

'During your stay at Leigh Court,' Clarke asked Bird, 'did you attend on Lord Colin from day-to-day?'

'From day-to-day.'

'When did you pay your visits to him?'

'Generally after breakfast, between half-past ten and eleven o'clock.'

'What sort of visit did you pay?'

'I dressed him and talked with him for some time.'

'When did you see him again?'

'After luncheon.'

'Apart from attending on Lord Colin, had you any occupation at Leigh Court?'

'None at all.'

Questioned by Lockwood, Annie Duffy offered her views on Tom Bird's activities:

'Did you see Mr Bird and Lady Colin much together at Leigh Court?'

'I did.'

'Did Lady Colin occupy the same bedroom as her husband?'

'No.'

'Did you ever see Mr Bird in Lady Colin's room?'

'I did.'

'More than once?'

'Yes.'

'Do you remember seeing him and Lady Colin on one occasion in the morning room?'

'Yes.'

'She was playing the piano?'

'Yes. He was sitting on a stool quite close to her.'

(Lady Colin was an excellent pianist.)

'Did you ever see Mr Bird and Lady Colin out walking together?'

'I did.'

'Did that happen frequently?'

'Frequently.'

'Do you remember anything in connection with Mr Bird's case of instruments?'

'Yes. The case was left on Lord Colin's bed, and I accidentally knocked it to the floor. In picking up the instruments and replacing them in the case, I noticed a small, very old letter which fell out of one of the pockets of the case. It was in Lady Colin's handwriting and was signed "G. E. B."'

'Did Lady Colin seem to be in good health at Leigh Court?'

'Yes. She seemed to be in robust health.'

'Did she take walks?'

'Yes, long walks with Mr Bird.'

During Russell's cross-examination, Duffy gamely hung on:

'When did you see Mr Bird in Lady Colin's bedroom?'

'I saw him once in the evening before dinner and once afterwards.'

'You have seen Mr Bird go into her bedroom?'

'I did not see him go in, but having occasion to go to Lady Colin's room I saw Mr Bird there.'

'The door being open?'

'I opening [sic] the door.'

'The door being unlocked?'

'All I can say is that I was told to go in, and I went in.'

'Was there any attempt at concealment with reference to Mr Bird's visits to Lady Colin?'

'No.'

'You did not attach much importance to these visits?'

'No.'

'Then nothing occurred at Leigh Court to excite your suspicion of any misconduct on the part of Lady Colin?'

'I think she was more intimate than a lady should be with a doctor who

[131]

was attending her husband. He was always in her society, walking out with her, and in her bedroom.'

'Did she not walk with other visitors to the house?'

'I never saw her walking with others.'

'Did you think there was anything wrong in what you saw?'

'Only what I have told you. Usually doctors don't devote so much of their time to a lady.' (Laughter)

'You thought she was too intimate with Mr Bird?'

'I thought her manner was not a lady's.'

'You formed a very poor estimate of Lady Colin Campbell?'

'I thought her manner very different from that of any lady in any house where I had worked.'

'You did not form a high opinion of her?'

'I cannot say that I did.'

As for the letter that Duffy saw, Bird was asked about it by Clarke:

'Until Mrs Duffy gave her evidence had you any recollection of the letter which she mentioned?'

'None at all.'

'After hearing her evidence, did you open the pockets of the case to see if you could find the letter?'

'Yes.'

'And you found it?'

'Yes.'

Bird produced a letter.

'Read it aloud, please,' Clarke said.

'The date is December 4, 1868. There is a little drawing of holly and ivy, and underneath, the motto "Friendship and Durability." Then follow the words, "My dearest Mary, detestable little animal, many happy returns of the day. Gobble up all the lollipops, if you please, but keep the box. Your humble but not too humble servant, Gertrude Lily Blood."'

'Lady Colin was ten years old when she wrote that?'

'Yes.'

'Do you know who "Mary" was?'

'Yes, Mrs Bolton, her sister. She was about to tear the letter up, and I said, "Don't destroy it. I shall have some fun with it." In that way it came into my hands.'

'Did you ever carry about a letter signed "G. E. B."?'

'Certainly not.'

Bird's explanation might seem to make Duffy look bad. But does it, really? Did she imagine, or lie about the initials 'G. E. B.'? Had Lady Colin's handwriting remained unchanged since she was ten-years-old?

And why was the childhood letter in the case?

Cross-examined by Finlay, Bird was asked about his fondness for walking:

'Did Lady Colin often accompany you on walks at Leigh Court?'

'Yes.'

'And alone?'

'And alone.'

'Did you walk in a wood with her?'

'Yes, but it was in the depth of winter.'

'How long were your walks?'

'Not very long. About an hour.'

'Were you constantly out walking with Lady Colin?'

'Not "Constantly." Perhaps three times a week.'

'Was it not more like three times a day?'

'No.'

The inferences intended to be drawn from these woodland walks elicited this response from the Solicitor-General:

'I don't think you will forget the way in which Mrs Duffy set her thin lips together and began to tell the story which she hoped you would accept as a disgrace to Lady Colin Campbell.

'It is against Mr Bird that her evidence is principally levelled. He was the doctor in charge of the case for which she was engaged as nurse. She had never nursed under him before and did not form a very friendly opinion either of him or of Lady Colin. And so that woman with nothing to do for many long hours sat by Lord Colin's bedside weaving together all the little suggestions of evil she could rake up with regard to Mr Bird and Lady Colin's bedroom.

'From her window she saw Mr Bird and Lady Colin go out for the exercise that was necessary for both, and that was a matter of suspicion. What was Lady Colin to do at a country house where her husband was ill? Was she not to go out for a walk? If she did go, with whom could she more properly go than with Mr Bird, who was in attendance on her husband?'

Finlay, in response, said to the jurors, 'Mrs Duffy is very much like other nurses, and it is for you to say whether she looked like a decent woman or not.'

CHAPTER 32

Tom Bird's Coat

Tom Bird was 38 and looked older. During the trial, when he was 42, he was frequently judged by reporters to be about 50. He was balding, and the hair he had was becoming white. His face was pale, with a heavy gray moustache drooping over his mouth. He was of medium height and rather stout. He looked like the quintessential professional man, the endearing family physician, a slightly younger version of the best known of all Victorian medical men, the central figure in Luke Fildes's painting *The Doctor*. Personally, he was quiet, dignified, pleasant mannered, a popular figure in Mayfair's social circles. His enjoyment of walking is not surprising since he was athletically inclined: he had been captain of his college boat club, and he was an expert skater.

Bird was a general surgeon, but recently he had become increasingly involved in a new field, anaesthetics. Being an anaesthetist in 1882 was not what it is today. He used chloroform, discovered 50 years earlier, and ether, which had been available for only 35 years. Without any of the modern refinements, the procedure required painstaking care from the practitioner. In his field Bird had a fine reputation. He was consulting anaesthetist at the East London Hospital for Children; he was visiting anaesthetist to the London County War Hospital; he was Instructor in the Use of Anaesthetics at Guy's Hospital; he was Administrator of Anaesthetics in the Hospital for Women in Soho Square; and he was the author of articles in medical journals.

It was not yet possible to be a full-time anaesthetist, and so Bird maintained a moderate-sized general surgical practice.

For years he had been a friend and medical advisor of the Miles's, who in 1878 introduced him to Gertrude Blood.

After a few weeks of tending to his patient at Leigh Court, Bird returned to London.

Lady Colin was also sometimes in London.

'When you came up to London,' Inderwick asked her, 'did you come to sing at concerts.'

'Yes, with two exceptions I always came for this purpose.'

'I think there were ten concerts at which you sang while you were on the Leigh Court visit?'

'Yes, about that number.'

'How long did you generally remain in town?'

'I would come up on the day of the concert or the evening before and return the day after.'

'Did Lord Colin know of your engagements?'

'I never went to one without his knowledge.'

Lady Colin's singing was also dealt with by Lockwood:

'Did your concerts interest Lord Colin?'

'No, he does not care for music.'

'You do, very much?'

'Yes.'

'May I take it that the concerts were a source of great pleasure to you?'

'They were a source of great fatigue.'

'My question was whether there was not a pleasure to you in discharging that duty?'

'There was a certain amount.'

One particular concert was of more than routine interest. It took place on 25 January 1883. Lockwood asked Amelia Watson about that evening:

'Do you remember when Lady Colin came home in a brougham with Mr Bird?'

'Yes.'

'Did anything happen in regard to a coat?'

'Yes. Lady Colin said that Mr Bird had left a fur-lined coat in the concert hall.'

'Did she say what she had done in regard to it?'

'Yes. She said she had written to Mr Bryant to bring it up.'

'Did she say anything further?'

'She said I was to take it to an address in Brook Street [where Bird lived] in a hansom.'

'Was the coat brought to the house?'

'Yes, it was brought by a man the next day who said, "I have brought Lord Colin's coat."'

'Had he a letter or anything of the sort?'

'Yes, he showed me her ladyship's letter.'

'What was in the letter?'

'"Dear Mr Bryant – I left Lord Colin's coat in the hall last night. Will you please look out for a fur-lined coat? The night being cold, I took it for a rug." '

'What happened on the evening before the coat was brought back?'

'The night of the concert Mr Bird had tea in the drawing-room. When his carriage came I went up to tell him and found he had gone to Lady Colin's bedroom. I knocked, and when her ladyship came to the door she turned round and said, "Keep your hand on that dose, doctor." This was the first time I ever heard her call him "doctor." '

'Did they go out shortly after that?'

'They started at eight o'clock.'

'Do you know what time Lady Colin got back?'

'No. I always went to bed before she came back.'

'Before that evening did you know that Mr Bird was a professional man?'

'No, I did not.'

Tom Bird was asked by the Solicitor-General to respond to Amelia Watson's evidence:

'Did you go to a concert on January 25, 1883?'

'No.'

'Had you been to a concert before with Lady Colin?'

'I had not.'

'Do you know anything of an incident of a fur coat?'

'Nothing.'

'Do you have a fur coat?'

'Yes, but I only wear it when I am travelling by railway. It is a Russian coat, with a collar reaching down to the arms. It is too heavy for ordinary use.'

Lady Colin's version of this particular evening was given to Inderwick:

'Did you go to a concert at the Bow and Bromley Institute on the 25th January 1883?'

'I did.'

'Was that for the purpose of supporting the Convalescent Home for Working Men?'

'Yes.'

'Who went with you?'

'A friend of mine, Miss Gordon.'

'Did you take anybody with you and pass him off as Lord Colin?'

'Certainly not.'

'At the end of the concert did Mr Hamilton Hoare hand you and Miss Gordon into a cab?'

'Yes.'

'Did you leave behind a fur coat?'

'No, it was a fur rug. I wrote to Mr Bryant, the manager of the hall, to return it as I needed it for travelling.'

'Did you tell Mr Bryant that you had left Lord Colin's coat at the hall?'

'I never said anything of the kind. I merely asked him to send the rug back, and it was brought the next day, after I had left for Leigh Court.'

'Is it a fact that Mr Bird was with you at the concert?'

'Certainly not.'

Judge Butt asked, 'Do you recollect that Mary Watson swore she was instructed to take the coat to Mr Bird's when it came?'

'That may very well have been so. Mr Bird was in the habit of coming down to Leigh Court to attend my husband. He came nearly every Saturday till the Monday. I may have directed it to be sent to him to bring it down, as I was leaving before it would come.'

Hamilton Hoare, organizer of the event, said that after the concert he had seen Lady Colin and a female companion to their cab. Asked if there was a gentleman with them, he said, 'No. If there had been I should not have escorted them to the cab.'

The assistant to the manager of the hall, George Birch, was questioned by Russell:

'You recollect the concert on January 25, 1883?'

'Yes.'

'Do you open letters for Mr Bryant?'

'Yes.'

'Did you open a letter from Lady Colin after that concert?'

'Yes, on the day following the concert.'

'Tell us, as far as you can remember, what it said.'

'It was to this effect: "Dear Mr Bryant, Having left a rug at the concert last evening – one that I use for travelling – will you kindly forward it as quickly as possible."'

Birch was cross-examined by Finlay:

'You have a considerable correspondence with regard to your entertainments?'

'Yes.'

'Can you give the contents of all the letters you have received?'

'No.'

'There was nothing very remarkable about this letter?'

'No.'

'And you had no special recollection of it?'

'Not until I found I had to come here.'

'When did this happen?'

'About twelve days ago.'

'From January 1883 down to twelve days ago have you ever thought of that letter?'

'No.'

After the trial had ended, the London correspondent for the Liverpool *Post* provided a postscript to this episode:

'You will remember the fur coat of Dr Bird. [Surgeons were often mistakenly called "Dr"] A few days ago a messenger went to his house to say that Mr Lewis, the solicitor for Lady Colin, wanted the coat. It was delivered, and you know the sequel. Dr Bird sent word to politely ask whether Mr Lewis had done with the coat, which is worth upward of a hundred pounds. The reply, of course, was that Mr Lewis had never sent for the coat. The disgust of Mr Lewis was great when he saw that there were people still innocent enough to be taken in by a trick so stale.'

CHAPTER 33

Charity Concerts

The concert on 25 January 1883, like most of Lady Colin's recitals, was for charity. This one was held on top of London Bridge Station, at the Bow and Bromley Institute. With 800 dues-paying members, the self-supporting Institute sustained evening classes, reading rooms, a lending library, lectures, recitals, and entertainments. It served the East End, which an American observer, without much hyperbole, called 'the most appalling place on earth.'

The East End had begun early in the century with the docks, and then came other industries – tailoring, boot-making, furniture trade, silk manufacture, women's sewing, coach and carriage building, and the fur trade. The workers in all of these industries laboured in sweat shops and lived in hovels.

In the East End it was not unusual for a family of ten or more persons to live their entire home life – eating, drinking, cooking, washing, and sleeping – in one or two small, poorly ventilated rooms. There was no privacy or cleanliness and so little water that, in one courtyard, 250 people shared one tap that was open for 25 minutes a day. The district was without one bookshop, art gallery, theatre, or cultural institution of any kind.

The Bow and Bromley was one of numerous organizations that tried to alleviate this state of affairs. Because the upper classes strongly opposed governmental intervention, everything was privately financed. There was no shortage of private philanthropic organizations. In September 1883 *The Times* enumerated the charities in the area of greater London: 23 foreign missionary societies; 56 home missions; 93 institutions affording general relief; 162 pensions and institutions for the aged; 101 education institutions; 17 general hospitals; four Bible societies; 13 home and foreign missions; 54 orphanages; 94 voluntary homes; 27 special hospitals; 69 reform institutions; 35 societies for social improvement; 20 hospitals for women and children; 24 charities for the blind; three institutions for idiots; eight consumption hospitals; 44 convalescent institutions; nine charities for incurables; six church and chapel building societies; 33 general dispensaries; eight charities for deaf mutes; five ophthalmic hospitals; 16 nursing institutions; four skin hospitals; and three orthopaedic hospitals.

Few of these establishments could have survived without the help of volunteers, mostly privileged women doing the only work they could properly perform. This wasn't said just by men. The noted activist Henrietta Stanley, who helped to establish the first women's college at Cambridge and the first medical college for women, once wrote, 'I have often heard it regretted that ladies have no stated employment, no profession. This is a mistake: charity is the calling of a lady; the care of the poor is her profession.'

One person who would have agreed that charity was 'a,' although probably not 'the,' calling of a privileged woman was Lady Colin Campbell.

'Did you,' Inderwick asked her, 'take a considerable interest in a number of charitable undertakings?'

'Yes.'

'Did you sing at concerts for charitable purposes?'

'Frequently.'

'In 1882 and 1883 did you sing at as many as forty concerts for charitable objects?'

'Yes, I did.'

'Did Lord Colin ever go with you on these occasions?'

'Never.'

'Was that on account of his illness or his attendance at the House of Commons?'

'I just don't think music interested him very much.'

Inderwick read a list of forty concerts at which Lady Colin had sung in different parts of London.

'How did you get to these places?' he asked.

'I hired a brougham or a hansom. Sometimes they sent for me. Once, when going to Whitechapel, I went to the Mansion House by train and then took a cab.'

'So much for the concerts. Did you also take an interest in teaching night classes?'

'Yes.'

'Did you go to Nine Elms for this?'

'Yes, to some factory girls.'

Nine Elms, a district of tenements south of the Thames, was as dirty and dismal as the East End.

'When were these night classes?' Inderwick asked.

'Every Friday evening.'

'Did they go on for some time?'

'Practically down to the present time.'

'In addition to teaching night classes, did you visit the poor?'

'Yes.'

Cross-examining, Lockwood asked, 'Apart from organized charities, did you pay individual visits?'

'Yes.'

'Can you mention any?'

'Yes. I went several times to see poor people. There was a poor woman in Westminster who lived in a lodging-house. I paid her rent.'

'I suppose you met a poor woman in the street who touched your heart, and you went and paid her rent for her?'

'Oh, no.'

If Lockwood was sceptical about Lady Colin's charitable activities, he did not stand alone.

After the trial the *Weekly Dispatch* editorialized, 'The way in which women of fashion help the poor by travelling 200 miles to sing at a concert or dance at a ball, instead of sending the amount of their first class ticket to a soup kitchen, is one explanation of why so little is really done.'

A more basic reason for so little being done to help the poor was suggested by a writer for *Leisure Hours*: 'We should look to the causes of the misery. A great deal of charity is only pumping against social leaks.' This points to the root cause of the problem. Instead of trying to change and improve the structure of social institutions, the charities with their condescension and paternalism were only perpetuating the status quo. To have done otherwise, as George Bernard Shaw noted in his early play *Widowers' Houses*, would have interfered with the sacred rights of property, which in Victorian times had priority over the rights, the health, even the lives of human beings who lived on that property.

Robert Finlay didn't deal with philosophical questions. He merely said, 'A married woman with a husband is better employed looking after him than in attending forty charitable concerts in the course of a year.'

CHAPTER 34

Lady Colin's 'Cruel Message'

In the autumn and winter of 1882–83, Lady Colin went to London, 'with two exceptions,' to sing. In his cross-examination of Lord Colin, Russell referred to one of these exceptions:

'Did you hear in the autumn of 1882 of a rumour that Lady Colin had eloped with Lord Blandford?'

'Certainly. Lady Miles told me about it when I was lying ill at Leigh Court.'

The source of the rumour was Mark Bouverie, who told friends of what he had seen in the waiting room in Fenchurch Street and on the platform at Purfleet. A gossip columnist for a widely-read society newspaper promptly informed his readers that Lady Colin Campbell had eloped with Lord Blandford.

'Was not that rumour,' Russell asked, 'the subject of conversation between you and Lady Colin?'

'On the contrary, she maintained complete silence on the subject after I had written to her about it.'

'Where from?'

'Leigh Court.'

'When?'

'Immediately after Lady Miles had told me of it.'

'Is it not a fact that when this rumour came to your ears it was arranged that your family should take the biggest box they could get at a theatre in London to show that there was no foundation for the story?'

'I know nothing about that whatever.'

'Do you not know that Lord Walter and his wife, and Mrs Bolton, and Lady Colin herself, and such members of your family as were in town, took the largest box they could get to show the public there was no truth in the rumour that Lady Colin had run away?'

'Lord Walter told me that he had taken her to the theatre so that she might discredit the report that she had run away.'

'That is exactly what I am asking. Did you forget it?'

'My brother told me. I had no knowledge of it at the time. I was not a party to the arrangement.'

'Did you not know your wife was coming to town?'

'She frequently came to town.'

'You did not know she was coming that afternoon?'

'No.'

'Of course we must take your answer.'

His answer was not that of his wife, who said that they had talked about the rumour and about her impending trip to London to attend a play with his relatives.

The Campbells' theatre party took place early in October. On 25 November Lady Colin again travelled to London for a theatrical performance, the opening night of Gilbert and Sullivan's *Iolanthe*, the first work to have its premiere in the Savoy Theatre. Lady Colin was the guest of Arthur Sullivan, and she sat next to Captain Shaw, recently returned from America.

Early in Act II, the Fairy Queen stretched her arms toward the fire chief and the woman beside him. She sang a song that contained these suggestive lines:

> 'O Captain Shaw
> 'Type of true love kept under!
> 'Could thy brigade
> 'With cold cascade
> 'Quench thy great love, I wonder!'

Lord Colin meanwhile had his own sources of news from London, one of which was mentioned during Inderwick's examination of Lady Miles:

'When Lord Colin was at Leigh Court, do you know whether he received any letters from Mary Watson?'

'Yes, he received several letters from her.'

'How did you know they were from Mary Watson?'

'Because he told me.'

'Did you see any of these letters?'

'Yes.'

'How were they signed?'

'Your affectionate Mary.'

Amelia Watson was questioned by Inderwick on her letters:

'Did you write to Lord Colin at Leigh Court?'

'Yes.'

'Did you sign yourself "Your affectionate Mary"?'

'Never in my life.'

'Or anything to that effect?'

'No.'

'Did you sign your letters "Mary"?'

'Yes, "Yours respectfully, Mary."'

'How many times did you write to him at Leigh Court?'

'Four or five times.'

'What did you write about?'

'About a puppy dog he had sent up and entreated me to fetch at Paddington.'

It was a sign of the times for a housemaid to be literate. This would have been unlikely not very many years earlier.

Soon Amelia Watson could communicate directly with her master. On 10 February 1883 the Campbells returned to London.

For the first time Annie Duffy entered 79 Cadogan Place. She was asked by Lockwood about the living arrangements:

'What room did Lord Colin occupy?'

'The dining-room.'

'Was it fitted as a bedroom?'

'Yes.'

'Where was Lady Colin's room?'

'In the bedroom above the drawing-room, the front room.'

'How long did Lord Colin use the dining-room as a bedroom?'

'As long as I remained there, until July 1883.'

Lord Colin was asked this question by Lockwood:

'Between June 1882 and February 1883, did you make any overtures to Lady Colin to resume cohabitation?'

'Certainly not. It would have been impossible.'

That was all right with Lady Colin. Lady Miles, who was soon in London, recalled for Inderwick a memorable scene:

'In February 1883, did Lady Colin give you a letter to be read or shown to Lord Colin?'

'Yes.'

[143]

'Did Lady Colin ask you to read it to Lord Colin?'

'Yes.'

'Did you read it to him?'

'No, because I did not promise to do so. After I read the letter to myself three times over, I made a statement to him.'

'Did you give him its contents?'

'Yes, much softened.'

'What did you say?'

'I told him that Lady Colin had decided not to live with him as his wife.'

'Was anything said about this being kept secret?'

'Yes. I said that I would be the only one who knew.'

'Did you tell Lord Colin the cause of the separation?'

'Yes.'

'What did you say?'

'I said she had complained of being miserable and had told me all the particulars.'

'What did Lord Colin say in answer to that?'

'He was very much shocked and pained. He said it was very hard on him and he could not live with her on those terms. He said that she could never have cared for him to ask such a thing.'

'How did you reply to this?'

'I said that she did care for him and loved him dearly.'

'What happened after this?'

'He carried on for some time in the same strain until at last he decided to leave her alone. For two years he would not ask her to return to him.'

'Did he write a letter?'

'Yes, and I took it to her.'

The letter contained this passage: 'I am very sensitive about what would be said at the clubs if it got out that my wife and I occupied separate bedrooms. I do hope you will not be the means of fastening a cruel libel on me – that I am not fit to lead a proper married life.'

Right after receiving the letter, Lady Colin told Inderwick, her husband spoke to her:

'Did you have a conversation with Lord Colin in reference to your taking back what he called your "cruel message"?'

'Yes, I did.'

'What did you say in reference to your message?'

'I told him I would take back the words of the message, but I entreated him for God's sake to let me alone.'

In 'this dreadful state of affairs,' Russell said, 'Lady Colin found life with Lord Colin absolutely revolting, and she could not continue to endure his embraces.' Even so, Lady Colin was well ahead of her time. A wife was expected to submit unquestioningly to her husband's wishes.

CHAPTER 35

Smoking Cigarettes

In this month of February 1883, Lady Blandford was in the Divorce Court seeking an end to her marriage. Her principal advocate was that veteran of this arena, Frederick Inderwick. In the Campbell case, Inderwick spoke gently of the Duke of Marlborough when he spoke of him at all. But in Blandford v. Blandford, he said this in his opening statement:

'In June of 1875, the Blandfords had words at the breakfast table about Lady Aylesford, and he struck his wife on the face, she being within two months of a confinement.... In October 1875, Lady Blandford wrote telling him that the infant had a mark on the back of his head as a consequence of the blow.

'Blandford showed no interest in the child, whom he did not see for more than two years after his birth. Even though he had deserted her, living for a while with Lady Aylesford, Lady Blandford, for the sake of the children, put off her divorce action.

'There was a reconciliation in the autumn of 1878, and the Blandfords lived together in Cadogan Square until April 25, 1882. Lady Blandford then removed from the sitting-room a photograph of Lady Aylesford, and Lord Blandford spoke to her insultingly because of this. Then when Lady Blandford learned about Lord Blandford's son by Lady Aylesford and a settlement upon the son, she began the divorce action.'

Lady Blandford was granted a divorce and custody of the couple's four children.

Lady Colin in the meantime had resumed her familiar lifestyle. Annie Duffy was questioned on this by Lockwood:

'Do you remember whether any gentlemen called at Cadogan Place during the months of March and April 1883?'

'They did.'

'Whom did they see?'

'Lady Colin.'

'In what room?'

'The drawing-room.'

'During this period did Lady Colin pay much attention to her husband?'

'None whatever. I did the entire nursing without any help from Lady Colin. It was very seldom she sat with him.'

'Did she stay at home and read to him?'

'Very, very seldom.'

'Do you know whether she went out and about?'

'She went out in the morning, came in to lunch, went out in the afternoon, came in to dinner, and went out again at night.'

'Does that fairly describe her life whilst Lord Colin was ill?'

'It does.'

Duffy was soon joined by another newcomer to Cadogan Place. At this time more than half of all housemaids stayed with one family for less than two years, and so it was not surprising when on 22 March 1883 Amelia Watson left after seventeen months with the Campbells.

Servants now moved about. Watson at once entered the service of a Mrs Ellis in London, stayed for a year-and-a-half, and then spent nearly two years with a Mrs Robertson in Brighton.

Watson was replaced by an attractive, pleasant young woman with large eyes and an oval face, Ellen Hawkes. The new housemaid quickly learned about her mistress's ways. By mid-March, Lord Colin could go to the House of Commons, and Ellen Hawkes was asked by Lockwood about a night when he was at the House:

'Did you know Mr Bird?'

'Yes.'

'Did he visit during the time you were there?'

'Yes, very often.'

'Did he generally come when Lord Colin was attending the House of Commons?'

'Yes.'

'How long did Mr Bird stay at one time with Lady Colin?'

'I know he was there very late one night, but I cannot say at what time he came. It was in the afternoon.'

'In what room did they sit when he came to see Lady Colin?'

'In the drawing-room.'

'Do you remember their smoking together once?'

'Yes.'

'Mr Bird and Lady Colin?'

'Yes.'

'What did they smoke?'

'Cigarettes.'

In the 1880s in England it was relevant to ask if a woman had been smoking. Although some countries were tolerant on the subject, most English people had not accepted the notion of a respectable woman smoking. Men did not smoke in 'a room inhabited by ladies,' and in public places frequented by women smoking was not generally permitted. A man who smoked and met a woman afterwards often changed his coat, and he might also rinse his mouth and brush his teeth. But not all women were against smoking, and some even argued for their right to indulge freely in the habit. Among them was Lady Colin Campbell. Seven years after her divorce trial, the *English Illustrated Magazine* published her 'Plea for Tobacco.' This is from the article:

'I find no difficulty in answering affirmatively the question "Should women smoke?" The growing prevalence of smoking amongst women is one of the most satisfactory proofs of the development of common sense in the female sex; it is regrettable that the common sense of the opposite sex has not also advanced, and that in this conservative country where prejudice dies slowly many men are still shocked to see a woman enjoying a cigarette.

'Men never weary of justifying their love of tobacco on the ground that it soothes overworked brains and nerves, that it adds enjoyment to well-earned repose, that it smooths their path through life. Why should women not share in this gift of the gods? If smoking were to be reserved for one sex, it would be logical to hand it over to women. Women's nervous organisations are far more delicate and acute than those of most men; trivial things which affect them will leave men unmoved; life's thousand and one little irritations have been known to cause nagging fits of hysterics. Is it too much to suppose that a daily dose of cigarettes would eliminate this sense of irritation and induce a more philosophical frame of mind to the benefit of husbands and the world at large?

'It is impossible for the most irritable person to continue in a bad temper with a cigarette between his or her lips. The nerves relax; the tingling sensation of the skin and at the roots of the hair gives place to a feeling of being in a delicious bath of milk; a more charitable view of the male gradually asserts itself, until the last trace of temper is wiped out by the wily suggestion that the manifest superiority of the female intellect should deal tenderly with the stupidity and denseness of the male, and by the time the cigarette is finished peace once more reigns supreme.

'What an extension of communion there is between husband and wife when they both smoke! When the gracious presence of our Lady Nicotine is felt in a household there reign peace and understanding. The ugly imps of bickering and nagging, impatience and recrimination, spread their wings and fly away.

'The modern woman is hung upon wires. Restlessness is her element. She can not be still for five minutes. From morning till night she is "on the ramp." Repose is unknown to her. She will not find the restfulness of strength that gives new life until she is taught wisdom and tobacco. The pleasure to a tired man to go from his office to a quiet drawing room where lamps are lit under transparent shades, where a fire makes the hearth brilliant with blue and violet flames, where deep arm-chairs invite the tired limbs, and a well-stuffed bolster supports the nape of a weary head, and where a low-voiced woman welcomes him rising out of the billowy silken cushions of the sofa, a cigarette just removed from her lips – is it too much to say, oh! my brothers! that such an experience when you sink into the chair, a cigarette between your lips, your favourite drink, at your elbow, and your wife smoking opposite you, is a foretaste of a paradise that outdoes that of the sons of the Prophet?

'Why should women have to hide like criminals to enjoy a cigarette? Why should not this innocent enjoyment be theirs, when and where they please? Think of it, oh! my brothers! for, bundles of nerves as we are, we need more than you do something to enable us to bear the *sturm und drang* of existence. When next you see your wife watching with envious eyes as you smoke your cigarette, encourage her to share your enjoyment.'

Nothing in the trial record suggests that Lord and Lady Colin ever sat together smoking.

CHAPTER 36

Cuddling in a Cab

On 7 March 1883, Lord Colin wrote to Tom Bird, 'I wish to consult you on an important matter, continuing with Mr Allingham. I do not feel sufficient confidence in him. I like Mr Allingham, but I cannot help feeling that he has not been sufficiently successful to enable me to feel confident in following his advice. I know in your profession rules of etiquette make the question a difficult one, but I ask you as a friend to help me decide. I believe your position is one which gives you a bird's-eye view (forgive the apparent pun).'

Lord Colin liked Tom Bird, as a doctor and as a man. While at Leigh Court, he had sent Bird more than 100 letters, sometimes as many as four in one day. In several of them he referred to his wife as 'Gerty.' Bird had not yet aroused Lord Colin's hostility. He could see Lady Colin openly, as he did on 5 April 1883.

On 5 April, Lady Colin was not well. In her own words, she was 'exceedingly ill, suffering most acute neuralgia.' But she had a singing engagement which she did not want to miss. Because of her condition, it was desirable for someone to accompany her. Asked by Russell if he could have gone, Lord Colin said, 'I took as much rest as I could and never went anywhere unless I was obliged.' And so late on that afternoon Lady Colin took a cab to Brook Street.

Mayfair's élite Brook Street is where Handel composed his *Messiah*; where the wealthy man-about-town of *Dombey and Son*, Lord Feenix, lived; where Claridge's, described in an 1879 guidebook as 'the hotel *par excellence* for foreign ambassadors, princes, and so forth,' is located. And, except for Harley Street, it was the favourite address of Victorian medical men. Among its medical residences-come-offices was that of Tom Bird.

Lady Colin went to Brook Street so that Bird could escort her to the concert. Asked by Russell if he would have objected to their going to the concert together, Lord Colin said, 'I don't think so.'

Together Lady Colin and Bird travelled by cab five-and-one-half miles to the concert hall, which was in New Cross.

New Cross, through which the ancient road to Canterbury passed, is a district in south-east London, three miles south of London Bridge Station. In the late nineteenth century it had two concert halls. The principal one, on New Cross Road, was large and luxurious, seating 2000. The more modest New Cross Hall, on Lewisham High Road, had 780 seats. It was here that Lady Colin sang.

The concert programme contained advertising by a pawnbroker, a fruit merchant, a cabinet maker, a piano tuner, and a man who was proud of his artistry:

'Artificial Teeth
'Mr. E. Smith
'Qualified and Register Dentist
'474 New Cross Road
'Supplies artificial Teeth on the best principles, defying detection

without extracting stumps or painful operations at half the usual
charges, he being the actual maker.
'Old teeth bought. Consultation fee.'

The concert would benefit the Convalescent Home for Working Men.
The patrons included the Bishop of Rochester, Baron de Worms, MP,
Viscount Lewisham, Sir Charles Miles, Lady Folkestone, and Lady Colin
Campbell. One of several performers, Lady Colin had been booked for
two songs. She broke down during the second selection.

Lady Colin and Tom Bird left immediately. They entered the cab that
had brought them to New Cross. The cabman had sat waiting for them.
His name was Charles Watson, and he drove a two-wheeled hansom.

The omnibus was the cheapest, most widely used form of transit, but
Lady Colin never used that proletarian vehicle. She always rode in that
most distinctive Victorian vehicle, the cab. 'Our gondolas,' Disraeli called
London's cabs. In 1883 10,000 were licensed for hire, 3500 four-wheelers
and 6500 two-wheeled hansoms. Four-wheelers carried four passengers
inside and a fifth alongside the driver. They were slow and uninteresting.
The carriers of romance and excitement were the two-passenger
hansoms, named after their designer, Birmingham architect Joseph
Hansom. For young people, the hansom furnished the thrills that in later
days would be provided by convertibles and sports cars. Readers of
Sherlock Holmes stories know how hansom cabs could dash around
corners and through crowds of pedestrians at the reckless speed of fifteen
miles an hour. (According to the Holmes authority William Baring-
Gould, one of the most popular of the stories, 'The Adventure of the
Speckled Band,' occurred on the day after Lady Colin's New Cross
concert.)

The hansom cab had a square body and large wheels. The driver sat
above and just behind the body. A sliding trap door let him communicate
with his passengers. Like today's London taxi driver, he was closely
examined on his metropolitan geographical knowledge before he was
issued a license. Rarely, even on foggy nights, was a cabman lost. Cabs
could be obtained at numerous stands on main roads, could be hailed in
the street, and, as on this occasion, could be reserved.

Cab driver Charles Watson was a moustached, sly, rakish-looking man
in his early forties. He was questioned by Finlay:

'You have frequently driven Lady Colin?'
'Yes.'
'Do you remember driving her to New Cross Hall in April 1883?'
'Yes.'

'Why did you go?'

'I got a postcard asking me to call, as Lady Colin had admired my horse and cab.'

'What time did you go to Cadogan Place?'

'About three.'

'And from there?'

'To 38 Brook Street.'

'From there?'

'To New Cross Hall.'

'Did anyone join her at Brook Street?'

'Yes, a gentleman.'

'You drove them together?'

'Yes.'

'And did you drive them back?'

'Yes.'

'Did anything happen on the way home?'

'Yes. While driving along the Peckham Road, the cab began to roll, and thinking something was the matter, I looked through the trap.'

This had to have occurred early in the journey because the Peckham Road is near the site of the concert.

'What did you see?' Finlay asked.

'I found the lady and gentleman caressing each other.' (Laughter)

'Just describe it.'

'The lady had her head on the gentleman's shoulder. (Laughter) Like this.'

There was much laughter as the witness, in the words of a reporter, 'suited the action to the word.'

'What did you see them doing?'

'I don't know how to express myself except to say they were caressing each other as I should do if I was courting.' (Loud laughter)

'Where did you drive them?'

'Back to Brook Street.'

'Did they get out there?'

'Yes. The lady paid me and said she would not want me any more. The gentleman went in with a latchkey.'

'What did she give you?'

'She gave me half-a-sovereign.'

A half-sovereign was valued at ten shillings, 50 pence in today's money. This included the fare and a generous tip.

'Did you go away?' Finlay asked.

'Certainly not.'

'Where did you go?'

'I went to a public house opposite because I thought she would want to be driven home.'

'How long did you wait?'

'About an hour and a half.'

'Did you stop till the public house closed?'

'Yes.'

'What time would that be?'

'Half-past twelve.'

London's licensing laws were less stringent than in more recent times. Because many drivers idled away their time in pubs, a Cabmen's Shelter Fund was started in 1875. In the late seventies and eighties, numerous shelters were built and served as club rooms for drivers, with newspapers, inexpensive food, and non-alcoholic drinks. There was one in Pont Street, near Cadogan Place, but none in the vicinity of Tom Bird's home.

'During the best part of the time that you were in the public house,' Finlay asked, 'you were on the watch?'

'Yes. I was gone for a few minutes, and I said to a man, "You keep your eye on number 38. I shall have a lady coming out presently."'

'When you came back, did you give him anything.'

'Yes, tuppence.' (Laughter)

'All that time, except when the man was watching for you, you were watching for her ladyship to come out.'

'Yes.'

'You left at half-past twelve?'

'Yes.'

'She had not come out by then?'

'No.'

Going from New Cross to Brook Street took 45 minutes, and so the cab arrived at Bird's residence at about 10.30. Watson, then, was in the pub not for ninety minutes, but for two-and-a-half hours. Supposedly during all of that time he was vigilantly watching the entrance to Bird's home. But did not this garrulous cabman engage in conversation with barkeepers, barmaids, and fellow tipplers? Did he not visit the lavatory? Did he not ask for refills? Might he not have been just a little tipsy? How conscientious indeed was Charles Watson as an observer of the house across the road?

Both parties were asked about the cab ride. Bird was questioned by the Solicitor-General:

'What happened at the concert?'

'She broke down, and on the way home I suggested that she should come to Brook Street, and I would give her something.'

"Was Lady Colin in a condition of ill health?'

'Yes, she had been for several months.'

'Had she complained that night?'

'Yes, she complained very much.'

'What was the mixture you gave Lady Colin at your house?'

'Fothergill's solution of hydrobromic acid.'

'Was that then a new preparation?'

'It was not easy to get.'

'Is it beneficial?'

'Yes, very beneficial.'

'What happened after you gave Lady Colin the medicine?'

'I put her into another cab within five or ten minutes. She told me she had paid the cabman who brought us from New Cross and then sent him away.'

'Is it true that in the cab you were caressing Lady Colin?'

'Certainly not.'

'Was there anything at all of that kind?'

'No.'

Lady Colin was questioned by Inderwick:

'Is it true that you caressed Mr Bird in the cab?'

'It is utterly untrue.'

'Why did you go to his house?'

'Because he wished to give me a dose, and the chemists' shops were closed. I went in and took the medicine.'

'Did you discharge the cabman?'

'Yes. I had, at his request, paid him his fare and discharged him. He said his horse was tired.'

'Had you noticed that the horse was tired?'

'Yes. I had previously complained of his driving so slowly.'

'How long were you in Mr Bird's house?'

'About five minutes.'

'And then you went home?'

'Yes. I went in another cab, getting home before eleven.'

Cross-examining, Lockwood asked Lady Colin to read aloud her diary entry for 5 April 1883: '"Concert at New Cross Hall, Bird went with me. Very ill. Too ill to sing. Stopped at B's house for some medicine to make me sleep. Neuralgia dreadful."'

'Was there anything extraordinary in your going to Mr Bird's house?'

'I attached no importance to my stopping at his house to get medicine.'

'Why then did you put an entry in the diary about it?'

[153]

'I have entered many things of far less importance in my diary.'

'I am bound to put this to you, Lady Colin. Was this entry entered in the diary long after the event took place?'

'Certainly not.'

'Look at the colour of the ink. Does it not strike you as different?'

'Different to what?'

'From the other entries.'

'It is written in a different pen.'

'Different ink?'

'No.'

'Does it not strike you as looking fresher?'

'No.'

Another questionable matter was noted by Finlay:

'The cabman was sent for by postcard. She then said the horse was so tired the cab had to be discharged. Is it likely that a cabman would bring out a horse so dead beat that it would be tired out by a drive of three-quarters of an hour, with an interval of two hours?'

It is a fact that cabmen's horses sometimes worked for as long as fifteen hours at a stretch.

Even apart from the New Cross concert, Lord Colin should have remembered the night of 5 April 1883. Clarke questioned him on this:

'Do you remember anything that occurred on the evening of April 5?'

'No, I do not.'

'Do you remember anything that took place in the House of Commons on that evening?'

'No, I do not keep a diary.'

'Have you ascertained from other sources what took place?'

'No, I have no sources of information.'

'But are there not plenty of sources of information on what took place in the House of Commons on 5 April 1883?'

'Certainly, the records of the House.'

'I will tell you. It was the Budget Night, Mr Childers' Budget. Now do you remember?'

'No, I never attended during a Budget Night.'

'Can you not say where you were on that evening?'

'No.'

'Have you no means of refreshing your memory?'

'No, I cannot say that I have.'

'Since you heard this story of your wife's doings on the 5 April, have you made no attempt to find out what you were doing?'

'I was probably resting in my own home.'

'You were in the front room on the ground floor?'

'I was in the dining-room fitted up as my bedroom.'

'With Mrs Duffy?'

'Sometimes.'

It is strange that Lord Colin should have had no recollection of this date, which was crucial to his case against Tom Bird. Despite his unconcern, Budget Night in Parliament was, and is, a big event. Also, since his bed was on the ground floor, could Lady Colin have slipped into the house at a late hour undetected?

CHAPTER 37

Colonel Butler

Less than a week after the New Cross concert, Lord and Lady Colin saw the fourth man who would become a co-respondent in Lord Colin's petition. It was on the evening of 11 April in the Egyptian Hall of the Mansion House.

In the Victorian period, the Mansion House was the setting for many gala affairs, usually in the large-roofed central courtyard known as the Egyptian Hall. On 11 April 1883, a reception was held there to honour Admiral Lord Alcestor, GCB, for recent accomplishments in Egyptian waters. *The Times's* partial guest list ran to more than forty lines. It included the names of His Royal Highness the Duke of Edinburgh; his Royal Highness the Duke of Cambridge; his Serene Highness Prince Edward of Saxe-Weimar; and numerous lords and ladies, generals and admirals. On line 32 was the name of Captain Eyre Massey Shaw, CB, and line 34 had the name of a Colonel William Butler, CB.

Unlisted in *The Times* but present in the flesh were Lord and Lady Colin Campbell.

'Do you recollect,' Russell asked Lord Colin, 'your wife introducing you to Colonel Butler?' (By the time of the trial Butler had become a Brigadier General.)

'No, on the contrary, I was particularly struck with the fact that she did not introduce me.'

'Did you want to be introduced?'

'Not particularly, but I was surprised that she did not.'

'You had no suspicions against Colonel Butler?'

'No.'

'Did your wife, in your presence, invite Colonel Butler to call at your house the next day?'

'I don't remember.'

At the time of the Mansion House gathering, Lord Colin did not know of a recent discovery by Ellen Hawkes. She was asked about it by Lockwood:

'Do you remember a photograph of Colonel Butler in the house at Cadogan Place?'

'Yes, her ladyship had one in her bedroom. It was an old one in a plush frame. I found it under her pillow one morning.'

'How came you to find the portrait?'

'It happened when I made up her ladyship's bed.'

Later Lockwood questioned Lady Colin on this:

'You remember hearing the servant speak of having found a photograph of Colonel Butler under your pillow?'

' "On the bed," I think she said.' (All reports of Ellen Hawkes's testimony contain the words 'under her pillow.')

'What do you say to that?'

'I say there was a shelf over the bed where photographs were kept, and if anything fell it would fall on the bed. Things were constantly tumbling down as the shelf was so small.'

Colonel Butler, 44-years-old in 1883, had had a distinguished military career going back to the Crimean War and the Indian Mutiny and including service in Burma, Canada, and Africa. Tall and strong, he was, like the other co-respondents, energetic and highly literate. He had written several published books, including two military biographies.

Butler's wife was the painter Elizabeth Thompson, sister of poet-essayist Alice Meynell. Noted for her pictures of military life, Thompson became famous in 1874 with *Calling the Roll After an Engagement, Crimea*, popularly known as *The Roll Call*, exhibited at the Royal Academy and purchased by the Queen. This led to her meeting, and, in 1877, marrying William Butler. Lady Colin frequently worked in the studio of Elizabeth Thompson, an intimate friend of hers.

Two days after the Mansion House reception, Butler visited 79 Cadogan Place. Annie Duffy, the nurse who doubled as household servant, answered the door. Lockwood questioned her:

'At about two o'clock did a hansom cab drive up?'

'Before two o'clock.'

'Who was in the cab?'

'A gentleman.'

'Who was that gentleman?'

'He gave the name of Colonel Butler.'

'Where did you show him?'

'Into the drawing-room.'

'Who was there?'

'Lady Colin.'

'Was anybody else in the room?'

'No.'

'Do you remember a lady in a carriage calling that afternoon?'

'I do.'

'Did you answer the door?'

'I did.'

'Did you tell Lady Colin that a lady had called?'

'I had no occasion to do that. Lady Colin came out and called, "Ellen, Ellen." Ellen was the housemaid, and it was her place to open the door. [At the moment no male servant was on the staff.] Her ladyship said, "Not at home." I said, "Not at home, my lady?" She said, "Yes," and returned to the drawing-room.'

'After you had these instructions, what did you do?'

'I went to the door and said, "Lady Colin is not at home." The carriage drove away.'

'When Lady Colin said "Not at home," was she over the banister?'

'Yes, looking down at me.'

'Did you notice her appearance?'

'I did.'

'Describe it.'

'Her hair was disordered, and her face was flushed.'

'What time did Lord Colin return home that afternoon?'

'As near as I can remember, the usual time, about four o'clock.'

'Tell us what passed when Lord Colin came home.'

'He asked the usual question, "Has her ladyship been at home?" These were always the first words he put to me on letting him in. I said. "Yes." Then he asked, "Is she alone?" I said, "No." He then said, "I am very tired." I advised him to go to bed, as he was in a bad state of health. I undressed him and put him to bed and gave him his writing materials. He then said, "Is it a lady or a gentleman?" I said, "A gentleman." He then asked, "Who is it?" I replied that I did not know – as I always did on such occasions.' (Laughter)

'Did you hear Colonel Butler leave?'

'First I heard her ladyship go upstairs into her bedroom. During the time she was there Colonel Butler came downstairs and let himself out.'

'What time would that be?'

'Four, or a little after.'

'When did you next see Lady Colin?'

About a quarter of an hour afterwards.'

'Did she come down to Lord Colin's room?'

'First she came from her bedroom to the drawing-room, where she commenced playing. [Actually the piano was in a small room at the head of the stairs, alongside the rear section of the drawing-room.] Lord Colin called to her to come down to his bedroom. She said, "I did not know you were in." He said, "You had a visitor?" She replied, "He is an old soldier who has known me since I was a child."' (Butler was nineteen years older than Lady Colin.)

Ellen Hawkes corroborated all of Duffy's testimony, and, questioned by Lockwood, she added some details:

'Did you see Colonel Butler leave?'

'I saw him in the hall when he let himself out?'

'Did he make much noise coming downstairs?'

'Not much. He went out on his toes.' (Laughter)

'How long did that visit last?'

'About two hours.'

'During the two hours was anybody else with Lady Colin?'

'No.'

'Do you remember other occasions when Colonel Butler was at the house?'

'Yes.'

'Do you remember him ever being at the house and seeing Lord Colin?'

'No.'

Lady Colin's evidence, given during Lockwood's cross-examination, differed from that of the nurse and the housemaid:

'Do you remember coming out of the drawing-room when Colonel Butler had called and saying to Ellen Hawkes that you were not at home?'

'Certainly not.'

'You deny that you came out of the drawing-room?'

'I absolutely deny it.'

'Was there another time when you came out and gave instructions that you were not at home?'

'Never.'

'But you were alone with Colonel Butler?'

'No, we were not alone.'

'You were not alone? Who was with you?'

'My sister, Mrs Bolton.'

'Mrs Bolton is now dead?'

'Yes, she is now dead.'

'Colonel Butler knew she was there?'

'Certainly.'

CHAPTER 38

Tom Bird's Protracted Visit

Only hours after Colonel Butler had left, Lady Colin was struck with a serious illness. Annie Duffy, questioned by Lockwood, described its earliest stages:

'Do you remember going out on the night of Colonel Butler's visit?'

'Yes, I went out at about eight and returned just before ten.'

'When you got in, did you find Lord and Lady Colin together?'

'I did.'

'In what room?'

'In Lord Colin's bedroom.'

'Did Lady Colin say anything?'

'Nothing whatever. She sat with a fur rug around her, looking very ill. Lord Colin said, "Her ladyship is in great pain. Please put her to bed and put on a hot bag." '

'Did you put her to bed?'

'I did not.'

'Next morning did you notice her appearance?'

'Yes. I met her in the hall, and she was doubled with pain. I said, "You are very ill. You had better go to bed." She said, "I am all right," and went into his lordship's room.'

'Had you further conversation with her on her condition?'

'Not till late in the evening, almost seven o'clock, in the drawing room. I was sent by Lord Colin with a message.'

'How did you find her?'

'Wrapped in a muslin wrapper on the sofa, looking very ill. I delivered the message, and I said, "You are still suffering. Why not go to bed?" She said, "I will presently." I think she went to bed soon after.'

'Did you have any conversation with her as to what was the matter with her?'

'Yes, as she passed out of the front drawing room to the back. Am I obliged to say this in a public court?'

'Yes, you must tell what you know.'

'Lady Colin said that her usual illness had come on and that accounted for her suffering.'

'How did she appear at that time?'

'The pain seemed excessive, and there was more than the usual haemorrhage.'

Soon afterwards, Lady Miles arrived in London and, questioned by Inderwick, told of her cousin's suffering:

'What was Lady Colin's condition at this time?'

'She was in bed, very, very ill.'

'Was she in pain?'

'Yes, she was in violent pain.'

'Was it a continuous pain?'

'No, it came on at intervals.'

'How did she appear during the intervals of pain?'

'Her condition was most shocking. She would writhe on the ground and gnaw the carpet while her limbs stiffened all over. I don't think she could have lived if it had lasted for a long time. I had never seen anyone in such pain.'

'Do you know if Lady Colin was under morphia?'

'I heard that she took a considerable quantity.'

Lady Colin was reluctant to undergo medical treatment. Lockwood asked her about this:

'You had been attended by Sir Oscar Clayton?'

'Yes.'

'I believe he was anxious to make an examination?'

'Yes.'

'You refused?'

'I did.'

'Why?'

'Because the idea was repulsive to me.'

'Sir Oscar Clayton occupied a high professional position?'

'I believe so.'

'His age, I believe, was about sixty?'

'I don't know. He looked younger.' (Laughter)

Still alive at the time of the trial, Sir Oscar Clayton was born in 1816. He had been a Fellow of the Royal College of Surgeons since 1853, and his patients included the Prince of Wales and the Duke of Edinburgh.

'Did you know Sir Oscar Clayton socially?' Lockwood asked.

'I had met him.'

'Would it have been painful for you to be examined by him?'

'Very.'

'You would have preferred to be examined by someone you did not know socially?'

'I should have preferred it not to take place at all.'

'That is not quite an answer to my question. I asked whether you would prefer an examination conducted by a person whom you did not know socially?'

'It would make no difference whether I knew the person or not. It would have been repulsive in either case.'

Lady Colin's disinclination to submit to a pelvic examination, which was not included in routine health care, was not unusual. Many women hesitated to confide in a doctor, who almost certainly would have been a man. Lady Colin's attitude might have been different if she could have been examined by a female. There were women practising in Britain – Sophia Jex-Blake and Edith Peckey, who had been licensed in 1877 (28 years after Elizabeth Blackwell had become the first American female doctor), and a few others – but they were rare. Women who entered the medical profession were expected to be nurses.

Finally Lady Colin agreed on a medical examination. The examiner would be Tom Bird. Lockwood queried Annie Duffy on this particular doctor-patient relationship:

'Was Mr Bird attending her professionally?'

'Yes.'

'What was the duration of his visits?'

'He usually came about 10.40 in the morning and stopped for a couple of hours, and he would come again in the afternoon and remain for two or three hours.'

'Do you remember one occasion when he stayed longer than that?'

'I do.'

'When was this visit?'

'About eleven or twelve days after illness had commenced.'

'What time of day did Mr Bird come?'

'Between three and four.'

'Was Lord Colin at home?'

'He was at home when Mr Bird came, but not during the whole time of the visit.'

'His lordship was then attending the House of Commons?'

'He was.'

'About what time did he leave for the House of Commons?'

'He went out about five o'clock.'

'Was Mr Bird in the house when he left?'

'He was.'

'Did Mr Bird dine in the house?'

'He did.'

'In what room did he dine?'

'The room was the study, which was turned into a dining-room because the dining-room had become Lord Colin's bedroom.'

'After he had dined, what did he do?'

'He went back to her ladyship's bedroom.'

'How long did he remain in her ladyship's bedroom?'

'Till past eleven o'clock.'

'At what time did Lord Colin return?'

'About eleven.'

'Had anyone else been in the room with Lady Colin?'

'Not that I know of.'

'And from about four o'clock, except for dinner, he had been alone with Lady Colin in her bedroom?'

'Yes, as far as I know.'

'What took place when Lord Colin returned?'

'He said to Mr Bird, "It is rather late for you to be here. Is she so ill that she requires your attention when we have a trained nurse in the house?" Mr Bird said, "I went to sleep and forgot the time."'

Lord Colin gave his recollection of the evening to Lockwood:

'Tell us about the occasion when Mr Bird paid Lady Colin an unusually long visit.'

'I found Mr Bird in Lady Colin's room in the afternoon, and I left him there at four o'clock. I went downstairs, and I remember going up again near dinner-time. I said it was getting late, and I asked him whether he would dine. He hesitated for a long time, and I got rather impatient. I asked, "Will you dine or not? Please say if it will be convenient or not." After some more hesitation, he said, "I think I will dine." I went downstairs and told Mrs Duffy to see that Mr Bird got dinner, and that I was going to dine at the House of Commons. I returned from the House of Commons at about eleven o'clock, and I found Mr Bird still sitting in my wife's room. I gave him the best hint I could, and very soon afterwards he left the house.'

'Did he say anything to account for his being there so late?'

'No, he did not.'

'Had you said anything to Lady Colin about Mr Bird's visits?'

'Yes. I noticed that Mr Bird came to my house without any consideration for me. He went to my wife's room and did not see me.'

The doctor was questioned by Sir Edward Clarke:

'On the occasion of your long visit to Lady Colin, did you dine at Cadogan Place on Lord Colin's invitation?'

'Yes.'

'After dinner did you return to Lady Colin's room?'

'Yes.'

'Lady Colin was under the influence of opium?'

'I had given her some that afternoon.'

'When you went up to her room after dinner what happened?'

'I stayed with her some time, and then Lord Colin came in.'

'At what time?'

'At about eleven o'clock.'

'What was said?'

'I cannot tell. I had gone to sleep, and he woke me up.'

'You had gone to sleep in Lady Colin's bedroom?' Judge Butt asked incredulously.

'Yes.'

'What did Lord Colin say?' Clarke asked.

'He seemed surprised, but I don't remember that he said anything.'

'Did he complain about your being there?'

'No, but he seemed surprised.'

Bird was cross-examined by Finlay:

'Have you ever before or since gone to sleep in the bedroom of a lady patient?'

'No.'

'Did it not strike you as very odd?'

'I could not help it.'

'Were you there from four to eleven o'clock?'

'No, from a quarter-past four to half-past seven. Then Lord Colin asked me to stay to dinner. I said I wanted to go home to do something, but I would see Lady Colin at eleven. He said, "Oh, come and dine," and I said, "I would rather not." He again said, "You had better stay," and I did.'

'Did not Lord Colin say he wished to know, one way or another, whether you were going to dine?'

'No, he would not have spoken to me like that.'

'After dinner you went up to Lady Colin's bedroom and fell asleep?'
'I did.'

'How was it that you fell asleep?'

'The light was low, Lady Colin was very drowsy, and I fell asleep. I cannot tell you why.'

'And Lord Colin was surprised when he came home?'

'Well, the room was dark, and I thought he was surprised.'

'You were calling upon Lady Colin at this time tolerably often?'
'I was.'

'You paid her visits of one hour or one-hour-and-a-half. Is not that unusual?'

'No, I think not.'

'Are you in the habit of paying visits of that duration to lady patients when no nurse is present?'

'I have had lady patients with whom I have stayed longer than that.'
'Alone?'

'Alone.'

'Is it not exceptional?'

'It is.'

In his summing-up, Finlay agreed that this episode was exceptional: 'Generally speaking, when a medical man makes a call, he gets away as soon as he can, but time was no object to Mr Bird. His practice must have gone to the dogs. (Laughter) Mr Bird's devotion to his fair patient was extraordinary. He was not a doctor. He was more than a doctor. He remained in her bedroom for hours without any light in the room. (Loud laughter, at once silenced by an usher) When a man spends hours with a young, beautiful married woman in her bedroom in the dark, it presupposes an intimacy that is likely to lead to mischief.'

CHAPTER 39

A Miscarriage?

On 23 April, Bird called in another medical man to examine Lady Colin.

The new doctor, a little, bald, white-whiskered man, was one of the world's most eminent obstetricians, Braxton Hicks. His credentials were impressive: Fellow of the Royal College of Physicians; Fellow, the Royal society; Fellow, the Linnaean society; Fellow, the Obstetric Society of London; Honorary Fellow of the Societies of Edinburgh and Berlin, and the American Gynaecological Society; consulting physician to four leading hospitals; author of numerous articles and books. For more than a century his name has been attached to the 'Braxton Hicks contraction,' a valuable method of diagnosing pregnancy.

Questioned by Russell, Hicks confirmed Bird's diagnosis of the cause of Lady Colin's suffering as 'an acute attack of inflammation which might almost be called peritonitis.' He was then asked a couple of questions that might seem surprising:

'Was there any indication in Lady Colin of pregnancy or miscarriage?'

'None at all.'

'You are certain that she could not have been pregnant or have had a miscarriage?'

'Yes, I am certain.'

The questions had been prompted by an accusation voiced by Annie Duffy when he was examined by Lockwood:

'You have had a long experience as a nurse?'

'Yes.'

'In the course of that experience have you had knowledge of the ailments of women?'

'Yes, I have had ample opportunities of observing their ailments.'

'From what you saw of Lady Colin's illness, did you form an opinion?'

'I did.'

'What was that opinion?'

'That she had had a miscarriage.'

[165]

All accounts of the trial reported 'Sensation in court.'

Duffy was cross-examined by Russell:

'When did you first suspect that she had had a miscarriage?'

'About a week after she was taken ill.'

'What caused you to come to this conclusion?'

Duffy responded to the question, but her answer was not reported anywhere.

'Did you say anything of your suspicions,' Russell asked, 'to Lord Colin?'

'Never, till he put great pressure on me.'

'Why did you not say anything?'

'I did not want to be mixed up with any trouble which might take place.'

'Was that honest?'

'To my patient it was honest, in his condition of health, not to disturb him.'

'Did you say anything of your suspicions to Mr Bird?'

'Never.'

'Or to Dr Braxton Hicks?'

'Never.'

'Why not?'

'It was no business of mine. I asked Mr Bird if I should be present when Dr Hicks was there, and he replied that there would be no need for me to be in the room, and that if I were wanted he would call me.'

'If you had suspicion, why not mention it to Mr Bird or Dr Hicks?'

'Because I knew that Lord and Lady Colin had not been living as man and wife, and I thought it right to hold my tongue while in the house.'

'You knew that they were skilful professional men?'

'I knew they were supposed to be. I have never worked for them, so I cannot speak to that.'

On the alleged miscarriage, Lady Miles was questioned by Inderwick:

'How did you learn about the supposed miscarriage?'

'Two or three days after Lady Colin had seen Dr Hicks, I came down from her room and went into Lord Colin's room. He asked me how I had found her. I said, "Exceedingly ill." He then said, "Oh, yes, there has been foul play going on." I asked, "What do you mean?" He replied, "She has had a miscarriage." I said, "A miscarriage! It is impossible. She has not been near you for months. Who could have told you such a foul statement?" He said, "It is all very fine, mother" – sometimes he called me "mother" – "You are getting angry, but it is a fact. That Tom Bird's a sharp fellow, and they have managed it between them." "Why, Colin," I said, "Dr Hicks has been there too. It could not be." He said, "Hicks is a friend of Bird's and would do as he was told. Mrs Duffy told me of her suspicions." I said, "What did she tell you?" He said, "From her observations of the linen left in my wife's room she knows it to be a miscarriage."'

'Was Mr Bird in the house at the time?'

'Yes.'

'Did you have a conversation with him?'

'Yes. I called him to the back room and had a very animated conversation with him.'

'Tell us about it.'

'I said to him, "How dare you deceive me?" He said, "What are you talking about?" I said, "Lady Colin has had a miscarriage, and you have concealed it from me. You should have told me." He said, "Good God! Who said that?" I replied, "Lord Colin told me, and his nurse told him." He then took God to witness that it was not true, that Lady Colin was suffering from a complaint exactly the contrary.'

'What did he say was the cause of her suffering?'

'That she was suffering from a contraction of the womb.'

'Did he say anything on her condition generally?'

'He said, "Poor creature, she has been suffering frightfully and is fearfully ill. After what she has gone through, it is very bad to have the additional suffering caused by this accusation."'

'Did he make any reference to Lord Colin?'

Yes. He said he would not attend Lady Colin any longer unless Lord Colin apologized and withdrew the allegation.'

'Did you report that to Lord Colin?'

'Yes, I told him exactly what had happened.'

'What did he say to that?'

'He pooh-poohed it and made out that he did not mean all that he had said.'

'Do you recollect his words?'

'He said, "I have been told these things, and when one is told things one believes them, but perhaps they are exaggerations." He spoke as if he wanted to get out of it.'

'What did you say then?'

'I said, "It is all very fine, but Mr Bird won't return to your wife unless you apologize and withdraw your charge."'

'What did he then say?'

'He said, "Well, you can tell him I apologize."'

'Did you speak to Mr Bird?'

'Yes.'

'What occurred between the two of you?'

'I told him that Lord Colin apologized and wished him to continue attending Lady Colin. Mr Bird did not accept the apology.'

'But did he continue to attend Lady Colin?'

'Yes. He said that she was so exceedingly ill he could not refuse to attend her.'

Lady Miles was cross-examined by Finlay:

'Did you believe Lord Colin when he said that Lady Colin had suffered from a miscarriage?'

'Yes. He spoke so forcibly.'

'You knew that, if true, this miscarriage was the result of Lady Colin's intercourse with another man?'

'I could hardly believe it, but Lord Colin took me completely by surprise.'

'Did you go upstairs believing that Lady Colin had been unfaithful to her husband?'

'I went upstairs full of surprise and indignation. I cannot say what I believed.'

Lord Colin was questioned by Lockwood:

'Is it true that you deputed Lady Miles to convey an apology to Mr Bird in respect of the alleged miscarriage?'

'It is absolutely false.'

'What conversation had you with her on the subject?'

'I told her about my wife's illness and my anxiety. Then she said, "Colin, it looks uncommonly like a miscarriage."'

Sir Edward Clarke cross-examined Lord Colin:

'Who mentioned the miscarriage to you?'

'Lady Miles.'

'Did Mrs Duffy say anything about it?'

'No.'

'Do you mean to say that Lady Miles originated the idea?'

'Certainly.'

'At the time you had no suspicion of your wife?'

'Certainly not.'

'Did you speak to Mr Bird about it?'

'No, I did not.'

'Why not?'

'It was a very delicate question. Then Lady Miles came to me and said, "Colin, I am mistaken. It is not a miscarriage."'

Clarke also questioned his own client on the affair:

'During the time of Lady Colin's illness, was any suggestion made of its being a miscarriage?'

'Yes.'

'Who mentioned it to you?'

'Lady Miles.'

'What did she say?'

'She said that the nurse and Lord Colin had told her there had been a miscarriage.'

'What did you say.'

'I said it was an infamous accusation and that I should withdraw from attending Lady Colin unless he withdrew the suggestion.'

'What took place upon that?'

'Lady Miles came to me and said Lord Colin pooh-poohed the affair and wished me to continue in attendance.'

'Did you continue your attendance until she recovered?'

'Yes.'

In light of Dr Hicks's assertion that no miscarriage could have taken place, Clarke and Russell characterized this episode as an invention of Annie Duffy. Clarke called her 'malicious' and Russell said, 'If ever a witness had a fixed expression of malevolence and ill-will Annie Duffy was that witness.'

Finlay, however, was not intimidated by the celebrated obstetrician: 'His evidence would have been more important if he had been called in earlier, and if he had approached the case from an independent point of view. He is, I submit, a thorough partisan in the case and would leave no stone unturned to help Mr Bird.'

As for the incident itself, Finlay said, 'Lady Miles went upstairs convinced that Lady Colin had had a miscarriage. What a revelation that is! Lady Miles is a most intimate friend of Lady Colin's, has known her since childhood, and she thought it possible that there had been a miscarriage. I ask you if Lady Colin had led an irreproachable life would Lady Miles have so readily believed that she had been guilty of unfaithfulness? Does not this speak volumes?

'After Lady Miles had communicated Lord Colin's suspicions to Mr Bird, the latter said, "I will take my oath in the name of God it is nothing of the kind." It was said a long time ago by a shrewd judge of human nature, Lord Chesterfield, that if a man affirmed what was probable in itself with violent oaths and asseverations, it might be presumed that the fact affirmed was a lie. Why should Mr Bird have recourse to such an affirmation if there was no colour for the suggestion?'

CHAPTER 40

The Cabman's Letter

'During her illness,' Lockwood asked Annie Duffy, 'did notes frequently come to Lady Colin?'

'They did.'

'Did you ever take them in?'

'I did.'

'How were they brought?'

'Sometimes they were dropped into the letter box, and sometimes they were left by a hansom cabman.'

'An ordinary cabman?'

Lockwood's surprised response was due to the fact that cabmen were not licensed to deliver messages. This regulation, however, was not strictly enforced, and sometimes, when the price was right, a cabman would carry a letter to the door of a house. But it would have been extraordinary for him to enter a private home and unbelievable if he ascended the stairs.

'Do you remember one particular instance when a note was brought into the house by a cabman?' Lockwood asked.

'Yes.'

'When was that?'

'About halfway through her illness.'

'Did you see the cabman?'

'I did. I opened the door to him, and he gave me a note for Lady Colin, which I took up.'

'Had the cabman another note?'

'Yes.'

'Did he show it to you?'

'Yes.'

'Who was it addressed to?'

'Lady Miles.'

'What did you do?'

'I took the note to Lady Colin, who was in bed.'

'What did she say?'

'I handed her the note, and she said, "Who brought this?" I said, "A cabman, and he is waiting for an answer." She said, "Give me my writing materials." I got them, gave them to her, and then left the room, saying, "I'll go to my room and wait for an answer." While I was waiting, the front door slammed., Lady Colin called me into her room and said, "Is that his lordship come in?" I said, "I don't know. I have not been downstairs." Some time after that she said, "I want to see the man who brought this note." I said, "The cabman, my lady?" She said, "Yes, show him up." '

"What did you do?"

'I went downstairs and called the boy up from the hall.'

For a few months, a page boy, James French, was on the Campbells' domestic staff.

'What did the boy do in the house?' the Judge asked.

'He ran errands and cleaned the boots and knives.'

'What did you tell the boy to do?' Lockwood asked.

'I told him to go into the street and hold the cabman's horse.'

'Then what happened?'

'The boy went out and held the horse, and the cabman came inside.'

'And then?'

'When I got the cabman into the hall and shut the door, I told him that her ladyship wanted to see him, and that he was to follow me upstairs.'

'Did he do so?'

'He did. He stopped at the drawing-room door and said, "Is she in here?" I said, "No, she is in her bedroom." He said, "She is not in bed, is she?" I replied, "Yes." He then said, "I cannot go in there." I said, "Her ladyship wants to see you." He said, "What can I do?" I replied, "The best you can." (Laughter) I opened the door and said, "The cabman, my lady." '

'Did he go in?'

'He did. (Laughter) I shut the door after him.' (Renewed laughter)

The fun continued during Russell's cross-examination:

"You showed the cabman into the bedroom?'

'I did.'

'Did you go inside as well?'

'I did not.'

'I hope the cabman did not look flushed and excited when he came out?' (Laughter)

'He looked very confused when he went in.'

'I hope his dress was not disordered and his hair disarranged?' (Laughter)

[171]

'Not any more than any other cabman's.'

'Why did you not go in?'

'When a lady tells you to show a cabman in, you leave the room. Had I not, I should have been told to leave.'

'Were you told to leave?'

'No, I left out of politeness. Her ladyship might have something to tell him which she did not want me to know.'

'Your delicacy prevented you from going into the bedroom?'

'My politeness.' (Laughter)

'But your politeness did not prevent you from looking at the envelope the cabman had after he came out?'

'I could not help seeing it.'

'Do you mean he thrust it under your nose?'

'He was holding it out, and I was standing by his side. He was reading it, and I looked at the same time.' (Laughter)

'Accidentally or intentionally?'

'A little of both.' (Laughter)

Lady Colin's version of the incident was brought out by Inderwick:

'Tell us the story of the cabman.'

'I had sent my maid out to get some things I needed. Whilst she was out, Mrs Duffy brought me a note, saying a messenger had brought it and another note for Lady Miles. It was from Lord Blandford, saying he had heard that I was dangerously ill and asking if that were the case. If I could not answer it, would I send the note to Lady Miles, who would no doubt answer it. I was very angry and very much under the influence of narcotics. I said, "Go and tell the man not to take the note to Lady Miles." Mrs Duffy said, "Oh, is he to take it on, or is he to take it back again?" I said, "Don't be so stupid. Send the man to me." He came up, and I said, "Take this note to Lord Blandford," and I gave him back the note for Lady Miles.'

'Did Mrs Duffy close the door and leave you together?'

'She did not. She was in the room all the time.'

While cross-examining, Lockwood naturally brought up this episode:

'Was it not an out-of-the way thing to have a cabman brought up to your bedroom?'

'Most out-of-the-way.'

'Do you account for it by the fact that you had been so much under the influence of narcotics?'

'Greatly, and to my irritability, which was owing to the great pain which I was suffering.'

'You hardly knew what you were doing?'

'Precisely. I hardly knew what I was doing.'

'You were able to write a note?'

'Such as it was. The general outline was very much blurred.'

'Is there any chance of our getting that note?'

'I haven't the slightest idea.'

'Do you know if Lord Blandford kept any of your letters?'

'I haven't the slightest idea.'

'You have never asked him?'

'Never.'

'When did you write the note?'

'While Mrs Duffy had gone downstairs to fetch the man.'

'Why did you not send it down?'

'Because of Mrs Duffy's stupidity.'

'Was there no one else in the house?'

'I don't know.'

'Did you inquire?'

'Certainly not.'

'Did you give the man a message?'

'I simply told him to leave the message for Lady Miles with me and to take the one I gave him back to Lord Blandford.'

'All that was to be done was to take one note from the cabman and give him another?'

'Yes.'

'And Mrs Duffy was too stupid to do that?'

'Her stupidity lay in not understanding what I said.'

'I need hardly say that you would have preferred that the cabman should not come into your room when you were in bed?'

'Certainly.'

'It was an unpleasant occurrence?'

'It was. You keep exaggerating the whole occurrence.'

'But it was extraordinary for a lady of your position to have a cabman sent up to your bedroom?'

'Yes, it was.'

The Duke of Marlborough, formerly Lord Blandford, was questioned by the Attorney-General on his role in the event:

'Will you tell us what you know about what has been called the "cabman incident"?'

'One day I met Mrs Bolton in the street, and she told me that Lady Colin was dangerously ill. I then sent by a cabman two notes – one to Lady Colin and the other to Lady Miles – telling him that if he did not receive an answer to the note for Lady Colin to take the other on to Lady Miles at Cornwall Gardens. The purport of the notes was simply to inquire after Lady Colin's health.'

'Did you get an answer from Lady Colin?'

'I got a short note stating that she was not so very bad.'

'Did you keep that note?'

'Oh, dear, no. I suppose it went straight into the fire.'

'Had you any reason for keeping it?'

'No.'

Asked by Finlay if Lady Colin had written 'a perfectly innocent letter which might have been published on the housetops,' the Duke replied, 'Oh, yes.'

But Finlay would not accept this answer. 'I put it to you, as men of common sense,' he told the jurors, 'whether a married woman, having written a letter to a man like Lord Blandford, would take such an extraordinary step as calling a blushing cabman to her bedside without some strong reason? Could she have any reason for such extraordinary precations except that she was very much afraid that the letter might get mislaid and its contents become known?'

CHAPTER 41

The New Duke's New Home

Early in June, Lady Colin was on her feet, resuming friendly relations with old friends like Tom Bird.

By the end of the month, Bird had become *persona non grata* with Lord Colin, who was questioned about it by Clarke:

'When did you ask your wife not to see Mr Bird?'

'At the end of June 1883.'

'Why did you tell your wife this?'

'I was not satisfied with Mr Bird's conduct.'

'In what respect.'

'He came to my house frequently, and he treated me with no consideration at all, and I was displeased because he sat so long in my wife's bedroom.'

'Do you remember at the beginning of June receiving a letter from Mr
Bird with regard to his fees?'

'Perfectly well.'

'Did you answer it and thank Mr Bird for his kindness and attention,
which, you said, placed you under deep obligation to him?'

'Yes.'

That letter was dated 5 June. What happened between then and the
end of the month to cause you to instruct Lady Colin not to admit Mr Bird
to the house?'

'I had heard that he had been at a bazaar with my wife.'

'At a bazaar? This is something new?'

'Yes.'

'Who told you about that?'

'Mrs Duffy.'

'What did she say?'

'That he was lounging about with my wife at a bazaar.'

Central London had numerous bazaars with covered walks and rows of
stalls stocked with all kinds of articles. The best known were the
Burlington Bazaar, Piccadilly (site of the present Burlington Arcade); the
Crystal Palace Bazaar, in Oxford Street; the Baker Street Bazaar; the
Opera Colonnade, in the Haymarket; and, the oldest and most popular,
the Soho Bazaar, in Soho Square.

'Did you,' Clarke asked, 'have any other objection to Mr Bird?'

'Yes. I did not think it right for a medical man to remain in attendance
upon a lady for five or six hours when there was a trained nurse in the
house.'

'Why did you not speak to Mr Bird about this?'

'I left it to Lady Miles to tell him. Her view on this matter was the same
as mine.'

'Were there other occasions when Mr Bird remained with your wife for
five or six, or at least several, hours?'

'Yes, there were several occasions.'

'And you said nothing to Mr Bird?'

'I gave him my opinion through Lady Miles.'

'Did you ever tell him face to face?'

'No, I did not take that step. I took a gentler course.'

Bird was banned from 79 Cadogan Place, but Lady Colin continued to
see him. She also saw Lord Blandford, whose title changed on 5 July 1883,
when his father died unexpectedly at the principal family residence,
Blenheim Palace. Lord Blandford became the eighth Duke of Marlborough, Marquis of Blandford and Dorset, Earl of Sunderland, Baron

Spencer of Wormleighton, Warwickshire, and Churchill of Sandridge, Herts, in the peerage of England, KG, and Prince of Mindelheim, in Suabia, in the Holy Roman Empire.

The new duke already had a new home in London. Late in June he had moved to 44 Queen Anne's Gate, immediately south of St James's Park. A short street of four-storey red brick houses, Queen Anne's Gate was populated largely by people who were associated with engineering. The residents of the 55 houses included 16 civil engineers, 12 architects, six surveyors, two railway engineers, one electrical engineer, one telegraph engineer, one contractor, and six who just called themselves 'engineers.' There were also three MP's, two solicitors, one barrister, one lithographer, one artist, and one surgeon. Blandford lived between the surgeon and one of the engineers. (Number 44 still stands, but several nearby houses were torn down to make room for the headquarters of the Home Office.)

Two doors from Blandford's house, on an extension of Queen Anne's Gate known as Queen Anne's Mews, was the home of Sir Charles Forster, Bart., MP. Attached to the home was a stable, and the groom was a man named George Baker. Because his job allowed him a great deal of free time, Baker became a witness in the Campbell trial. He was examined by Finlay:

'During June and July 1883, were you standing about the entrance to the mews frequently?'

'Yes.'

'During these months did you notice a lady coming there?'

'Yes, on several occasions I saw one come out.'

'Come out, did you say?'

'Yes, and get in a cab and drive off.'

'Come out from where?'

'From Number 44.'

'Whose house was that?'

'The Duke of Marlborough's.'

'What time of day was it?'

'About half-past three.'

'Was the lady accompanied?'

'Yes, by a collie dog.'

'Did you ever see the lady go into the house?'

'Yes.'

'How often did you see her go in and come out?'

'Six or seven times.'

'How did she come and go?'

'In a cab.'

'Do you know this lady by sight?'

'Yes.'

'Is she in court now?'

'Yes.'

'Who is she?'

'Lady Colin Campbell.'

George Baker was cross-examined by Russell:

'When did you first notice this lady?'

'It must have been in the middle of June.'

'What did you notice about her?'

'I have seen her with her collie dog come out of Number 44 and get into a cab, and I have seen her go to the house.'

'Was she alone?'

'Yes, with the exception of a collie dog.' (Laughter)

'I suppose you were lounging about at the entrance to the mews when you saw her?'

'I was standing, not lounging.'

'Don't laugh, sir. This is no laughing matter. How did you know she was Lady Colin Campbell?'

'A gentleman outside told me who she was.'

'Who was the gentleman?'

'I can't say.'

'Where does he live?'

'I don't know.'

'What was he?'

'I can't say.'

'Do you mean you stopped a gentleman in the street and asked him who a certain lady was?'

'No, a gentleman stopped me and said, "Do you know who that is – that is Lady Colin Campbell."'

'Was he a real gentleman?' (Laughter)

'He was dressed like one.'

'With a top hat?'

'Yes' (Laughter)

'Where was he when the lady came along?'

'He was passing. He came from the direction of the Underground railway station.'

'Had you ever seen him before?'

'No.'

'Had you ever seen this lady?'

'No, but I have seen her several times since that day.'

'He was walking along from the Metropolitan Railway and stopped to talk to you. Did he address you by name?'

'He didn't know my name.'

The man must have come from the St James Park Underground station, opposite the entrance to Queen Anne's Gate. The London Underground, the first of its kind in the world, had begun operations in 1863. The initial line was the Metropolitan, and for a time the whole system was known as the Metropolitan Railway, but the St James's Park station is actually on the Circle line. For Victorians, the Underground provided easy, rapid, economical travel, with the average fare only twopence and the highest fare, for the longest journey, one shilling. There was a station near the Campbells' home, at Sloane Square, but neither Lord nor Lady Colin ever rode on a train of the London Underground.

'Did you ask this gentleman,' Russell said, 'why he gave you, of all men in the world, this information?'

'I did not.'

'How long did you stand at the entrance to the mews?'

'I used to stand there about two hours-and-a-half at a time.'

'How long did you stand there on the day in question?'

'About an hour-and-a-half.'

'Is that your general occupation?' (Laughter)

'No. I stand there when I have nothing to do.'

'Are you a celebrated person, Mr Baker?'

'No, I am not.'

'A remarkable person?'

'No.'

'And yet a gentleman whom you did not know addressed you, whose name he did not know, and says, "Do you know who that is – that is Lady Colin Campbell." Why did he say that?'

'I don't know.'

For the Attorney-General it was clear why he had spoken: 'I suggest that this communicative individual was there for the purpose of making evidence in this case, and that that led Baker to believe he saw something of the kind.'

CHAPTER 42

The Lady and the Dog

The nearest cabstand to Queen Anne's Gate was in the Broadway. One of several drivers who regularly stopped there was Frederick Deane. He was questioned by Finlay:

'Do you know Lady Colin Campbell?'

'Yes.'

'Have you driven her?'

'Yes.'

'When did you usually drive her?'

'In the afternoon.'

'Over what period did your drives extend?'

'From the middle of July to the beginning of August 1883.'

'How often did you drive her?'

'About a dozen times.'

'Where mostly did you take her from?'

'From 44 Queen Anne's Gate.'

'Where did you drive her to?'

'To 79 Cadogan Place, and two or three times to 44 Beaufort Gardens.'

'When you took her at 44 Queen Anne's Gate, who called you?'

'A gentleman. He had a whistle.'

'Do you see him in court?'

'Yes, there he is (pointing to Marlborough, seated, as usual, just behind the second row of barristers).'

'The Duke of Marlborough! Where did he stand when he whistled?'

'At the door.'

'And then Lady Colin got into your cab?'

'Yes.'

'And drove away by herself.'

'Except for her collie dog.'

'Have you any doubt that the lady sitting there (pointing to Lady Colin) is the lady who rode with you?'

'None at all.'

Cabman Deane was cross-examined by Russell:

'When the gentleman called for you, was there any attempt at concealment about his action?'

'None at all. He used to come to the door, blow the whistle, and then the lady would come out.'

'Was the lady muffled, wrapped up, or concealed in any way?'

'No.'

'Had the lady always a collie dog with her?'

'Yes.'

'Am I to take it that the whole number of times that you drove the lady was in July or early August?'

'Yes.'

'Over how many days?'

'I should say it was from the middle of July to August. That would be about a dozen times within a fortnight or three weeks.'

When she was in the witness boxs, Lady Colin was asked by Inderwick about the Duke's new home:

'Have you ever been to Queen Anne's Gate?'

'Once.'

'When was that?'

'After I returned from Leigh Court in 1883. My sister and I met Lord Blandford one day at the Army and Navy Stores [in Victoria Street, not far from Queen Anne's Gate]. He said, "You have never seen my little house. Come and see it now." so we walked down, all three of us. We saw through his house. He gave us some tea, and we went away.'

'Was that the only occasion on which you were inside the house?'

'The only occasion.'

'Did you at any other time ever visit the house?'

'Yes. At the end of July I went there with the last parcel of books I had from Lord Blandford. I think the servant said he was out of town. I said it did not matter and handed the books to the servant with a note.'

The Duke confirmed Lady Colin's testimony. When cross-examined by Finlay, he admitted that a woman with a collie dog had visited him.

'Was this lady,' Finlay asked, 'the same lady that was with you at Purfleet?'

'Oh, no.'

'Do you mind writing her name down?'

The Duke wrote something on a slip of paper and handed it to Finlay. After looking at it, Finlay offered it to Judge Butt, who, told that the name was not Lady Colin Campbell, said 'I do not want to see it.'

'Do you say,' Finlay asked the Duke, 'that this lady was in the habit of taking a collie dog about with her.'

'Yes.'

'Habitually?'

'Yes.'

It may seem strange that Lady Colin and the woman who the Duke said visited him each owned a collie dog. Even stranger, if cabman Deane is to be believed, is that this woman should have asked him to take her to 79 Cadogan Place.

There were rebuttal witnesses who appeared for Lady Colin.

At the head of Queen Anne's Gate there was an actual gate, with a gatekeeper always on duty. One of the two principal gatekeepers, William Fowler, was questioned by Inderwick:

'From the gate have you a view of the house numbered 44?'

'Yes.'

'Do you remember the summer of 1883?'

'Yes, that was the summer that Lord Blandford was made Duke.'

'During that summer, when were you on duty at the gate?'

'From 1 p.m. to 8 p.m.'

'You have seen Lady Colin in court?'

'Yes.'

'Have you ever seen her go into Number 44, Queen Anne's Gate or come out of it?'

'Never.'

'Have you ever seen her pass through the gate, either on foot or in a cab?'

'Never.'

William Fowler's colleague, Edward Lay, also denied ever seeing Lady Colin. Under cross-examination, he admitted that his duty was not to watch visitors but to direct traffic.

Lady Colin, it should be noted, did not seem to have gone freely anywhere without being noticed.

Cabman Deane was one of four who regularly waited at the Broadway cabstand. Two of the others, with names that might suggest a comedy team, were Norton and Martin. They said that to the best of their knowledge they had never driven Lady Colin.

'The fourth man who uses this cab-rank,' Russell told Judge Butt, 'is in hospital, and with your Lordship's permission I will call him later.'

'Any other cabman will do as well, Sir Charles,' Finlay said.

'I object to that comment,' Russell said. 'I submit that this is material evidence to show how singular it is that one man, and only one man, should have driven this lady.'

In his summation, Russell returned to this point: 'Deane was one of four cabmen on that rank. I called the others to show that they had never driven a lady from or to Queen Anne's Gate. We must assume that the cabmen attend with equal regularity, and so on each occasion the chances are one in four that a particular individual will be engaged. I elicited from a senior wrangler [a top mathematics student at Cambridge] that the chances against one cabman being engaged for the twelve occasions on which a cab was required at 44 Queen Anne's Gate are 16,770,216 to one.' (Laughter)

Russell also noted that 'Cabman Deane said he sometimes drove Lady Colin to 44 Beaufort Gardens. But Mrs Bolton's number is 6 Beaufort Gardens, and who lives at 44 we do not know.'

At one point during her examination by Inderwick, Lady Colin said, 'From the time of the death of the Duke of Marlborough in July 1883 down to May 1884 I did not see Lord Blandford.'

Blandford confirmed this statement, and then, examined by Webster, explained why he could not have seen much of Lady Colin in London during the two pertinent months:

'After your father's death, where did you stop during July and August?'

'At Blenheim, continuously, except for one or two days.'

'Did you, during July or August, come up at all to Queen Anne's Gate?'

'I might have come up once or twice on business, but with that exception I passed my time entirely at Blenheim.'

To support his statement, another Watson entered the box. He was George Lindley Watson, for thirty years the Duke of Marlborough's resident agent at Blenheim. He was briefly examined by Marlborough's junior counsel, the tallest barrister in the case, six-foot five-inch Lewis Coward:

'The late Duke of Marlborough died on July 4, 1883, and his funeral took place on July 10?'

'Yes.'

'Do you have letters, books, and diaries for the months of July and August which enable you to speak with certainty as to whether or not the present Duke of Marlborough was at Blenheim during those months?'

'Yes.'

'During those months you had personal interviews with the present Duke?'

'Yes.'

'Will you give the dates during July and August of that year in which you had personal interviews with the Duke?'

'In July I saw him on the 7th, 8th, 9th, 10th, 11th, 12th, 13th, 14th, 16th, 23rd, 26th, 27th, and 28th. In August I saw him on the 1st, 2nd, 7th, 10th, 11th, 12th, 13th, 14th, 15th, 16th, 17th, 18th, 20th, 21st, 22nd, and 23rd.'

'When did you usually see him?'

'In the middle of the day.'

In answer to a question by Finlay, agent Watson said that coming up to London from Blenheim took about two hours.

CHAPTER 43

Lady Colin's Ultimatum

Until the summer of 1883, the Campbells maintained a measure of decorum in their personal relationships. But peace could not last forever. Eventually there would be an explosion. There was one. It came in July at a mansion known as Syon House.

Built in 1547 in Brentwood, Middlesex, a Thames River market town twelve miles west of London, Syon House was one of six residences of the Duke of Northumberland. Lord and Lady Colin were not strangers there because Northumberland's first son was married to Argyll's eldest daughter, Edith.

On 10 July, the Campbells were expected at Syon House, and Lockwood asked Lord Colin about this:

'Did you and your wife go to Syon House together?'

'No. I asked my wife to make no other engagements, but she did make other engagements, and I went to Syon House alone.'

'When did she follow you?'

'Six days later.'

'Do you know where she stayed while you were there?'

'She said she would stay at her sister's home.'

Lady Colin was not with her sister. She remained at Cadogan Place. Lockwood asked Ellen Hawkes about that week:

'Do you remember anything happening after Lord Colin had gone to Syon House?'

'Yes, a gentleman was in the house at four o'clock one morning. The place smelled of tobacco smoke, and I found half a cigar on the hall table.'

'What time was it that you smelled smoke?'

'At four in the morning. The dog barked, and I went downstairs to his lordship's room.'

Hawkes was cross-examined by Russell:

'Did you see anybody come home that night?'

'No, but I heard.'

'What did you hear?'

'Footsteps. I knew there must be a stranger because the dog barked. He barked only at strangers.'

'Did you learn who the gentleman was?'

'No.'

'Did you tell his lordship that you found the remnant of a cigar on the hall table?'

'Yes. I kept it and showed it to his lordship.'

'You kept it to give to him?'

'Yes.'

'You intended to tell him whether he asked you or not?'

'Oh, no.'

'What did you intend to do with the cigar?'

'Show it to Lord Colin if he asked me.'

'You kept the cigar, thinking that Lord Colin might ask whether you knew anything against his wife?'

'I did not think it could go on much longer.'

'Have you for the sake of sparing Lady Colin kept anything back?'

'(Smiling) Oh, no.'

The smile is understandable. Lady Colin was not popular with her servants.

This was Lady Colin's explanation of the smoke:

'I was at a ball that evening with my sister, my sister-in-law, and my brother. We stayed until nearly the end. My brother took me home. He may have smoked a cigarette, but I did not take much notice.'

Neptune Blood was questioned by Russell on that evening:

'Do you remember escorting your sister from a ball in July of 1883?'

'Yes.'

'At what time did you arrive at Cadogan Place?'

'About three in the morning.'

'Did you go inside?'

'I think it probable that I did. In fact I am sure I did.'

'Do you remember whether you stayed some time?'

'If I went in, I have no doubt I stayed some time.'

'Do you recollect whether you were smoking or not?'

'I really cannot say.'

'Is it a habit of yours?'

'Yes. If I went in, I probably smoked a cigarette.'

One might wonder why Lady Colin did not mention the ball to her husband, and why the dog barked at her brother. And if Neptune Blood smoked a cigarette, why did Ellen Hawkes find a cigar?

Eventually Lady Colin arrived at Syon House. She told Inderwick about what happened there:

'You went to Syon House on July 16, Saturday?'

'Yes.'

'On Sunday did Mr Allingham come to see Lord Colin?'

'Yes.'

'On the following day did Lord Colin make a communication to you as to yourself?'

'On the same day.'

'What did he say?'

'He said that Mr Allingham had pronounced him perfectly cured.'

'Did he make any request to you as to cohabitation?'

'Yes.'

'When was that?'

'That evening.'

'What did Lord Colin say or do?'

'When I was saying goodnight, he was very affectionate, and he asked me to come back to him.'

'What did you say in answer to that?'

'I made an excuse and said I was very tired.'

'Were you suffering from the complaint?'

'Yes.'

'Was any other reference made to resumption of cohabitation?'

'Yes, the next day.'

'What occurred?'

'Lord Colin taxed me with not caring whether he was cured or not. I said I did care, and he said, "Why did you not come to see me last night?" I said because of the message I sent him in February I could not do so. He said, "I shall not allow you to keep to that message." I said, "I shall keep to it." He said, "You have no right to send me such a message." I said, "It was not a determination made in five minutes. It was the result of intense suffering, physical and moral. I shall keep to it until the end of my life. If you force me to sleep with you, you will find me dead beside you on the pillow in the morning. I should prefer that to ever being touched by you again."' (Sensation in court)

'Was there any further conversation?'

'He said I had the feelings not of a woman but of a tigress.'

'Was anything said about separating?'

'He said he would separate from me if I did not give way. I said it was for him to decide that. I was willing to care for him, to keep the matter secret, as I had done up to that time, but if there was a separation, it must be open and public so that everyone should know the cause.'

'Did you give any reason for wishing the separation to be an open one?'

'I said I would not allow him and his family to go about giving what version they pleased of the matter.'

'Did Lord Colin make any charges of impropriety against you?'

'None whatever.'

'After this, did you go to town and see your mother?'

'Yes, on the next day.'

Lord Colin's recollection was given to Lockwood:

'Do you remember your wife coming into your bedroom at Syon House?'

'Yes. I remember going to bed early. I asked her to come and say good night when she had her dressing gown on. She said that she was tired and was going to bed.'

'Do you remember having a conversation in which you made complaints about her conduct?'

'Yes.'

'Tell us about it.'

'I complained of her neglect of me. I complained about having to go to Syon House alone. I questioned her about her right to send the message by Lady Miles. I questioned the right of a wife to send such a message to her husband. She said she would never cohabit with me again.'

'Did you express any suspicion as to her conduct with others?'

'Certainly. I told her that I was uncomfortable with her, in fact that I had some suspicion.'

'Do you remember what she said to that?'

'I have difficulty in remembering exactly what she said. I have the recollection that she was violent and very abusive.'

'Do you remember her saying anything as to how much she cared for you?'

'Yes.' I said, "You cannot care for me," and she gave me to understand that she cared more about many others.'

'Do you remember putting a specific question to her as to whether she had been unfaithful to you?'

'Yes, I do.'

'What did you say?'

'I said, "Have you always been faithful to me?" "Yes," she replied. "Do you wish to insult me?" She mentioned the Divorce Court and said, "If you take me to the court, you will get the worse of it." ' (Sensation in court)

'Lady Colin, I believe, left you at Syon House?'

'Yes.'

'Before she left, did you say anything with regard to the use of "never" in connection with your mode of life?'

'I said, "I can understand that you do not wish to cohabit with me now, but I deny the right of a wife to tell her husband that she will never cohabit with him again." '

On Lady Colin's rights, Russell made some far-reaching remarks: 'It was not unnatural that Lord Colin should assert his rights as a husband. When, therefore, Lady Colin told him of her firm resolve, his answer was, "If you do not yield to me, I will separate from you." Her answer was, "If you do separate from me, the world shall know the reason." I affirm that she was justified in saying that. If Lord Colin had been allowed to separate from her, and the world were not told why, upon whom would the condemnation fall? Upon whom in such cases does it always fall? Society has strange codes of morality as applied to the sexes.'

At this point, according to one report, 'Sir Charles spoke with great emotion.'

'When sin of this kind,' he went on, 'is committed by a man, the world affects to be shocked for a moment. But his sin is soon forgotten, and men and women who pride themselves on their virtue and highly moral tone are willing to accept the society of such a man. How is it with the poor, hapless, fallen woman? Is there any hope for her? Does society ever open its arms to receive her back again, however much there is to be said in mitigation of her offence, however penitent her life? No, it is not the charity of this world.

"Therefore," Lady Colin said, "If you leave me and tell the world in effect that you leave me for a fault of mine, then in self-respect, in self-defence, for myself and for those who honour my name and are close to me, the truth shall be known." '

CHAPTER 44

A Family Conference

Later on the day that Lady Colin left Syon House, Lord Colin spoke briefly with Annie Duffy. Russell asked her to recall the conversation.

'I found his lordship very ill,' Duffy said, 'and I implored him to tell me the cause. He said that Lady Colin treated him like a leper, and he asked me what was the matter with him. I said, "Nothing, it must be a mistake." He said, "I cannot understand why she is so cold to me. What is wrong?" I said, "What do you mean?" He said, "She has told me that she will never live with me again as my wife." Then he added, "Do you know anything about Lady Colin?" I replied, "No." '

'Why did you say that?' Russell asked.

'Because I did not want to be mixed up with any trouble which might take place.'

'Was that honest?'

'It was dishonest to tell a lie, but it was honest not to make mischief between husband and wife.'

Two days later husband and wife conferred at Thurloe Square. The meeting had been initiated by Lord Colin in a letter from Syon House to Mrs Blood. He wanted the conference to be limited to Lady Colin, Mrs Blood, Lady Miles, and himself, but when he arrived he found that Neptune Blood, Mrs Bolton, and Mr Blood were also present. Mr Blood was temporarily invalided and was mainly confined to a sofa, but occasionally his excitement would bring him to his feet.

'Was it a long meeting?' Inderwick asked Lady Miles.

'Not very long. Perhaps half-an-hour.'

'What were the relations between Lord and Lady Campbell?'

'Rather strained.'

'What did Lord Colin say?'

'He made several accusations. One was about having smelled smoke in the hall and finding a half-burned cigar. Then he spoke about a cabman bringing a letter to Lady Colin.'

'Did he mention Colonel Butler?'

'Oh, yes. He said Colonel Butler had been alone with her for four or five hours. Everybody laughed.'

'Did Mrs Bolton respond to this?'

'Yes. She said that this could hardly have been the case since she had been with Lady Colin for the whole time of Colonel Butler's visit and outstayed him.'

'Did Lord Colin say anything more on that point?'

'No. He seemed to accept what Mrs Bolton said.'

Mrs Blood confirmed what Lady Miles had said about Mrs Bolton.

Lord Colin, however, during Russell's cross-examination, expressed a different opinion on what had been said:

'You recollect Mrs Bolton saying that she had been there during the whole of Colonel Butler's visit?'

'No.'

'Nothing of the kind?'

'No.'

'Kindly think, Lord Colin, before you say that?'

'I am bound to say what I believe. I say "No," to the best of my knowledge I deny that statement.'

'I am obliged to put it to you. Do you undertake to swear that Mrs Bolton did not make that statement?'

'I will undertake to swear that there is not the smallest trace of it in my memory.'

Mrs Bolton had died just before the start of the trial. This question of whether or not she had been at Cadogan Place on 13 April 1883 was of great importance. Had she been there, especially if she had been there all afternoon, there would have been no case against Butler. Annie Duffy and Ellen Hawkes, it will be remembered, never mentioned Mrs Bolton in connection with this incident. They both insisted that during the whole visit the Colonel and the lady had been together alone. From the standpoint of the trial, Mrs Bolton's death had been most untimely.

Continuing with his examination of Lady Miles, Inderwick said, 'Describe the temper of the meeting.'

'Mrs Blood was angry. They were all very angry. Everybody was talking at once.'

Inderwick read from a letter Lady Miles had written to Lord Colin, telling of how Lady Colin had said that she knew at least twelve men whom she preferred to him.

'Where,' Inderwick asked, 'did Lady Colin say that she preferred twelve men to her husband?'

'She said this at Thurloe Square. She was very angry at the time.'

'Were those her exact words?'

'I think her exact words were "a dozen men."'

'Were you angry with Lord Colin?'

'I was angry with all of them. We were all angry with one another.'

Lord Colin gave Lockwood his recollections of the meeting:

'Who was the first person to speak?'

'Mr Blood.'

'What did he say?'

'He said, "I understand you have come to say something. We are ready to hear what you have to say."'

'Yes?'

'I said, "Gertrude, tell me whether it is true or not that you have been in correspondence with Lord Blandford." She said, "I have written to him once or twice." I said, "Once or twice! Will you not go beyond that?" She said, "No." I then said, "From whom did you receive those notes when you were ill in April, notes which arrived sometimes two or three in a day? Were they from Lord Blandford?" She admitted that they were from him. I asked her how it was that she was in such close correspondence with Lord Blandford. She said, "He wished to know how I was." I then said, "Do you remember when you were ill in April, a cab coming to the door, and you receiving a note which was taken to your bedroom? Do you remember that after you read that note you ordered the cabman – a common cabman from the street, an entire stranger to you – to be shown into your bedroom, and that you wrote a note in his presence and gave it to him to take to Lord Blandford?"'

'Yes, what then?'

'She said, "Yes, I remember the circumstances perfectly, but my maid was in." I said, "I have other information. Your maid was not in." About that time I was interrupted by Mrs Blood, who said it was plain I had come to insult her daughter. I said to Mrs Blood, "I have not come to make charges against Gertrude. I have come to ask for explanations, and if those explanations are satisfactory, nobody will be more glad than I shall be."'

'Did you say anything about 44 Queen Anne's Gate?'

'Yes. I asked her whether she had visited Lord Blandford at 44 Queen Anne's Gate, and she replied, "Yes, I have been there once or twice at tea with my sister." I asked her whether she had been there alone. She said she had not. I asked her also about Colonel Butler's visit and why she was at home to him and to nobody else. I asked her also about her correspondence.'

'With whom?'

'Generally. I said, "Why are you so careful about your correspondence? How is it that you will not allow anyone to sort the letters but your maid? Why are you so angry when by chance a letter of yours gets amongst mine? Why this secrecy and guardedness about your correspondence?" In reply she said, "I am no more annoyed by a mistake of that kind than by anything else that goes wrong in the house." I asked her about her correspondence with Colonel Butler. I said, "Is it a fact that you heard from him every day? Will you have any objection to showing me this correspondence?" She said, "I do not keep my letters."'

'Did you say anything about the period when you were at Syon House alone and she was still in London?'

'I did. I said, "Why did you not go to your sister's, as you had said you would? Why did you remain at Cadogan Place? Why did you remain there and write your letters from Number 6 Beaufort Gardens?"'

'Did Lady Colin answer these observations?'

'I really cannot remember what her answer was.'

'Well, please go on.'

'I asked her whether she had brought anyone back from the ball and whether she had had a smoking party in my bedroom.'

'Did she make any answer to that?'

'She denied it to the best of my recollection.'

'What happened next?'

'Mr Blood got up, shook his fist in my face, and told me that I had made infamous charges against my wife. He said it was not the first time I had told him untruths – I think the word he used was "lie" – because before my marriage I had told him that I had not had a specific disease.'

'Yes? Go on,'

'I said, "Mr Blood, it is impossible for me to discuss this question with you in this matter. I have come here not to make charges against my wife, but to ask for an explanation, and I shall not reply to you in the same tone that you assume towards me. I have no recollection of your asking such a question, but if I did reply in the way you have said, I spoke the perfect truth."'

'If I might put this to you, Lord Colin, is it a fact that you have never been affected that way in your life?'

'Never in my life.'

'Now please go on with the interview.'

'I then said I had finished. My wife said, "What about the other question?" implying the question of her resolution never to sleep with me again. She said, "Unless you sign a paper binding yourself never again to molest me, I will place this matter in the hands of my solicitor, Mr George

Lewis."'

'Yes?'

'I said, "Gertrude, I am not afraid of your taking such a course, if you are determined to take it. You will not succeed because I can bring medical evidence to prove that the charges which you are insinuating against me are false."'

'Did she reply to that?'

'Yes. She said, "Well, Colin, it is not the very best way to show that you are not afraid to begin by saying you are not afraid." I said, "I shall not be intimidated. I decline to sign any paper." I then asked Lady Miles to go into another room with me, and we went downstairs.'

Because of rules of evidence, Lord Colin could not report on his conversation with Lady Miles when they were alone together.

'When you got back,' Lockwood asked, 'What did you or Lady Miles say?'

'Lady Miles said, "Colin wishes me to say that he has not made any charges against his wife, that he has only asked for explanations." She also said, "Colin has never been suspicious of his wife." I then said to my wife and her family, "I am perfectly willing to submit this question to a commission. I shall appoint two or three medical men, and you will appoint two or three. I will undertake that if the result of the commission is favourable to me, as I anticipate, I shall take no undue advantage of you. But you, on your part, must undertake to give up this correspondence with Lord Blandford." She said, "Anything of that kind you must say to my solicitor, Mr George Lewis."'

'Anything further?'

'Yes. I asked her to see me alone, and she refused. She said, "I shall only see you in the presence of my solicitor."'

'Did Mrs Blood make any observation about Lord Blandford?'

'Yes. She accused me of having placed spies on her daughter, which I denied.'

'Did she make any other accusations?'

'She certainly made some insinuations with regard to my health of a very offensive kind.'

'Did she make a direct accusation as to your health?'

'I do not know if she used the specific name of the disease, as Mr Blood did, but the impression left on my mind is that she charged me with having the disease mentioned by her husband.'

'Did Mr Blood make a specific accusation?'

'I recollect distinctly that Mr Blood shouted out the name of the disease which he alleged I had been suffering from before all the ladies in that drawing-room.'

CHAPTER 45

George Lewis

After the abortive meeting in Thurloe Square, Lady Colin consulted her solicitor, George Lewis.

Lewis's office was on a short street, just off Holborn, called Ely Place. In 1883, Ely Place was almost 600 years old. It was a unique backwater in the heart of the metropolis. With a large gate at its entrance facing Holborn which was shut every night at nine o'clock, Ely Place was still governed by an act of Parliament, and it was the only place in London where a porter called out the hour throughout the night. Its most ancient building, the Gothic church of St Ethereda, was there when the street came into being (and was restored after being hit by wartime bombing). Alongside the church, toward Holborn, was the busiest building in the road. It contained the offices of George Lewis.

The place in which Lewis worked, and was born, and for many years resided, was a three-storey, 22-room red-brown Georgian house with large double glass doors numbered 10 and 11 below a brass-lettered sign "LEWIS AND LEWIS" (the founders of the firm, George Lewis's father and uncle). George Lewis was easily the most celebrated member of his profession in the nineteenth century. He was known as Society's solicitor since his roster of clients was a veritable who's who of socially prominent women in trouble. He could have been his era's greatest historian, but as a historian he remained mute. He kept no diary, and, with an encyclopaedic memory, he seldom took notes. The epitome of tact and discretion, he never violated a confidence, and when he died his secrets died with him. Because he was Jewish, Lewis could not obtain a university degree, but there was no barrier between him and the inhabitants of Mayfair, his clients and his friends.

George Lewis was of medium height, thin, grey-haired, and white-moustached. He wore a monocle, which, along with a fur coat, was one of his two trademarks. (In Victorian productions of Gilbert and Sullivan's

Trial by Jury, the solicitor was always dressed to look like Lewis.) His non-legal pleasures included collecting china, attending first nights, playing cards, and smoking cigars. But in his office and in a courtroom he had no diversions; he was totally dedicated to the interests of his clients.

On the morning of 23 July 1883, his latest client entered his office. A genial man, he greeted Lady Colin Campbell warmly and grasped her hand firmly. The two of them then spent all morning together.

Early in the afternoon Lewis sent a letter to Lord Colin. It was read aloud in court by Finlay, who often paused for a personal commentary:

'"My Lord, Lady Colin Campbell has consulted me with reference to the interview you had with her on Friday last, and has reported to me the result of that interview. She has further consulted me on the course of cruelty you have pursued toward her since her marriage, and in order to fully place the facts before me, it was necessary for her to make me aware of the disgusting state of your health." His state of health had been communicated to Mrs Blood, and was known to Miss Blood before their marriage, in spite of which Mrs Blood urged the marriage upon her daughter so that she might become Lady Colin Campbell.

'The letter continues: "The deception you practised on her family." A more infamously false charge it is impossible to conceive, and those who instructed Mr Lewis must have known it was false. Continuing, "The overtures that you have so repeatedly and cruelly made to her whilst in that state of health, and your refusal to live with her unless she submitted to your demands for marital rights." Again, infamously untrue. In a letter to Lady Miles, Lord Colin promised not to press Lady Colin to have relations with him until her inclinations went that way.

'Continuing, "I need hardly point out to your lordship" – you will observe how full of civility the letter is – "how essential it may be for your own interests that such facts may not become public, and Lady Colin is prepared to make any sacrifices to prevent the life of misery she endured with you from coming to light. At the same time she will not submit further to your demands, nor will she suffer any longer your insults." Gentlemen, Lord Colin said that he would make no demands on his wife. He said only that he refused to enter into a degrading bond that they would not live together as husband and wife.

'The letter continues: "Lady Colin is prepared, should you refuse her reasonable conditions, to apply to the Court for a decree of judicial separation on account of the cruelty she has suffered at your hands." Now we come to the "reasonable conditions," and I beg your special attention to this passage: "Unless you are prepared to abstain," for all time, whatever his health, "from demanding marital rights and to admit that at the time of your marriage you were suffering from the results of a loathsome disease" – which is utterly untrue – "and that you have had operation after operation performed ineffectually, and you are still under care of medical advisors, and, further, that during your married life Lady Colin attended you with care and affection" – utterly untrue again, for she neglected him if ever a wife neglected a husband.

' "Notwithstanding the constant scenes that have taken place owing to your condition, she will file a petition for separation. But if you will admit in writing the facts herein stated, and make the required promise, Lady Colin will live with you and keep secret the past life she has endured. As this matter weighs heavily upon her mind and is very much calculated to injure her health, I ask for a prompt reply." '

Lord Colin sent a prompt reply: 'Sir, your letter appears to have been written to intimidate me. The assertions which you have been instructed to make are untrue. I shall not sign the paper which you and Lady Colin have forwarded, and Lady Colin must act as she may be advised.'

CHAPTER 46

Another Dismissed Servant

Less than a week after receiving Lord Colin's reply to his letter, George Lewis filed a petition for judicial separation. Grounds for a decree of separation, as stipulated in the Matrimonial Causes Act of 1857, were desertion for two years, adultery, and cruelty. Judicial cruelty was any action that might endanger one's life, limb, or health. Knowingly communicating a venereal disease was regarded as cruelty, and this lay at the heart of Lady Colin's petition. She alleged that Lord Colin had consistently treated her with great unkindness; that he had sworn at her and abused her; and, the salient charge, that he had forced her to share his sleeping quarters when he was suffering from syphilis and threatened to continue to do so.

Lady Colin had been staying with her parents, but once the petition had been filed she returned to Cadogan Place.

Lord Colin tried to eject his wife from their home. His solicitor wrote to George Lewis, stating that nothing but unhappiness could result from their living together, and asking that Lady Colin be advised to leave Cadogan Place and seek alimony. The letter also said that Lord Colin objected to her seeing tradesmen and continuing to draw on their bank account.

Acting upon Lewis's advice, Lady Colin refused to leave. Had she departed, she could not have sued for separate maintenance. Not until 1886 could a British wife take this action.

Safely entrenched in Cadogan Place, Lady Colin continued to have problems with her domestics. Now the troublesome servant was Ellen Hawkes. She was questioned by Lockwood:

'Do you remember Lady Colin on the return from Syon House having an interview with you?'

'Yes.'

'What did she say?'

'She wanted to dismiss me at once, without a character, but as I had not done anything I refused to go.'

'Did she give any reason?'

'No. She offered to pay a month's wages in advance.'

'I believe they did eventually turn you out?'

'They turned my boxes out into the street, and I sat in the hall all night. Lady Colin threatened to send for a policeman in the afternoon because I refused to go.'

'Who threw your boxes out?'

'Young Mr Neptune Blood.'

'Had you done anything to deserve such treatment?'

'No, except I had spoken to his lordship about Lady Colin.'

'That is a very important exception,' Russell said, in beginning his cross-examination. 'Did you speak to Lord Colin about Lady Colin after he came back from Syon House?'

'Yes.'

'What did you say, or what did he say to you?'

'His lordship said, "You do not know anything against her ladyship?" '

'Well, what then?'

'I said, "Yes, I do, my lord." '

'What did you then say?'

'I told his lordship all that I know.'

'What did you tell him?'

'I have almost forgotten. It is so long ago.'

'Oh, no, that won't do. Out with it.'

'I told him about Colonel Butler coming.'

'Tell us what you said.'

'I said that Colonel Butler had called one afternoon when Lord Colin was out and stayed two hours, and that a lady called and Lady Colin refused to see her.'

'Was that all you said about Colonel Butler?'

'I believe I also told his lordship that I saw Colonel Butler walking up and down outside the house.'

'When?'

'One afternoon, and then he came to the door. I let him in and showed him to the drawing-room.'

'Is that all you told him about Colonel Butler?'

'That is all I can think of.'

'Did you not tell him about the photograph under the pillow?'

'I think I did, and I said I saw Lady Colin bring down one of Colonel Butler's photographs into the drawing-room and put it into a new plush frame. I think I told him about that.'

'Did you tell him anything else?'

'Yes. I told him about a gentleman coming home with Lady Colin at four o'clock in the morning.'

'Do you say that without giving you any reason or finding any fault Lady Colin turned you out of the house?'

'She found no fault with me except that I had spoken to his lordship.'

'Did Lady Colin order you on one occasion to bring up some hot water for her maid?'

'Yes.'

'And you refused?'

'Yes.'

'Why did you refuse to get the hot water?'

'Because I was not engaged to do it.'

'Did Lady Colin then and there give you notice?'

'She offered me a month's wages.'

'You said you would not go by her orders?'

'Yes, I did.'

'Did Lady Colin send for her brother, Mr Neptune Blood?'

'Yes, he came.'

'Did he ask you to go?'

'He did, and I said I would only take orders from Lord Colin.'

'Did he then say that if you did not go at once, your luggage would be put outside?'

'More than that. He put it outside.'

Lady Colin answered Inderwick's questions about her servant's

[197]

departure:

'Did you dismiss Ellen Hawkes because she had said something to Lord Colin?'

'No, that was not so.'

'Why did you dismiss her?'

'She refused to obey my orders.'

'What was the order that she refused to obey?'

'I desired her to bring some hot water for my maid, and she declined to do so.'

'What did you say in answer to that?'

'I said, "I will allow nobody to disobey me in this house. If you will not obey my orders, you shall leave." She refused to go. I dined at my mother's that day, the 7th of August, and spoke to my brother about it. He then insisted on her leaving.'

Lady Colin revealed that the cook was also dismissed, 'because she backed up Ellen Hawkes.'

Here we see another sign of changing times. A generation earlier it would not have occurred to a servant to refuse to carry out a task that she had not been hired to perform.

CHAPTER 47

A Letter to Argyll

Ellen Hawkes left Cadogan place on 8 August 1883. One week later Lady Colin sent a letter to her father-in-law:

'My dear Duke,   I hope you will not think it ill-fitting for me to give some explanation, painful as it may be to both of us, of the causes which have led to the deplorable state of affairs between Colin and myself.

'It is some months since Colin agreed to a personal separation, and I hoped that, notwithstanding the sad and cruel experience and disillusions of my short married life, we might still keep our affairs to ourselves and not take the public into our confidence. His late conduct seems entirely to preclude this. He has told me plainly that he will separate from me unless I consent to cohabit with him, and he persists in this decision. In justice to myself, I cannot consent to a private separation. If we are to live separate, the reasons for my refusal to live with him as his wife must be known openly.

'It is not only of his health and the deceit he practiced upon me that I will tell you, but rather of his personal treatment of me, which I have kept to myself. The present crisis makes such reticence no longer possible.

'Girls have illusions, and to be initiated in the mysteries of matrimony by being given a cutting from a doctor's letter, in which marital intercourse was recommended as a salutary prescription would be a shock to any girl.

'Throughout, the idea of my usefulness seems to have been the principal one to Colin. On the very eve of an operation I had to give way because he said "it was good for him." At no other times than these did he show me any of the affection a young wife has the right to expect. If I tried to interest him in anything I have seen or heard, or if I tried to do some little thing to please him, my efforts were met with absolute inattention. But if any trifle put him out, I was the scapegoat. Many times, about such trifles as my wearing a linen collar or a serge dress, he has sworn at me and ordered me to leave the house as if I were a servant, and this before we had been married a month. My giving in to him did no good. The next time I happened to err, no matter how trifling the matter might be, I was treated in the same way. Last year he did not speak to me for five whole days, after ordering me to leave because I happened to put on a new bonnet which did not please his fancy. There has been one constant dropping of ill-temper, impatience, insult, and sulkiness on my unhappy head. I have put up with it and have given in to him in every way that I could. I have submitted to not being mistress of my own home. Even over the servants I have allowed myself to be passed over, and to be considered of no account in the household.

'I made allowances through it all on account of his illness, but all human patience has its limits, and he has come to the end of mine. His treatment of his nurses alone would have been enough to arouse most women. I was made into a go-between when he ill-treated them, even striking and knocking them down. I was sent to soothe and console them, to try to persuade them to excuse his behaviour and return to him. I have had to leave my room at night and sit with the nurse for hours, with my arms round her, when she was sobbing from his personal violence, and make excuses for him in every way that I could imagine. Then after one of these outbursts he would think nothing too good for these women, and he would go from the extreme of positive violence to that of familiarity.

'The whole of last autumn and winter I used to sit in his room from the time I got up till I went to bed, except for my daily drive for one-hour-and-a-half. I did all I could to amuse him in every way, and all the result was that he told me he did not consider I had ever taken care of him at all. Short of dressing the wound, I could not do more or show more care for him than I did through these many months. I am not a jealous woman in any way, but even I could not fail to remark the difference between the absolute ignoring of my presence in his room and his effusive delight when anyone else came in.

'Forgive me for writing so long a letter, but I thought it only right and fair that you should have some idea of what the real state of things has been. I have left out entirely the question of how much my health has suffered in every way, but I hope you will see that the one thing I ask for – personal non-molestation – is, under the circumstances, not an outrageous request. If Colin persists in his refusal, the whole question, with all its details, will have to be decided in open Court. He alone has forced me to this course against my will. There is none other open to me which, in justice to myself, I can pursue. If he will not grant me protection I must obtain it otherwise – believe me, your affectionate G. E. Colin Campbell.'

Lady Colin's father-in-law answered her letter promptly. This, in its entireity, is his reply:

'The Duke of Argyll has received Lady Colin Campbell's letter. He has also heard from his son, Lord Colin, of the accusations which Lady Colin has brought against her husband, in the form of a petition to the Divorce Court. The Duke has heard from Lord Colin, and has reason to know from other sources, that these accusations are false. The Duke therefore can only regard Lady Colin's letter to himself, threatening further legal proceeding, as written in pursuance of the attempt at intimidation which has already been tried unsuccessfully with Lord Colin. Under these circumstances Lady Colin will understand that the Duke must refuse further correspondence with her ladyship.'

Never again was there a communication of any kind between the Duke of Argyll and Lady Colin Campbell.

CHAPTER 48

Lady Miles's Correspondence

On 7 August 1883, just after Lady Colin's petition had been filed, Lady Miles began an extended correspondence with Lord Colin. The first letter was read aloud, with comments, by Finlay:

'This letter was written by the cousin, friend, and confidante of Lady Colin, to Lord Colin upon charges which had been put forward for the first time: "Now what on earth could make her bring those charges founded on falsehood and perjury? It is very dreadful. She could not prove cruelty on your part. Few husbands give their wives the liberty and indulgence you give her."'

Actually Lady Miles's last sentence may have been true!

As to the charge of cruelty, Lady Miles said that she had understood cruelty to mean 'personal violence.'

Continuing, Finlay referred to this specific point: 'So far the letter might be open to the idea of a charge of cruelty in the ordinary sense of beating, kicking, and swearing. But the passage which follows destroys any comfort which anyone could derive from that theory: "I could not but loathe the present proceedings against you. Any honest woman could but shrink from the course this family is taking." Lady Miles writes this, having been associated with Lady Colin on the most intimate terms and with a fuller knowledge upon the situation than any other human being could possess. "Has Blandford anything to do with it?" That is not an answer to a question by Lord Colin. It is a question put by herself, a suggestion of her own. What was in her mind when she wrote it? Simply that this charge was put forward in consequence of Lord Colin's suspicions of infidelity. "I never heard," she wrote, "of her having any disease of the kind you mentioned, and do not believe she ever had, as no mention was made to me of it when she spoke of separating from you. I told her Mr Bird's opinion was that you could impart to her nothing of the kind." Mr Bird, who had been attending professionally upon Lord and Lady Colin, expressed that view, and it was put in writing by Lady Miles

[201]

in August 1883.'

Four days later Lady Miles wrote again: 'Dear Coco, – you are quite mistaken if you think I know anything that could be brought against G. She has always been very close about most things, but she used to talk to me about what she considered were her grievances against you. She also spoke very strongly about Shaw and Blandford, but there never seemed anything harmful to you in what she said. Indeed, I always thought her too cold to please any man or be pleased by any man, and so I was surprised by the cabman's story. I think if she was in any way compromised I would have known about it. At the same time, dear Coco, I would certainly stand forward and say that you were a very lenient and good husband, and I do not suppose anyone can contradict that. Any of the servants could prove that you never ill-treated Gertrude. What a pity you ever met such a woman. She is not of a nature to make a man happy. It is a cold, pitiless, cruel nature with no fear of God to guide it.'

'Is that your estimate of Lady Colin's character, your cousin whom you have known since she was a child?' Finlay asked Lady Miles.

'When I wrote that I was extremely angry, and women say many things when they are angry that they would not say otherwise.' (Much laughter from the spectators, all of whom were men.)

Russell questioned Lord Colin on what underlay this letter:

'Had you written to Lady Miles to see whether she could put you on the track of any information against Lady Colin?'

'Well, yes, certainly I had.'

'You were therefore treating Lady Miles as a friend in whom you could repose confidence?'

'I hoped so.'

'It must have been so, because you were writing to her asking whether she could give any information against your wife?'

'I had a very strong idea that Lady Miles was able to give me information.'

Lady Miles's next letter, dated 17 August 1883, came from the sailing yacht *Shah*, moored in the harbour of Cowes, then, as now, an élite Isle of Wight resort.

'My dearest Coco, – I saw a paragraph in *Truth* saying you were not going for a divorce, but a separation. Dear little boy, it seems as if you are never to be at peace, neither in body nor in mind. I think all that [Blood] family have gone mad.

'You had better keep the whereabouts of the servants in view as there must be some sufficient reason for sending them off without any beat of the drum. [This referred to the recent discharge of two of Lady Colin's

[202]

servants, who out of pique might speak against her.] Any one of them could prove that you never ill-treated Gertrude.

'I told her the reasons she had given me were not sufficient, and I also said that no man could live with a wife in the way she insisted on. I said I thought you would send her home to her parents, and she replied that she would not consent to this arrangement. She is living in a most senseless, indelicate manner, and I think she has no right to do anything in your house. She never had any brains and is acting most unwisely for her own reputation. I now think, dear Coco, that you will be much happier when all this is at an end, and that you ought not to live with a woman who said before her whole family that she preferred twelve other men to you. Now, my dearest Coco, with much love and blessing from your very true and faithful friend in affection, Muzzie.'

Asked about this conclusion, Lady Miles said, 'I always treated Lord Colin as my son. I was extremely fond of him.'

On 22 August, Lady Miles's letter enclosed an excerpt from a letter by Lord Colin.

'This is the extract,' Finlay said. ' "I was given to understand that the [marital] duty was repugnant to her, and that she had no feeling, no desire, no inclination. I took this to be a *bona fide* feeling which any man was bound to respect. I recollect her saying that anything of the kind made her feel like a wild beast." Is there one word here about communicating a disease? Your eyes, gentlemen, are being opened to the true facts. Women are differently constituted, and from my painful experience in the Divorce Court I know that a dislike of her husband's bed is one of the best symptoms of a woman's infidelity.'

On 21 September, Lady Miles wrote, 'I wish this horrid affair could be amicably arranged. It would be much better for G. to have separate apartments than to have such a tissue of unpleasantness brought before the public. It is not as if truth would only be told, but lawyers twist every word out of its meaning. [Much laughter] Even if she offered to come back as your wife, you would hardly care for her after what has happened. You might let her be your housekeeper and look after your house, as she is economical and careful. You need have but little to say to her.'

In his response, Lord Colin said, 'I cannot entertain the proposition you hint at. I should be much obliged if you will see my solicitors. If you will let me know, I will arrange an appointment.'

This raised a point which was developed during Lockwood's examination of Lord Colin:

'Did you show Lady Miles's letters to your solicitors?'

'I showed every one of her letters to my solicitor.'

[203]

'Did you consult your solicitor before answering them?'

'I consulted him about that correspondence, letter by letter.'

Russell asked Lady Miles, 'Did you write your letters in the most private way as Lord Colin's friend?'

'Yes. The letters were written privately and in perfect friendship. I had no idea that the correspondence would go beyond his eyes. He never gave me a hint that it would. I thought I was writing to a man of honour. A lady's letters should be sacred.'

CHAPTER 49

A Legal Separation

While Lady Miles was posting letters to Lord Colin, Lady Colin was also doing some writing. A friend persuaded her to submit an essay to the editor of the *Saturday Review*. He liked it enough to ask her to become a regular contributor to the magazine. Early in October 1883, she sent her first article.

Founded in 1855, the *Saturday Review* – its full title was *Saturday Review of Politics, Literature, Science, and Art* – was an important weekly journal with influential book reviews and articles on a variety of topics. It was significant because of the quality of its writers. Before the end of the century they included Thomas Hardy, H. G. Wells, Arthur Simons, Max Beerbohm, Edmund Gosse, Hilaire Belloc, and, soon after Lady Colin began writing for it., a young drama critic who signed his reviews 'GBS.'

George Bernard Shaw notwithstanding, the *Saturday Review* was a conservative publication, especially regarding women. Its 'ideal woman,' it editorialized, was 'a creature generous, capable, and modest; something franker than a Frenchwoman, more to be trusted than an Italian, as brave as an American, but more refined, as domestic as a German, but more graceful; a girl who can be trusted alone if need be, because of her innate purity; a girl who, when she marries, will be her husband's friend and companion, but never his rival; a girl who is content to be what God and nature have made her.'

Lady Colin was questioned by Lockwood on her affiliation with this magazine:

'When you wrote for the *Saturday Review*, what subjects did you take?'

'I wrote on many subjects, sometimes two or three articles a week.'

'Two or three articles *a week?*' Judge Butt asked.

'Yes, my lord.'

'Did you ever write on scientific subjects?' Lockwood asked.

'It depends on what you mean by scientific subjects. I wrote on anatomy and the globes.'

'Did you also write on ordinary subjects?'

'I wrote on any subject that was given to me.'

This exchange was not part of Lady Colin's direct examination. It is from her cross-examination. Her husband's advocates knew that the all-male jury would not be favourably impressed by a woman of intellect.

Lady Colin must have been a dynamo to have two or three articles a week published in the *Saturday Review*, but she often did just that. Her work for one issue might include a general article, a short leader, and a book review.

She frequently reviewed volumes written in European languages. Because of her excellent reading knowledge of Italian, French, German, and Spanish, she was admirably qualified to deal with most of the foreign language books received by the magazine.

Lady Colin's first article appeared on 20 October, 2500 words on the recent South Kensington fisheries exhibition. This is an excerpt: 'As to the importance of the great sea fisheries, there cannot be two opinions. It is not only that every year we become dependent upon them for a considerable portion of our food supplies, but the pursuit furnishes a means of subsistence for an ever-increasing number of our population; while they form the nurseries of a brave and hardy race of seamen, trained from their earliest youth to seek their livelihood from the stormiest and most tempestuous of seas. Our inland fisheries are only of less interest and consequence because they are less extensive and more under our command; but their value lies not only in the food they furnish, but in the harmless and healthy recreation they afford.'

When Lady Colin was beginning her journalistic career, a friend was in the news. This appeared on 23 October in *The Times*: 'Captain Shaw, CB, chief officer of the Metropolitan Fire Brigade, has received a remarkably handsome timepiece, accompanied by a letter, in which Sir Henry Personby stated that the Queen had commanded him to send the clock as a present from Her Majesty. The gift contained an inscription plate: "Presented to Captain Shaw, Superintendent of the Metropolitan Fire

Brigade, by Victoria, RI, 1883." It is an ebonite marble clock, surrounded by a gold helmet, and bronze hatchet and belt with a gold buckle.'

Six months later at an awards ceremony, the gift was a Bible. It was thus inscribed: 'To Lady Colin Campbell, from the London Cottage Mission, thanking her for her kindness to the poor, expressing the sincere prayer that God's richest blessing might attend her all her life.' It was presented by the director of the mission, located in the East End community of Stepney.

Lady Colin's earlier work in the East End had not included Stepney, where she went for the first time in December 1883. Until about 1800, Stepney had been a quiet riverside village, but in the nineteenth century immigrants poured in uncontrollably so that by 1870 its population was about 275,000. The overcrowding produced streets that were human sewers. Here in 1865, fittingly, William Booth founded the Salvation Army.

Stepney became a West End conversation piece in 1883 with the publication of the widely-read *Bitter Cry of Outcast London*. Perhaps this book stimulated Lady Colin to go there.

'On what day of the week did you visit Stepney?' Inderwick asked her.

'Wednesdays, and later on I used to go on Sundays as well to sing.'

'What was your appointment on Wednesday?'

'I served soup.'

'Was it a soup kitchen?'

'Yes.'

'What time did you go on Sundays?'

'Sometimes in the morning and sometimes in the evening.'

In Stepney, Lady Colin worked in Salmon Lane, at a religious mission. The 'objects' of the mission, an official said in giving evidence for Lady Colin, were 'the religious teaching of the people and the provision of penny Irish stew dinners.' The managing director, Walter Austen, spoke of Lady Colin's conscientiousness in visiting the neighbourhood and distributing dinners.

'Was her work substantial and good?' he was asked.

'Thoroughly so. An article was written on the subject in *All the Year Round*, by Charles Dickens, the younger.' (Laughter)

Charles Dickens, Jr., proprietor and editor of the magazine that his father had started, visited the Stepney mission on a Wednesday when 500 children were provided with dinner. He reported on his experience in a long article.

'Salmon Lane,' he began, 'is a most prosaic thoroughfare. Its small houses are of the most ordinary, square-box, plain, back-slummy order of architecture. Miles of similar dull, dreary, dismal, dirty little tenements surround it on all sides, and one may look vainly for relief from the sad, wearisome monotony. To one who had been trudging through the slushy little streets, courts, and alleys in the neighbourhood, the sight of the New Cottage Mission Hall, with its cheerful white brick frontage and clean, well-kept aspect, was pleasant to the eye.'

Inside, there was an enormous dining hall with fourteen tables, each with fourteen chairs. The children were fed in three shifts. Each of them had brought a bowl and a spoon. Two gigantic tureens on casters were wheeled out, and the attendants passed around filling the bowls with Irish stew. Unlike Oliver Twist, these boys and girls could ask for 'more.' They could have as much as they desired.

'There was no cause to complain of the sluggishness of waiters,' Dickens wrote. 'Miss Napton, the kind lady who presides over the feasts [and who gave evidence for Lady Colin], and the young ladies who come every Wednesday to help, are deft and active. One of these lady helps is a lady by title as well as by courtesy and gentle birth and bearing. All gratitude and honour to lady helps like these, who bring to the East End the gracious manners of the West, and lend a kindly hand to bridge the social chasms which are said by some to yawn between the rich and the poor.'

During Lady Colin's tenure at Stepney, there was a particularly glittering affair at Leigh Court. For several days, beginning on 28 January 1884, the guest of honour was the Prince of Wales. His fellow guests included Mrs and Mrs George Bolton, but not Mrs Bolton's sister Gertrude. Lady Miles could hardly have invited a couple who would soon be battling in court.

The trial in which Lady Colin sought a decree of judicial separation took place on March 27 and 28. It was to be held in an open courtroom with a special jury, but on the morning of the 27th Charles Russell (he had not yet become Sir Charles), representing Lady Colin, asked for a hearing *in camera*, without a jury and with the press and public excluded. The motion was granted.

All charges against Lord Colin had been dropped except that of passing on a venereal disease. Lord Colin entered a simple denial. He said nothing about his wife's alleged unfaithfulness. In the divorce trial, he was asked about this by Russell:'Did you, Lord Colin, in the last trial, say one word as to charges of infidelity against your wife?'

'I was advised by counsel to say nothing against my wife.'

'It would have been very important to show that Lady Colin's petition for a judicial separation was an attempt to anticipate charges of infidelity against her?'

'Certainly it would.'

'Again I ask you, did you say one word relating to infidelity on the part of your wife?'

'On counsel's advice I did not.'

'Do you recollect your counsel saying, "There is not one single charge of any kind made against Lady Colin."?'

'I heard that.'

At the time of the separation hearing, Lord Colin's solicitors had obtained full statement from, among others, Amelia Watson, Rose Baer, Annie Duffy, Ellen Hawkes, Sarah Ann Bristowe, Elizabeth Wright, and Albert de Roche. One person who had *not* made a declaration was James O'Neill.

After two days of unreported testimony, Lady Colin was granted a decree of separation. The Judge must have been convinced that Lord Colin had in fact infected her with syphilis. When the decision was upheld on appeal, the question was settled.

Lady Colin moved in with her parents. Thanks to the Married Women's Property Act of 1882, which gave married women absolute power over their own possessions, she could retain her modest separately-owned financial resources secure in the knowledge that they could not be legally touched by her husband.

CHAPTER 50

Detectives in Paris

After the trial, Lady Colin and her parents visited Italy and France.

'Did you have a very serious attack of fever in Italy?' Inderwick asked her.

'Most serious.'

'It laid you up for two months, I think?'

'Yes.'

'I think that your life was despaired of?'

'Oh dear, yes.'

Lady Colin received good medical treatment in Florence, and, in Russell's words, 'regained the health which she had never had since her marriage and at last rid herself from the pernicious, contagious influence of cohabitation with her husband.'

But she was not wholly free from his influence.

Lord Colin told Lady Miles that in the judicial separation trial he had been 'very badly used.' His 'pride,' Russell said, 'was humbled in the dust. Whatever his feelings toward his wife had been, whatever his kindliness was, all was lost in the overwhelming feeling that possessed him that by some means or other he must wreak vengeance for the verdict against him. He did not hesitate to exhaust every means which ingenuity, money, and social influence could furnish to endeavour to rake from the gutters some manner of charge.'

Before the trial, Lord Colin had hired detectives to follow his wife and also the Duke of Marlborough. Presumably they had found nothing incriminating. After the decree had been granted, the surveillance was intensified. Lady Colin was spied on even when she was critically ill in Florence.

'Was your wife watched continuously from 1883 to 1885?' Webster asked Lord Colin.

'Not continuously. She was watched in 1883 and after the separation.'

'And the Duke of Marlborough?'

'He was watched after the separation suit. Before the separation suit, in the autumn of 1883, I had suggested to my solicitors that he should be watched.'

Lord Colin's investigators were particularly active in Paris, where his wife and her parents went after she had recovered from her illness.

'In Paris,' Russell said, 'Lord Colin did some things that are almost incredible.' Less partisan observers agreed. The Birmingham *Daily Mail* said that he had become 'overwhelmed by his eagerness to turn the tables upon his unfortunate wife.' The *Standard* called him 'the victim of his own morbid fancies.' And *Truth* saw a 'diseased imagination that belonged to some guardian of an Eastern harem rather than an English gentleman.'

Opening this phase of the narrative was Alfred Davis, a private detective, thus described by one reporter: 'He has a large breast-pin stuck in an ample white scarf with black spots. He wears a cut-away coat and has red hands and close-cropped hair. He reminds one of a race track rather than Scotland Yard.'

'In May 1884 were you living in Paris?' Lockwood asked him.

'Yes.'

'Did you receive instructions to watch the movements of Lady Colin Campbell?'

'Yes.'

'Do you remember where she was staying when you first saw her?'

'She was staying at the Hotel Windsor, in the Rue de Rivoli.'

'Did you watch the Hotel Windsor?'

'Yes, every day.'

'Do you remember seeing her leave the hotel?'

'Yes, several times.'

'On these occasions did you follow her?'

'Yes.'

'Do you remember on one occasion following her to the entrance of the Hotel des Invalides?'

'Yes.'

'After a discussion involving Judge Butt and the leading barristers, Davis was permitted to read from notes he had written on the job in 1884;

'The first memorandum I have is dated the 31st May: "Mr Blood came out of the Hotel Windsor about nine o'clock and went towards the Rue Bastille. Lady Colin Campbell came out about ten o'clock and walked sharply to the Grand Post Office. She asked for letters. Then she walked through the Rue St Honoré and other streets to the Hotel Continental, going in by the back entrance. She went up to the first floor and stayed ten minutes. Coming down, she asked the concierge where the telegraph office was, and, on being told, went to the Rue Cambronne, where she remained five minutes. Then she went to Grand Hotel, and on leaving went by way of the Place de la Concorde to the Place des Invalides, where the cab stopped and she remained in a corner of it.

'"As I passed by, I saw her in the cab. I then watched through the gardens at the corner of the Boulevard des Invalides. She stayed in the cab twenty minutes and then got out, looking about. She then walked towards the entrance of the Hotel des Invalides, still walking up and down two or three times, when I saw a gentleman (Laughter) come up and speak to her. They both got in and drove round the Boulevard des Invalides until they came round to the back of the Jardin des Plantes, where they walked out together, the cab waiting for them. They stayed nearly an hour, and then they drove along the bridge and stopped at the Prefecture de Police. Lady Colin got out. She walked across to a cabstand close by, took another cab, and drove towards the Hotel Windsor. She took her cab at 10.45, and the Duke of Marlborough paid for it. (Laughter. This was the first time that Davis named Lady Colin's companion.) I left off following the lady and followed the gentleman."' (Laughter)

Davis was cross-examined by Russell:

'Who employed you?'

'Mr B. Rae, a solicitor in Paris.'

'Is he an agent for Messrs. Humphreys?'

'I believe they are connected in some way.'

After losing in the separation trial, Lord Colin sacked his solicitor and turned his affairs over to the Messrs. Humphreys.

'You were very diligent in pursuing Lady Colin?'

'I was engaged to look after her, and I did my best.'

'So zealous were you that you jotted down memoranda in a cab and sent it off by fast messenger to the post office?'

'Yes. I endeavoured to send reports before the post left for London. Letters had to be posted before six.'

'On one occasion you hired a horse to follow Lady Colin?'

'Yes, but she went too fast for me.'

Alfred Davis was not alone in giving evidence on Paris in 1884. George Lewis and Charles Humphreys went there and, before a local judicial officer, questioned two men who could not conveniently travel to London. Under these circumstances solicitors may examine and cross-examine witnesses, who in this instance were British subjects living in Paris, the Boyd brothers, Herbert and Aubrey. Their testimony was taken by deposition and read into the proceedings in London.

Herbert Boyd had been a solicitor's clerk in Paris for twelve years. He said he had seen Lady Colin for the first time on 6 June and received instructions regarding her and the Duke of Marlborough. He was cross-examined by Lewis:

'What were your instructions?'

'My instructions were to take out a warrant for the arrest of Lady Colin Campbell.'

'If she had been arrested, what would have happened?'

'She would have been sent to the prison of St Lazare, the only prison for women.'

'Who had the brilliant idea of putting Lady Colin into prison?'

'I do not know. I believe Mr Humphreys first spoke to me about obtaining a warrant. I was then instructed in the presence of Mr Humphreys by Lord Colin himself on June 9. A complaint was then drawn up.'

'Were you aware that she had obtained a decree of judicial separation from her husband?'

'I cannot remember. It never entered my head when I received my instructions to ask whether she was a lady living with her husband or not.'

'What was the crime for which she was to be arrested?'

'The warrant was issued for adultery.'

'Was there evidence to support this?'

'The warrant was issued on a complaint but not on evidence.'

'Who made the complaint?'

'The complaint was made by the husband. No other person could make such a complaint.'

'And the warrant was issued without any proof of adultery?'

'Yes, it was issued on the complaint of the husband without any proof. That is the method of proceeding here.'

'How is it that Lord Colin and Mr Humphreys were in Paris?'

'On the 5th of June I telegraphed to them to come over because both Lady Colin and the Duke were in Paris.'

'Were you aware that Lady Colin was travelling with her father, her mother, and her maid?'

'I did not know that she was with her parents, but I was informed that her maid was with her.'

'Did you condescend to take the trouble to ascertain if her parents were with her?'

'No.'

'Did you think it a very serious step to arrest Lady Colin?'

'It never occurred to me to think about it.'

'Why was Lady Colin not put in prison?'

'Because she was not arrested.'

'Why was she not arrested?'

'Because she and the Duke were not found together in the same room alone.'

This was a ephemism for a rather more intimate personal relationship.

At one point in the examination, Boyd noted that 'Lady Colin had a collie dog with her.'

'What is your brother's occupation?' Lewis asked him.

'He is an accountant.'

'Did you and he work together in Paris?'

'I refuse to say whether we worked together. I object to the form of the question.'

'Where is your brother's office?'

'He has requested me not to give his address. I can't say where his office is. Actually he has no office. He works in his apartment.'

'Does he have his name over his door?'

'I cannot say, as I have not been there since it was furnished.'

'How did your brother become involved in these proceedings?'

'I gave him an addressed envelope on June 7. It was a dummy letter addressed to Lady Colin. It was a sham to get the door opened. I instructed him to say that he had found the letter in the street. I gave the letter a muddy appearance. It was soiled on purpose.'

'Whose idea was it to make the letter muddy and to tell the lie about it being picked up in the street?'

'I refuse to answer a question thus framed, as there was no lie in it.'

'Well, how did the letter get its soiled appearance?'

'The letter was thrown down by my brother, stamped on by him, and then picked up to obviate telling a lie.'

'What was the purpose of the letter?'

'It was a sort of credential or passport in case my brother was stopped inside the hotel and asked any questions.'

'What was the purpose of sending your brother to Lady Colin's hotel with the letter?'

'It was with the object of seeing if the Duke had gone to Lady Colin's bedroom.'

Aubrey Boyd made a statement which was introduced into the trial record:

'On the 7th June, 1884, I received from my brother an envelope addressed to Lady Colin Campbell. At the same time he gave me certain instructions. I took that letter to the Hotel Windsor at about midday, and I made an enquiry at the porter's lodge. In consequence of what I was told, I went to the third floor to room 69. I knocked at the door, and it was opened by a maid who spoke French. She asked me what I wanted, and I told her I wished to deliver a letter to Lady Colin Campbell. I refused to hand the letter to the maid and said I wished to hand it personally to Lady Colin. While talking to the maid, I saw the interior of the room. It appeared to be a sitting room. I saw a gentleman's tall hat on a piece of furniture, but I did not see a man in the room. The only person in the room besides the maid was an elderly lady sitting with her back to me.

'While I was speaking to the maid, Lady Colin came into the room from an inner room and told me to give the letter to the maid. I gave it to her. Lady Colin had on a white jupon chemise and stays. Her arms and neck were uncovered. There was a blue ribbon in the chemise or the stays. The maid gave the letter to Lady Colin, who opened it. She was in the doorway between the first and the second room. She remarked that it contained a circular. The door was then shut in my face.

'After the door was closed in my face, I knocked again, and the maid opened the door. I told her that it was not very polite and that she should have thanked me for taking the trouble to come up. While I was speaking to her, a gentleman came forward with the circular in his hand. I recognized the Duke of Marlborough from photographs I had seen. Lady Colin was still standing in the doorway, and the gentleman came in front of her. He asked me who had given me the letter. I told him I had found it. He then said "*C'est très drôle*" twice. The door was then shut, and I left.'

Asked why he had been sent to the hotel, Aubrey Boyd said, 'I understand that I was sent to see if I could obtain any evidence of adultery between Lady Colin and the Duke.'

Lady Colin spoke of this Parisian interlude during Inderwick's direct examination:

'In May 1884 did you meet Lord Blandford in Paris by arrangement at any time?'

'Oh dear, no. I met him purely accidentally.'

'Do you know why he was in Paris?'

'No, I do not.'

'Did you know that you were being watched by detectives?'

'Yes. I knew that I had been watched by detectives since August 1883, and I knew I was being watched in Paris.'

'When you saw Davis in court, had you the pleasure of seeing him for the first time?'

'Oh dear, no. I had had the pleasure of seeing him in Paris.' (Laughter)

'Did he follow you about like a shadow?'

'Very much so. He followed me wherever I went.'

'How did it come about that you and the Duke went to the Jardin des Plantes together?'

'He had come to call on us. On the day before I had been to the Jardin d'Acclimation, and I was speaking about the very poor collection of animals there compared to the Zoological Gardens in London. He told me the best collection was at the Jardin des Plantes and suggested that we should go there on the next day.'

'Boyd stated that at the hotel he saw you in a room with Lord Blandford when you were dressed only in your skirts and stays. Is that true?'

'Quite untrue. I had been riding in the morning, and the Duke called to see my mother. I went into my room to change my things. While my maid was dressing my hair, a man came to the door and said he had an important letter which he must deliver into my hands. My maid told him I was dressing, but he said he must give it into my hands. I had on my ordinary blue dressing-gown. I put my head outside the door and said I could not see him. He then handed in a circular. From where I was standing I could not see Lord Blandford, nor could he see me.'

The Duke was questioned on this topic during Finlay's cross-examination:

'Is it not rather roundabout to go from the Hotel Windsor to the Jardin des Plantes by way of the Hotel des Invalides?'

'It would be rather out-of-way in London, but not in Paris. One's time is occupied differently in Paris.'

'It is rather out-of-the-way?'

'I should say it is ten minutes longer.'

'Why could you not have driven over and picked up Lady Colin at the Hotel Windsor?'

'No reason at all.'

'Would it not have been a civil thing to do?'

'Not necessarily.'

'You preferred to have the lady wait for you at the Place des Invalides?'

'No, I had an appointment. I told her that I had this appointment and said, "Do you mind coming to the Place des Invalides and we will meet there?"'

'She did not mind?'

'Not at all.'

'Are you fond of zoology?'

'Not more than other subjects. I am a member of the Zoological Society, and I go to the Zoological Gardens in London very often.'

'Do you say that the only reason that you went to the Jardin des Plantes was to look at the wild beasts?'

'Certainly.'

'You left Lady Colin to go home alone?'

'Yes. I went to the florist's, and I got out of the cab and left her to return home.'

'Would it not have been civil again to have seen her home?'

'Yes, but one has so many commissions in Paris, and time is differently disposed of there.'

'Now I ask you, was not the appointment made to meet her at a place where you might not be seen together?'

'Oh dear, no, certainly not.'

Finally, Lord Colin defended his own conduct in Paris by saying that he had consulted his solicitors and had acted 'entirely under their advice.'

This didn't satisfy Sir Charles Russell.

'Can you believe this?' he asked. 'Lord Colin Campbell made a formal complaint to the criminal authorities in Paris to have a warrant issued upon which his wife might be arrested and lodged in the prison of St

Lazare, where women under police supervision are consigned, principally prostitutes.

'If documents did not prove it, it would pass understanding that any man could have so treated the wife whom, according to medical testimony, he had injured and degraded. But, no, Lord Colin's pride had been injured; it had been lowered into the dust. Feelings of revenge got the better of him, and nothing was too low to stoop to in order to gratify that passion. The punishment, if this warrant had been executed, would have not less than three months, and it might have been twelve months, imprisonment in St Lazare. The laws of this country were not good enough for Lord Colin Campbell. He must fly to a foreign land to seek the power of gratifying his revenge.'

And, in his summation, Judge Butt expressed his feelings of indignation. He said that he could not 'conceive of anything more infamous' than Lord Colin's attempt 'to consign his wife to prison with common prostitutes,' an action which was 'nothing short of an outrage.'

His principal advocate, however, stood by him. This is what he was paid to do. 'I will ask you individually,' Robert Finlay said to the twelve, probably married, jurors, 'to put yourself in the position of Lord Colin. He believed he had been treated infamously by his wife, and he believed she was living in adultery with Lord Blandford. Try, gentlemen, to imagine your feelings, if like Lord Colin, you were smarting under an intolerable sense of wrong because of what you considered a wicked judgement, and you had reason to believe that your shameless wife was living in adultery with her paramour. If that were your state of mind, do you think it would be wrong since these people were in Paris, to take, under advice, the usual course of action under French law of applying for a warrant which would take effect only if Lady Colin and Lord Blandford were found together *in flagrante delicto*, circumstances to give flagrant proof of guilt.'

CHAPTER 51

Petitions for Divorce

What the Campbells really needed to do was to obtain a divorce. On this matter Lady Miles was an intermediary between them. She was questioned on this by Finlay:

'Now, Lady Miles you opened a fresh correspondence with Lord Colin on the 12th of August 1884. Please follow me while I read from your letter: "G. is in London and has again taken up her East End work." This consisted in singing at concerts?'

'A great deal more than that,' Russell said.

Ignoring the interjection, Finlay continued to read from the letter: ' "If I were you I would get rid of her by letting her divorce you if you cannot divorce her." What did you mean by that?'

'I was referring to the story about Mary Watson.'

'But what did you mean?'

'I did not believe that Lord Colin could get a divorce because he had been unable to find anything against his wife. I knew he had tried but had never succeeded. He told me so.'

'Further on, you say, "I have heard them say that she would not accept alimony or costs if she could get a divorce. It is worth thinking of, and less hard than to be tied to her for life as you could get a nice little woman who would be a real companion. Poor dear, you will be entirely ruined by this abominable affair." What did you mean to suggest that Lord Colin should do?'

'Put me in a position to help him.'

'In what way?'

'So that he – no, that she – might get a divorce.'

'How was he to be helped by you?'

'By giving me permission to speak about Mary Watson.'

'Why did you not say so?'

'Because I don't like to put such things in letters. He knew what I meant.'

'I am sorry to have to put it this way, Lady Miles, but did you not mean to suggest that Lord Colin should commit adultery so that his wife might get a divorce?'

Lady Miles, it was reported, 'became excited and indignant, and spoke with warmth and emphasis.'

'No, certainly not!' she said. 'I could not suggest or even think of anything so heinous as that. How dare you ask such a question! How dare you make such a proposition as that! Sir, I am a woman of honour!'

This response, we are told, caused 'a great sensation in court.'

In his answer to Lady Miles's letter, Lord Colin said, 'I do not quite understand your suggestion. Have you any authority for saying that 'G' would not ask for alimony or costs if I allowed her a divorce. Let me know exactly how the case stands.'

In her next letter, Lady Miles said, 'I immediately acted to find out the opinions of the family, which I now state. They are very proud about this business. As "G" will never give you a chance of divorcing her, and as you are both young you would be much better free from each other than to bear the unsupportable dragging chain of your marriage. They are willing to support her and pay her costs and not come to you for a shilling for alimony or anything else if she is put in a position to divorce you. I think really that this would be the happiest conclusion for you. You would be much happier free. Also the expense will be awfully heavy, and it is better that her family should stand the expense.'

'What did you mean,' Finlay asked again, 'by suggesting that Lady Colin should be "put in a position to divorce you."?'

'I meant that if I were to tell the story of Mary Watson, the Blood family would proceed for a divorce. With my testimony, added to other matters, they would be certain to succeed.'

'Why did you not say so?'

'Lord Colin knew what I meant.'

'Why did you not say so plainly in the letter?'

'Because I wrote the letter, not you. (Laughter) Mr Finlay, you cannot dictate to me the terms in which I should explain myself. This was my letter.'

On 28 August, Lord Colin asked, 'May I take it that you are speaking for Gertrude and her family? What guarantees have I that I shall be relieved from all pecuniary obligations?'

Lady Miles replied on 30 August: 'You may take my word for what I say, that anything I write about will be confirmed. What I write is the only possible solution. If you agree, you have only to tell your lawyers to settle with Mr Lewis. I give you my word of honour that it will be as I have said. If you could divorce G., it would be better, but you can't. I cannot put things more plainly than I have done.'

[218]

Next, early in October, Lady Miles had a private meeting with Lord Colin in the St James's Place Hotel, London.

'What took place at the interview?' Russell asked her.

'We agreed that his solicitor and Lady Colin's solicitor should make an arrangement about money matters between the parties. I believed Lord Colin would then permit me to tell the solicitors about the Mary Watson affair.'

'Was the subject of Mary Watson mentioned?'

'It was the principal topic of conversation.'

Questioned on the meeting by Lockwood, Lord Colin said, 'Lady Miles went a little further than in her letters. She told me that the cost of the [judicial separation] trial would be refunded.'

Immediately after the discussion, the peripatetically fashionable Sir Philip and Lady Miles left for Newmarket, fifty miles north-east of London, famous for the Jockey Club and racing.

After a week with the other aristocrats in Newmarket, Lady Miles received news that sent her rushing back to London. Lord Colin announced that he would file a petition for divorce. She telegraphed him at once, 'Meet me at your solicitor's.'

Lady Miles joined Lord Colin in the thoroughfare whose completion in 1869 was one of Victorian London's most notable engineering feats, the Holborn Viaduct. Since 1882 the Viaduct had been London's only street where all the buildings were electrically lighted, including the Holborn Restaurant, whose lights made it a tourist attraction. A few doors from the restaurant was the office of Charles Humphreys and Son. Because of the elder Humphreys' illness, they met with his son William.

'What did you say?' Inderwick asked Lady Miles.

'I told Lord Colin that I had heard of his petition, contrary to our agreement.'

'What did he say?'

'That he had not filed a petition.'

'Please tell the Court of the ensuing conversation.'

'I told him that he was going to file a petition if he had not already done so. He said he had not yet made up his mind. I replied, "You are prevaricating." He hemmed and hawed and said, "Well, I am thinking of it." I said, "You must recall that petition." Lord Colin asked, "Why must I?" I replied, "Because of your adultery with Mary Watson." Mr Humphreys seemed very uncomfortable and wanted to leave the room. I told him, "Please remain and be a witness to what I shall say."'

Lady Miles then told them about what she claimed to have seen at 79 Cadogan Place on the night of 17 June 1882.

Questioned by Lockwood, Lord Colin gave his recollection of the meeting on the Holborn Viaduct:

'Lady Miles said, "Colin, I find that you have deceived me. You have been leading me to believe that you are willing to enter into an an arrangement, while all the time you were taking proceedings against your wife. I have information that a petition is about to be filed." I declined to tell her whether that was so or not. I said, "The time has come for an explanation from you. I received a letter from you last August in which you made a proposal which would ruin my reputation if carried out. From that moment I no longer considered you my friend, and I was determined to find out whether my wife or Mr George Lewis was a party to this disgraceful proposal." She said, "I can tell you this. Unless you instantly drop these proceedings, I shall tell George Lewis what I know against you." I said, "attempts have been made to intimidate me, but I am determined not to be intimidated. I challenge you to say what you know against me."'

'What did Lady Miles say to that?' Lockwood asked.

'She said, "When you were ill, I used to come and visit you in Cadogan Place. There was a very pretty housemaid in the house, and you said, 'What pretty hair that girl has got, and how much I would like to see it down.'" I said, "Even if that were true, and you gave the information to Mr George Lewis, do you suppose it would be of the slightest use to him? Go and tell him by all means. If you put it on paper, he will tear it up and put it in his waste paper box." I then left the room.'

Lady Miles took the short walk over to Ely Place, where by pre-arrangement she met Lady Colin in George Lewis's office.

Lady Miles told her cousin and her cousin's solicitor about what she insisted she had seen at Cadogan Place in June of 1882. George Lewis, who knew that a divorce petition was about to be filed against his client, wasted no time. On 6 November, the day after his meeting with Lady Colin and Lady Miles, his clerk rushed off to the registry office and filed a petition. A couple of hours later Charles Humphreys's clerk arrived with *his* petition. Since George Lewis had won the race, his client would be the 'petitioner.'

Lady Colin charged her husband with adultery plus cruelty. The cruelty consisted of knowingly passing on a venereal disease, and also treating his wife with neglect, unkindness, and ill-usage, and swearing at her. Lord Colin charged Lady Colin with adultery and named as co-respondents the Duke of Marlborough, Captain Shaw, and General Butler.

Lord Colin's petition did not include the name of Tom Bird. William Humphreys, a witness at the trial, was asked about this by Clarke:

'In the petition of November 6, there was no allegation made against Mr Bird?'

'No, I believe not.'

'At that time had anybody ever suggested any impropriety against Mr Bird?

'Not directly, no.'

Actually Tom Bird had been trying, without success, to collect his fee from Lord Colin for medical services performed. Finally Bird initiated a legal action against Lord Colin to compel him to pay.

On 18 May 1885, when Bird's suit was pending, Lord Colin filed an affidavit to amend his divorce petition. He asked that Tom Bird's name be added to the list of co-respondents, charging that his wife and Bird had committed adultery in Cadogan Place, at Leigh Court, and in Brook Street.

During Clarke's cross-examination, Lord Colin acknowledged that early in 1885, after the suit for non-payment of the medical bill had been filed, he had hired a detective to seek out evidence against Bird, and that the detective had found and taken a statement from the New Cross cabman, Charles Watson.

After the filing of Lord Colin's amended petition, more than a year and a half would pass before the start of the trial.

During the interval, Lady Colin was busy with charitable and creative work. She painted pictures, one of which would hang in a major exhibition while the trial was on. She wrote articles and oversaw the publication of her third and fourth books.

One of her new books brought together seven pieces she had done for the *Saturday Review*. Entitled *A Book of the Running Brook and of Still Waters*, it deals with the various fish in English waters which might provide food for the poor. In the preface she asks, 'Is it not a ghastly mockery that in a country surrounded by seas teeming with fish there should be found utter destitution in our cities?' The book demonstrates Lady Colin's knowledge of different kinds of fish and the methods of catching them. It also has a literary tone. Among the writers quoted accurately and relevantly are the Venerable Bede, Chaucer, Shakespeare, Michael Drayton, Ben Jonson, Carolus Linnaeus, John Keats, and, naturally, Izaak Walton.

Lady Colin's fourth book, which appeared in 1886, shortly before the trial began, was her most commercially successful volume. It would go through numerous printings, and during her lifetime 92,000 copies would be sold. It was called *Etiquette of Society*. There was nothing ironic about the book or the title. It was an all-inclusive guide for upper and middle class people on what to do on almost any conceivable occasion from birth to death. Here are a few entries selected at random from the index:

Affection, Excessive, to be avoided

Balls, Duties of Partners at
Breakfast, What to Serve for
Calls, When they should be paid
Conversation, Remarks on
Courtship, Etiquette of
Father-in-law, Interview with
Gentleman, Characteristics of a
Gloves, When to Wear
Hand, Different Modes of Shaking the
Letter, How to Write a
Picnics, Things not to forget on
Rooms, Temperature of
Voice, Cultivation of
Wines, Dinner

Lady Colin's method and style are embodied in a passage from Chapter 3, 'Etiquette and Social Observances.' She deals with the earliest stage of the relationship between a man and a woman:

'When a lady and a gentleman are introduced, the lady's permission should first be asked and obtained, and the office must be performed by a common friend. Always introduce the gentleman to the lady, never the lady to the gentleman. The friend says, "Allow me to introduce Mr Sinclair-Miss Grant, Mr Sinclair." Both bow, but do not shake hands, the introducer retires, and the introduced at once enter into conversation....

'It is always the lady's part to make the first intimation of recognition at their next meeting. A gentleman must not bow or shake hands with a lady until she has made the first movement; neither may he ever fail to return her courtesies. If he meet her in the street, and sees that she wishes to speak, he will immediately turn and walk in the direction in which she is going; it is never permissible for a lady to stand for any time while talking in a street ... A gentleman will get out of a carriage first and offer his hand to assist her to alight; he will not use slang expressions when conversing with her; he will never smoke in the presence of a lady without first obtaining her permission....'

As for Lord Colin, he finally did all that was necessary to become a legal advocate, and he was called to the Bar from the Middle Temple. In September of 1886 he became a fully-fledged barrister. Two months later, more experienced lawyers would be speaking for and against him in Campbell v. Campbell.

CHAPTER 52

The Trial: Campbell v. Campbell

This chapter summarizes the eighteen-day trial of Campbell v. Campbell, from the first opening statement until the retirement of the jury to consider its verdict. The participants, all of whom have taken part in the narrative, will be seen in the exact order in which they appeared in the witness box.

Day One: Friday, 26 November

The first morning was taken up by Sir Charles Russell's opening statement.

After he had been speaking for about fifteen minutes, and was discussing the melancholy honeymoon, there was a stir in Court. A tall, burly, fair-skinned man in his sixties entered, strode toward the solicitors' table and sat next to Lord Colin. The was the Duke of Argyll, who thought the case would be opened by his son's advocate.

The Duke arrived just in time to hear Sir Charles say, 'The first sexual experience was followed by shameful injunctions from Lord Colin which could not but shock a young wife. He advised her to take precautions to guard against an infection.'

Lord Colin turned around and protested angrily. His words were not clear. According to the *Telegraph* he said, 'You are not stating the fact.' The *World* heard 'It's a lie!' The Bristol *Mercury* reduced it to one word: 'No!' Whatever it was led an angered Judge Butt to say, 'If there is a further interruption, I will order the person causing it to leave the court.'

Resuming, Sir Charles said, 'The details are horrible and revolting enough in their bare truth to make unnecessary for me to resort to the slightest colouring of the facts.'

When Sir Charles charged that Lord Colin's ailment was syphilis, the Duke of Argyll looked at his watch, rose abruptly, and, without saying a word to anyone, hurried out of the courtroom.

Argyll missed the morning's biggest sensation. It came when Russell said that Lord Colin had tried to have his wife confined in the prison of St Lazare, 'where women under police supervision are consigned, principally prostitutes.'

While the courtroom buzzed, Sir Charles paused for a familiar ritual.

Russell was one of Britain's last prominent snuff takers. His black snuff box always rested on his desk, and occasionally he would halt momentarily and take a sniff. This occurred usually when he wanted the jury to digest what he had just said.

He lifted the box with his right hand, passed it to the left, and rapped it two or three times before opening it. After striking the side with two fingers, he brought away a pinch of white powder which he held for a second or two. Then with great solemnity he carried it to his nose and sniffed with both nostrils. Finally with a flourish he closed the box.

Now he could finish his address, which ended a few minutes before one o'clock. Judge Butt then called for a luncheon adjournment.

Near the Royal Courts of Justice were numerous eating places, such as the Old Cock Tavern, famous for steaks, chops, and whisky punch; the Ship and Turtle, with its popular turtle soup; the Cheshire Cheese, renowned for rump-steak puddings; several oyster bars; and, opened for only two weeks, opposite the main entrance, a vegetarian restaurant. For those not wanting to go out, food was obtainable at several locations within the building.

Wherever they may have eaten, they were all back in their places at two o'clock.

The morning session had been the overture. The drama itself began with the examination of the first witness. From her seat alongside her cousin, Lady Miles rose and walked confidently to the witness box. With a decorative bonnet rising from her carefully coiffured head, and a ruffled collar clinging to her neck, the one-time 'Venus of Miles' appeared not unlike a mature goddess. She held a Bible and swore by Almighty God that her evidence would be the truth, the whole truth, and nothing but the truth. Then, as required, she kissed the book.

Customarily witnesses stood, but for Lady Miles a chair was brought, and she sat down. Questioned by Frederick Inderwick, her direct examination filled out the afternoon.

Day Two: Saturday, 27 November

'One of the most miserable of stories is being laid bare before the eager gaze of the world,' the *Yorkshire Post* observed after the first day's proceedings. It was laid bare in great detail. Here are random samples of journalistic space given to Day One (at a time when newspapers had many fewer pages than today): Birmingham *Daily Post*, 1286 lines of newsprint; Bristol *Mercury*, 1071 lines; London *Echo*, 1064 lines; London *Globe*, 1115 lines; Liverpool *Post*, 1372 lines; London *Daily Telegraph*, 1395 lines; Sheffield *Daily Telegraph*, 1316 lines. The London *Evening Standard*, which along with the London *Evening News* provided the fullest coverage, had 1226 lines in an early edition which covered only the morning proceedings. Displaying some restraint, *The Times* gave the case 599 lines.

The second day would take up less space because Saturday sessions ended early in the afternoon. Again there were crowds outside and inside, and again the courtroom entrance was protected by barricades. Inside, the parties were seated as on Friday. Lady Colin wore a black silk dress and a high lace-trimmed velvet bonnet. She may have been advised by Russell, who regularly counselled female clients in divorce cases to dress in black because he felt that women charged with adultery should appear to be sad.

There was an air of excitement preceding the first cross-examination. The cross-examiner was Robert Finlay.

He tried to confuse and fluster Lady Miles, but she was a match for him. At one point indeed she scored a triumph.

In an effort to disconcert her, Finlay asked in rapid succession a number of questions relating to various dates.

After four or five questions, Lady Miles said, 'You confuse me, sir. You go first to 1882, then to 1885, then back to 1884. You must keep on, or I cannot follow you, especially when you don't let me have any notes to refer to.'

What followed was unprecedented. Visiting junior barristers began clapping, and this spread to the public gallery. The entire arena was applauding.

'I must ask for silence!' Judge Butt shouted. 'I will not have any clapping of hands. It is indecent in the extreme. I direct the ushers if they see anyone clapping to turn him out immediately or bring him forward to me.'

This was sufficient warning to young men who would hardly wish to be disciplined by the Judge.

Lady Miles's appearance in the box ended at 12.30. Russell then made a surprise announcement: 'My lord, we have presented the case for the petitioner.'

Lady Colin's entire case was contained in the evidence of Lady Miles. This did not, however, preclude the calling of further witnesses for Lady Colin, nor would it bar Lady Colin herself from stepping into the box. When the other side had ended its case, rebuttal witnesses would appear.

The rest of the abbreviated Saturday session was taken up by the start of Robert Finlay's opening statement. At two o'clock the trial was adjourned until Monday.

LADY COLIN CAMPBELL

Day Three: Monday, 24 November

On Mondays, Divorce Court proceedings started at eleven. Long before this hour the largest crowds thus far packed the Strand. And this wasn't the only focus of attraction. Morning newspapers carried this announcement: 'We are asked to state that 79 Cadogan Place is not now, and has not been for more than two years, the residence of Lady Colin Campbell.'

When he entered, Judge Butt carried a small parcel wrapped in brown paper. It had, he said, been sent from Leigh Court. A court attendant opened the package and removed a book bound in dark blue leather with gold edges and stamped with a gilded cross. Perhaps for the first time, a Book of Common Prayer was introduced into the proceedings of a divorce trial.

Finlay then resumed his opening address, which took up the rest of the morning.

During the address, Mrs Blood occasionally wiped her eyes with her handkerchief. Lady Miles sometimes had to be restrained by George Lewis. But Lady Colin kept her composure. Now and then she whispered to Lewis or to Russell, immediately behind her. Sometimes she fondled a silver-topped scent bottle. Once she drew from a small black bag a batch of letters, which she read or pretended to read. Mostly she just looked expressionlessly at the surface of the table.

As the luncheon hour drew near, Finlay said, 'Gentlemen, I leave in your hands, on behalf of Lord Colin, everything that is dear to a man. He has for more than two years suffered from the most odious calumnies, the result of an infamous conspiracy. He has strong influences arrayed against him: almost all the best counsel at the English bar and Lady Colin, who no doubt trusts to her beauty in the witness box to get a verdict. But Lord Colin has one thing on his side, the truth.'

After lunch, the two doctors who had examined Amelia Watson said that she was undoubtedly a virgin. They were followed by the young woman herself.

Amelia Watson was an object of interest. Tall, slim, attractive, delicate featured, simply dressed, she seemed intelligent and respectable. The *World* called her 'The Joan of Arc of Cadogan Place.'

Watson's direct and cross examination lasted for the rest of the afternoon. Tuesdays in the Divorce Court were devoted to hearing summonses and motions, and so when she stepped down the trial was adjourned until Wednesday.

On this particular Monday, Lady Colin was being talked about in more than one context. It was the opening day, in Suffolk Street, of the annual exhibition of Britain's second most important group of artists – after the

[226]

Royal Academy – the Society of British Artists. The show was the first under its new president, the feisty American James Whistler, whose main entry was a large, still unfinished full-length portrait of – Lady Colin Campbell. She is shown in a sleeveless white evening gown, and Whistler, who liked musical titles, called the picture *A Harmony in White and Ivory*. A weekly tabloid observed that 'these were hardly the colours Mr Finlay used to portray her ladyship.' (Another entry in the show was a small landscape by Lady Colin herself.)

Just before the opening, Whistler sent her a letter with these lines:
'You are of course Splendid! of the "Amazing."
'To be understood by you is my delight! To do beautiful things with you is my ambition.'

Day Four: Wednesday, 1 December

Even on a day of adjournment Lady Colin was newsworthy.

'Between one and two o'clock this afternoon,' a late edition of Tuesday's *Echo* reported, 'as a hansom cab containing Lady Colin Campbell was proceeding through Fetter-lane, the horse fell, and her ladyship suffered a severe shock. After a few minutes, she was able to proceed on foot to Holborn.'

Also on Tuesday, a letter signed 'R. T. W.' appeared in the Birmingham *Daily Gazette*, one of the few papers that did not print full daily accounts of the trial: 'I am relieved that you have exercised some discrimination in reporting the revolting Colin Campbell case, and have done your best to keep from under the noses of your readers the viler portions of this garbage. I am glad that one newspaper editor has the courage to run counter to those depraved tastes which seemed to devour the most vicious details with the greatest relish.'

R. T. W. was in a minority. As the Liverpool *Courier* noted on the next day, 'The interest in this unhappy case is, if possible, on the increase.' Before the start of Wednesday's proceedings, the *Evening News* reported, 'despite the cold, nipping air, a crowd larger than ever walked in front of the Palace of Justice to witness the arrival of personages in the case. Among the crowd animated conversation goes on.'

Inside, wearing a black morning coat with a small button-hole flower, the Duke of Marlborough was present for the first time. He sat with folded arms alongside his solicitor, two rows behind Russell. He was most attentive and sometimes leaned forward to hear the witness. Today, for the entire day, there was just one witness, Rose Baer, now Rose Baer Fisher.

Fashionably apparelled in a fur-lined dress and matching bonnet, she seemed self-possessed and imperturbable. She spoke softly and clearly, with only a trace of an accent.

During the explosive direct examination, Lady Colin wrote on a notepad with a gold pencil case attached with some keys to a large gold ring; she conversed with George Lewis, who took copious notes; and now and again she spoke to Russell. At one point, when she turned to Russell, she momentarily made eye contact with Marlborough. This occurred just when the witness said, 'I noticed that she had had her dress off while she was away.'

Finally, after the last question and answer – 'Have you any doubt that Lady Colin's dress had been off between your fastening it and her coming back?' 'No.' – the witness stepped down, and the trial was adjourned until the next day.

Day Five: Thursday, 2 December

Divorce Court Number One was now guarded by five officials and newly-fortified barricades.

Marlborough and his solicitor were again present, for a day which, to a large extent, was concerned with the village of Purfleet. Questions were asked of the Hon. Robert Villiers, the Hon. Mark Bouverie, and Cornelius Callingham.

Callingham was followed by the two men who had been butler to the Campbells – a bespectacled Alfred De Roche and James O'Neill.

While De Roche was being examined, a middle-aged, florid, white-moustached man entered. This was Captain Shaw. He shook hands with Lady Colin and her parents and sat down at their table.

When the day ended, O'Neill was in the box, being questioned by Russell on his 'keyhole performance.'

Day Six: Friday, 3 December

Because of the darkness of the day, gas lamps were lighted in the courtroom for the first time in this trial. Marlborough and Shaw were again in court, along with Tom Bird, who had been present since the beginning.

After Russell had finished cross-examining O'Neill, a cabman reported on rides that he said Lady Colin had taken with him, and Lady Miles's former head housemaid, Elizabeth Evans, testified on events at Leigh Court in the Spring of 1882.

The day's major witness was Annie Duffy. She came up with a shocker by insisting that Lady Colin had had a miscarriage.

During one stage of Russell's cross-examination, Duffy was closely questioned on Lord Colin's physical condition and on the operations performed by rectal specialist Allingham. As with O'Neill's description of Lady Colin lying on the dining-room floor, this was an instance in which all newspapers considered the details 'unfit for publication.'

The day ended with an extraordinary statement. Lord Colin's first post-marital nurse, Elizabeth Wright, said that Lady Colin, not Lord Colin, had syphilis and passed it on to her spouse!

Day Seven: Saturday, 4 December

Everyone was dumfounded by Wright's accusation. At the start of the proceedings, Finlay said, 'The witness took us very much by surprise. Lord Colin expressly repudiates the charge.'

Finlay's recantation had been preceded by a few minutes of excitement. For nearly half-an-hour before the Judge's arrival, a rumour spread throughout the courtroom and corridors: Captain Shaw had committed suicide! 'Is it true? Is it true?' everyone was asking. Then just seconds ahead of Judge Butt, George Lewis entered the courtroom and calmly remarked that he had just been conferring with a very much alive Captain Shaw.

The day was taken up by brief appearances by an assortment of witnesses: George Baker, the groom at Queen Anne's Gate; Frederick Deane, the cabman who said he had driven Lady Colin from Queen Anne's Gate; Margaret Lowe, housemaid at Argyll Lodge; Elizabeth French, caretaker at 79 Cadogan Place before the Campbells moved in; James Wilson, Lord Walter Campbell's coachman; Police Constable Edward Dalby; and Alfred Davis, the former detective in Paris, The last order of business was the reading of depositions by the Boyd brothers.

Day Eight: Monday, 6 December

Conservatively dressed Ellen Hawkes, Lady Colin's second housemaid, was today's first witness. She revealed that her mistress and Tom Bird had smoked together.

After Hawkes, there were appearances by the manager of the New Cross concert hall and by the cabman who had driven Lady Colin and her companion to New Cross, Charles Watson. Next came a witness who aroused more than a little interest, Lord Colin's father. The 63-year-old Duke of Argyll wore black broadcloth, with a black necktie and an old-fashioned gold chain around his neck. A little lame, he walked slowly up the stairs into the witness box, and without asking for permission to do so he at once sat down.

Calling Argyll was a blunder. His evidence contributed nothing to advance his son's cause, but his presence as a witness gave Russell the opportunity to quote Lady Colin's eloquent letter to her father-in-law and his chilly response.

As soon as Argyll had stepped down, Finlay called Lord Colin Campbell.

It was three o'clock when Lord Colin rose and trudged wearily up to the box. His physical condition was evident in his slow walk, his pale face, and his soft, indistinct voice.

Since his counsel stood directly behind the solicitors' table, Lord Colin could hardly not see his wife, but he tried not to look at her. As for Lady Colin, she sat with her hands crossed or toyed with her pencil case. Not once was there a meeting of the eyes between husband and wife.

Lord Colin was examined by Frank Lockwood. The contrast between them was striking: a pale, tired, sickly witness, and a handsome, tanned, broad-shouldered, physically robust Yorkshireman. But Lockwood was a gentle questioner.

When Lockwood was in the midst of his examination, it was time to adjourn. Before everyone left, Judge Butt presided over a brief conference. Frederick Inderwick said that he and Russell thought it would be desirable for the jury to visit 79 Cadogan Place. Finlay did not object, but the Judge was unenthusiastic, perhaps because he lived in Cadogan Place, but he did not reject the proposal. (It was ironic that this suggestion came from Lady Colin's counsel because the jurors would learn from their visit that it was possible to see through the dining-room keyhole.)

Day Nine: Wednesday, 8 December

The trial resumed after the usual Tuesday break. Lady Colin arrived with a large bundle of letters to which she would frequently refer, occasionally handing one to Russell. The letters were never identified, but it may be remembered that Lady Colin said, apropos of her correspondence with Blandford, that because of the size of her house she never kept any letters.

Today Lord Colin's answers were given more loudly and firmly than on Monday. The direct examination ended in mid-morning. Russell then began the first of the cross-examinations of Lord Colin. His wife, who had been writing a letter, put aside her pencil and paper and for the first time looked directly at the witness. Perhaps she hoped that the grilling would be painful.

Actually he held up rather well in answering Russell's questions and those that followed, by Captain Shaw's leading advocate, William Gully,

QC, and Sir Edward Clarke.

Day Ten: Thursday, 9 December

The morning session began with the conclusion of Clarke's cross-examination of Lord Colin. Then after a brief examination of the surgeon John Propert, Finlay said, 'That is Lord Colin's case, my Lord.'

Now each co-respondent was entitled to an opening statement, beginning with the Duke of Marlborough.

Sir Richard Webster's statement took up the rest of the morning and much of the afternoon. He was followed by Gully, a placid, sociable man, who, like Webster and Lord Colin, was a graduate of Trinity College, Cambridge, where he had been President of the Cambridge Union. After he had finished his brief address on behalf of Captain Shaw, Judge Butt called for an adjournment.

Day Eleven: Friday, 10 December

This was a 'letter to the editor' in *The Times*: 'Can you not induce other newspapers to be as careful as you are in editing the reports of divorce cases? I hear everywhere loud complaints as to the grave mischief caused by the details which some journals think fit to give of the Campbell case, and of the effect which these reports have on servants, on the young, and on working classes. Young lads devour the details as they go home to work. Servants sit up at night to read them. It is a scandal that the law officers of the crown (the Attorney-General and the Solicitor-General) should be engaged for parties in the case and unable to move on behalf of the public to prevent it from turning into the corruption of a nation.'

Papers like the *Evening Standard*, the *Evening News*, the *Echo*, and the *Daily Chronicle* would continue to provide full reports of the trial and to enjoy record levels of circulation.

Friday's session began with a statement from the chief counsel of Bridadier General Butler, 55-year-old John Murphy, QC, who at 18-stone was the heaviest member of the Bar. Murphy ended by saying, 'I believe you will agree that this charge ought never to have been made; that having been made, it should not have been persisted in; and that Lord Colin, when he found out what the evidence really was, should have withdrawn the charge.'

The final address was that of the Solicitor-General, who noted that a verdict against his client, a medical man, would be his professional ruin. The real reason, Clarke suggested, for including Bird, belatedly, on the petition was that Lord Colin did not want to pay his medical bill!

When Clarke sat down, at 12.20, it was the turn of Lady Colin's counsel to offer rebuttal testimony, to explain, counteract, or disprove the opposing evidence.

The first rebuttal witness was Lady Colin Campbell. When her name was called, she arose at once. She wore a tight fitting black jacket with a matching bonnet fastened under her chin with a thick black band. She turned, reached out close to her husband's shoulder, and received two small books from Inderwick. She then walked gracefully to the witness box, where she leisurely unbuttoned and removed the black kid glove on her right hand before taking the oath.

The woman who stood before the Court had been for more than a fortnight Great Britain's most highly-publicized human being. She appeared slightly nervous but generally well composed. Her voice was a little low, but clear, melodious, and refined. Perhaps because he was gentler than his leader, the questioning was done by Inderwick.

The rest of the day was devoted to Lady Colin's direct examination, which was still going on when the Court adjourned.

Day Twelve: Saturday, 11 December

Dressed again in black, Lady Colin smilingly walked back to the witness box. On Friday she had stood, but today, expecting a lengthy cross-examination, she at once sat down.

Inderwick's questioning ended after thirty minutes, and then the cross-examination began.

The cross-examiner was Lockwood. The *Yorkshire Post* explained Finlay's decision to hand this assignment to his junior: 'To have subjected the witness to severe brow-beating would have roused sympathy for the other side. Mr Lockwood knows the best means of extracting what he wants from a hostile witness, just as a skilful dentist will painlessly extract obstinate teeth from an unwilling patient.'

Lockwood's questions were asked with coolness and elaborate courtesy. Lady Colin generally replied in the same way. By the end of the day, the battle, it seemed, had ended in a draw.

Day Thirteen: Monday, 13 December

Today, Campbell v. Campbell became the longest of all British divorce trials. (It still holds the record.) Mrs Blood and Lady Miles showed one effect of the longevity; they brought cushions.

Monday's witnesses included Dr Hicks; two railway employees who told of the arrival of Lord Colin's grouse; Lady Colin's second personal maid, Valerie Kautzmann, and her second cook, Annie Brown; the Miles's family butler; the painter Frank Miles; Lady Colin's brother and sister-in-law; an associate in Lady Colin's charitable work; and Mrs Blood.

The day ended with Judge Butt asking whether, contrary to the usual practice, they should meet on Tuesday.

'Recollect,' he said, 'we are approaching Christmas. (Laughter) Nothing will induce me to let the case go over the holidays even if we have to sit till midnight.'

'It would sit like a nightmare on the holidays,' Russell said to the accompaniment of laughter. 'I think your Lordship will be able to commence your summing-up on Monday.'

Judge Butt then adjourned Court until Wednesday.

Day Fourteen: Wednesday, 15 December

After a few more minor rebuttal witnesses had appeared, Russell said that his client's case had been concluded.

Judge Butt nodded to the Attorney-General, who rose and called for his client, the Duke of Marlborough.

The impeccably but unpretentiously dressed Duke strode to the witness box. As he took the oath, he was the image of *savoir-faire* and *savoir-vivre*. He then stood with his left hand deep in his pocket and his right hand lying flat on the edge of the box. As a courtroom spectator he had been cynically amused, but now he was nervous and ill-at-ease. Webster at once threw out two questions:

'Have you ever committed adultery with Lady Colin Campbell?'

'Never!'

'Have you ever been guilty of any impropriety with Lady Colin Campbell?'

'Never!'

This was therapeutic. The Duke was relieved to get it behind him. For the rest of the morning and much of the afternoon he calmly answered questions by his and opposing counsel.

When he had finished, his place was taken by Captain Shaw, who denied all accusations and called O'Neill's story of the dining-room floor 'absolutely untrue from beginning to end.'

Shaw's cross-examination ended at 4.45, and the Court was told that because of illness Mrs Shaw would not be called. Whereupon Judge Butt called for an adjournment.

Day Fifteen: Thursday, 16 December

The morning was noteworthy for the first appearance since the start of the trial of that natural phenomenon which was so conspicuously a part of Victorian London, heavy fog. The metropolis was gloomy and dark. Suburban trains were late, and cabs crawled along the streets. Artificial lights glowed everywhere. Omnibuses, tram cars, and cabs carried lamps upon open pans. Costermongers, street hawkers, and newsboys held torches. And there were the inevitable accidents. Vehicles collided with each other and with pedestrians. It was a typical foggy morning.

Late arrivals among the jurors and other necessary personnel delayed the start of proceedings, but eventually everyone managed to reach the courtroom.

The first order of business was a question of added compensation for the jurors because of the length of the trial. Judge Butt said that when gentlemen had to make financial sacrifices it was customary to augment their fees, and it was agreed by counsel that the matter would be attended to promptly.

The Solicitor-General then called for his client. Tom Bird, like Marlborough and Shaw, categorically denied all charges.

The only co-respondent who did not deny everything was General Butler, who did not appear. For his absence he was roundly denounced. Responding typically, the Birmingham *Daily Mail* said, 'The conduct of a man calling himself an officer and a gentleman, who, when a woman's honour is in question, refuses to speak, cannot be too severely censured.' Butler was a Catholic, and a Roman Catholic journal, the *Tablet*, tried to explain his absence: 'He felt a most natural reluctance to go down into that well of defilement, that filthy pesthouse, the Divorce Court.' Butler's own counsel, John Murphy, and Sir Charles Russell were also Catholics.

The presentation of evidence ended when Bird stepped down. Now it was time for the final summations.

The Attorney-General was first. 'Wicked or immoral as the Duke might be,' he said with a frankness he could not avoid, 'I did not know there was any rule in society which says that a man is to be treated as a leper and regarded as an outcast. The intimacy of Lady Colin and the Duke is not denied; their friendship is not denied; but I ask the jury to conclude that, however great his former guilt, the Duke of Marlborough is innocent of the slightest impropriety with Lady Colin.'

Next came William Gully. This is the essence of his address: 'I ask the jury to say whether Captain Shaw's evidence is not that of a man of truth and honour – whether you have any reason to doubt the truth of his story as opposed to the tale told against him.'

John Murphy said, 'If you conclude that my client is guilty, you abrogate the maxim that a man is not called upon to deny an accusation until some ground is laid for it.'

After dealing, one by one, with the charges against his client, the Solicitor-General said he was confident that Bird would, in the jury's verdict, 'be absolutely cleared in the public mind of having been unfaithful to the trust reposed in him.'

Now came the spokesmen for the principal parties.

'Lord Colin is not a paragon of virtue,' Finlay admitted. 'He was wrong to put himself in the way of contracting a certain malady. All men should lead chaste lives, and Lord Colin has not done so. But I was astonished to hear the virulence with which the Attorney-General denounced Lord Colin's youthful indiscretions. The denunciation became ridiculous and grotesque when it is remembered that at that moment the Attorney-General was supposed to be expressing the sentiments of the Duke of Marlborough.' (Laughter)

Finlay had barely begun his address when, at 4.30, Judge Butt called for an adjournment.

Before the Court adjourned, there were two announcements. Because of the length of the trial, the jurors would receive one guinea per day of service instead of the usual payment, a guinea for the case. Also, the current residents of 79 Cadogan Place had agreed to allow the jurors to inspect the famous keyhole. The tenants hoped that there would be no public announcement of the visit. (It was dutifully reported by nearly all Thursday afternoon and Friday morning newspapers, and Cadogan Place was besieged by sightseers.)

Day Sixteen: Friday, 17 December

More fog, and the jurors' visit to Cadogan Place, delayed the start of this session. After the jurors had arrived, and the foreman gave his report, Finlay resumed his summation. For eight hours, the entire day, he held the floor. Here are several excerpts from his address:

'You have heard a great deal about the accomplishments of Lady Colin Campbell. I do not deny her abilities. I think there is no art in which she does not shine, especially one of the highest, the dramatic art, which she showed when she was in the witness box.'

'The only possible reason for General Butler's absence is that he dare not deny the charges against him. He sent two counsel to represent him, but when the time came to deny the charge he was not here. An honourable

[235]

soldier who knew that his evidence was vital to clearing the character of a woman would not be absent if he could give evidence without committing perjury.'

'There is not the slightest reason to suppose that Mr Bouverie would be mistaken as to the identity of Lady Colin Campbell. I do not think that anybody who has been introduced to Lady Colin would be likely to forget her.'

At the end, Finlay delivered his peroration: 'I ask you to consider all the circumstances. You have a picture of Lord and Lady Colin's married life, and a picture of what the Blood family think is right and wrong in society. You know the independent life she led, and how she lived entirely on her own account. Are we to tolerate such a code of morality as when she asserted that the Duke of Marlborough is a fair representative of the male sex. Take all these matters into consideration, and see whether you can reject the great body of evidence on behalf of Lord Colin. Does not every piece of evidence point to the same conclusion, and when they are all joined together, is not the inference irresistible?'

Day Seventeen: Saturday, 16 December

Sir Charles Russell had to discredit the allegations against his client and against each of the four co-respondents. He needed time, plenty of time. To accommodate him, the Court stayed in session all day on this Saturday, but still he did not finish.

These are extracts from his oration:

'Lady Colin led a very open and public life in what is called "fashionable society," and she could not move without attracting attention. Is it not odd that not one single witness from her class of life has been called to suggest any act of impropriety or indiscretion on her part? Is it not remarkable that the case is made up of gossiping stories of servants supplemented by fugitive observations of cabmen?'

'The stories of the witnesses consist in part of turning circumstances unsuspicious in themselves into circumstances of suspicion, and, in part, of exaggerating, multiplying, and quadrupling what has occurred. In part I suggest misrepresentation, and in part absolute fabrication.'

Day Eighteen: Monday, 20 December

All morning Russell addressed the jury. Here, succinctly, is how he evaluated the charges against the co-respondents:

'Lord Blandford has suffered for his sins. He has deserved to suffer. But do not let these consequences fall upon Lady Colin. The meanest creature, with a list of convictions as long as a brief, is entitled to have any charge against him tried without prejudice from previous convictions.'

'If there were a case against General Butler, I admit that his absence would strengthen it. But if there is no case, his absence does not make one where there was none before.'

'Should not Captain Shaw's character be of weight against the testimony of someone like O'Neill?'

'Mr Bird's name was added to the petition at a curious time. He asked for payment of his bill, and Lord Colin replied by a charge of adultery.'

Sir Charles appealed to the jurors' feelings: 'Some men believe all that is wicked of man and woman. If I thought that one of you approached this case in such a spirit, I would not address you. I wish you to approach it with a belief in human nature, with a belief in the purity of woman. I want each of you to approach this case not as a cynical, sneering man of the world, but as a man with faith in his kind and in the general purity of woman.'

In his final sentences, Russell said, 'If on calm, dispassionate consideration you believe that the case is made up of misrepresentation, exaggeration, and invention, and you feel that you cannot safely rely upon any evidence, you will take away no man's reputation. I will not speak of the effect of an adverse verdict upon others. I will only take note of the aged parents whose child has been their delight and comfort, whose heads will forever be bent in shame if you condemn their child. Gentlemen, with an earnest heart and a spirit of reverence I pray that your mind and judgment may be inclined to give a true, a just, and an honest deliverance.'

Russell finished at 2.15 p.m. As he sat down, some spectators began to applaud and were at once silenced by the ushers.

A luncheon adjournment of only thirty minutes was followed by the Judge's summation of the evidence, to guide the jury in its deliberations. He ended by saying, 'Before you find any of these persons guilty of the charges against them, you must be satisfied beyond reasonable doubt that the charge has been brought home. Gentlemen, you will now consider your verdict.'

CHAPTER 53

The Verdict

At 6.45 the jurors retired. For an hour and 45 minutes they deliberated, and then a call came from the Foreman. Had a verdict been reached? No. He wondered if they could have refreshments. They were given tea and coffee.

At 9.10 the Foreman reported that they were hopelessly deadlocked. Ten minutes later they were back in the courtroom.

Judge Butt asked, 'Is there no chance of your agreeing?'

'We are agreed upon one suit,' the Foremain said, 'Lady Colin's charge against Lord Colin.'

'The charge of adultery against Lord Colin?'

'Yes, my Lord. We are differing about Lady Colin.'

'Lady Colin might, in your opinion, have committed adultery with all or with none?'

'We differ as to whether she committed adultery with any or not.'

There was a murmur in the courtroom, immediately followed by muffled cries of 'Hush! Hush!'

'It does not seem to me,' the Foreman said, 'that there is any chance of our agreeing.'

'The only charge upon which you are agreed,' the Judge asked, 'is the charge of Lady Colin against her husband?'

'Yes, my Lord.'

'Very well. The next question is, are you agreed with regard to any of the charges involving Lady Colin and the four co-respondents?'

'My Lord, we cannot find that the co-respondents committed adultery with Lady Colin unless she committed adultery with them.' (Laughter)

'Lady Colin may have committed adultery with some and not with others.'

'That is precisely what we cannot agree about. We cannot agree that she has committed adultery with any one of them.'

'You cannot answer any of the questions?'

'No, my Lord, not at all. Some of the jury wish me to tell you how we are divided. I do not know whether it would be proper to say how we stand.'

'No, we had better not know that.'

One juror, in a low voice, said to the Foreman, 'We will have another try, if you like.'

Another jury man, also speaking softly, asked, 'Cannot we have something to eat?'

Some jurors then conferred briefly with the Foreman.

Judge Butt asked, 'Gentlemen, do you think it would be useful to retire any longer?'

One juror said, 'No.'

The Foreman said, 'Judging by some of their observations, it seems useless. Some of them won't alter their opinions.'

A court official spoke privately with the Judge.

The Judge asked the Foreman, 'Do I understand that you have been fasting all this time?' (Laughter)

'Well,' the Foreman said, 'I don't know how long we are to remain.'

Judge Butt said, 'I directed that you should be provided with provisions.'

The Superintendent of Courts appeared and said that he had sent out for refreshments because they were not available in the building. The jurors then held another consultation.

The Foreman said, 'Perhaps we should deliberate a little longer.'

'I think it would be wise,' Judge Butt said, 'It would be a calamity if you were to depart without a verdict.'

'We do see that, my Lord.'

'Well, have another try. Food will be sent to you. What would you like?'

A court functionary said, 'We can get tea, coffee, rolls, and butter.' (Laughter)

After directing the chief usher to obtain refreshments, the Judge said, 'Gentlemen, I ask you to talk it over a little longer, and I will take care that you have something to eat. I am sorry that we did not do this before. I hope you understand what I mean. No one should set up his opinions obstinately against the views of the majority, although I do not suggest that anyone who cannot conscientiously give way should do so.'

The Foreman asked, 'Suppose there is no majority to set it up against?' (Laughter)

'Perhaps,' the Judge said, 'you will try till ten o'clock, and if there is no chance of your agreeing I will authorize Mr Registrar Owens to release you.'

The jurors retired again.

The food had its effect. At 10.15 the Foreman reported that the jury had reached a verdict on all issues.

None of the barristers were present, and Judge Butt had left for the night. The Court was under the supervision of the Registrar, Robert Owen.

When the jurors had taken their seats, the Registrar asked, 'Gentlemen, have you agreed upon a verdict?'

'We have,' the Foreman said.

The Clerk of the Court asked, 'Do you find that Lord Colin Campbell committed adultery with Amelia Watson?'

'No,' said the Foreman.

'Do you find that Lady Colin Campbell committed adultery with George Charles Spencer Churchill, Duke of Marlborough?'

'No.'

There was applause in the courtroom.

'Do you find that Lady Colin Campbell committed adultery with Captain Shaw?'

'No.'

'Do you find that Lady Colin Campbell committed adultery with General Butler?'

'No.'

'Do you find that Lady Colin Campbell committed adultery with Tom Bird?'

'No.'

'Do you find that Lady Colin Campbell committed adultery with a person or persons unknown?'

'No.'

'That is the verdict of you all?'

'It is.'

The Foreman then asked for, and received, permission to read a statement: 'The jury desires me to give expression to an opinion which they formed. "The jury desire to express their opinion that in not coming forward in the interests of justice, General Butler acted in a manner unworthy of an English officer and gentleman and is responsible for the jury's difficulties in coming to a decision."'

Again there was applause.

The Registrar said, 'Gentlemen, you are discharged.'

Several of them asked, 'For how long?'

Lord Colin had abruptly departed as soon as he heard the verdict. Now Lady Colin, smiling broadly, rose, and, along with Lady Miles and George Lewis, received congratulations from all sides. (Mr and Mrs Blood and their daughter Francesca were not present.)

After receiving the last of the congratulatory expressions, Lady Colin and Lady Miles were escorted by Lewis through a side entrance. The women got into a cab. Lewis waved goodbye. This had been his longest case.

CHAPTER 54

After the Trial

The costs of the trial, including legal fees, were about £20,000 and by order of Judge Butt were born by Lord Colin. After his father had taken care of this, Lord Colin went to Bombay and became an undistinguished member of the Bar. On 19 June 1895 he died of pneumonia at the age of 42.

The Duke of Marlborough married again in 1888. He died, suddenly and unexpectedly, from heart failure on 8 November 1892 at the age of 48.

Captain Shaw continued as London's fire chief until his retirement in October 1891, whereupon he became a Knight Commander of the Bath. He died in 1908 at the age of 78.

General Butler served in Palestine and Africa, as well as England, and retired as a Lieutenant General in 1905. He became a Knight Grand Cross of the Bath. He died in 1910 at the age of 71.

Tom Bird was an unmarried anaesthetist and instructor of anaesthetics until well into the twentieth century. He died on 3 January 1932 at the age of 87.

Lady Colin Campbell lived a full life after the trial but her notoriety didn't end with the verdict. A booklet, *The Colin Campbell Divorce Case*, was a best seller in England, and another publication, *l'Affaire Campbell*, was widely read in France. The stigma of the affair would stick to her for the rest of her life.

She rarely mentioned the case. After her death, a lifelong friend recalled that only once had he ever heard her speak of what she called 'that horrible trial.' She was usually cheerful and always energetic, and she created for herself a new world.

Lady Colin had to rely on her own resources, which were not ample. Obviously she had to scale down her life-style. After staying for a few months with her parents in Thurloe Square, she moved into a large block of flats, Victoria Mansions, in busy Victoria Street, near the railway terminal.

Twenty of the flats in Victoria Mansions were used as engineering offices. The building also housed the editorial facilities of *Railway Engineer*, and it was the headquarters for several other commercial ventures. This was not a congenial place for a woman like Lady Colin Campbell, and she lived there for only a year.

Early in 1886, she moved a few hundred yards into the residence that would be hers for the rest of her life. It was a first-floor flat in one of two long, dreary five-storey red brick buildings known as Carlisle Mansions, situated on both sides of a short road which branches off from Victoria Street, Carlisle Place. It is literally a stone's throw from Victoria Station and not much farther from Pimlico. The dwellings, which still exist, were strictly residential, and were especially popular with retired military officers. It also provided living quarters for the Archbishop of Westminster and his staff, and, from 1901 until 1906, for a young writer named William Somerset Maugham, who shared a flat with an intimate male companion.

In 1901 Maugham was the 27-year-old author of two published novels who had given up medicine and was concentrating on writing. He had an annual inheritance income of £150, and he earned less than £100 a year from writing for each of the first ten years of his career. 'It was,' he said, 'a constant struggle against poverty. I hardly made enough to live.'

Living in Carlisle Mansions was economically expedient for Somerset Maugham and for Lady Colin Campbell, both of whom were trying to live off their writing.

In 1889, Lady Colin's second work of fiction was published, a 175-page novel, *Darrell Blake, a Study*. It is about a provincial journalist who comes up to London to edit a morning newspaper. His pregnant wife, devoted but dull, stays in the country, and Blake has an affair with a judge's wife, Lady Alma Vereker. He is swept off his feet, but she is only trifling with him. She becomes bored with him and ends the relationship. In answer to a telegram from his wife's parents, Blake rushes home to find that she and her prematurely-born baby have died. He quits his job and goes off to the colonies.

Britain's most important literary weekly, the *Athenaeum*, said that *Darrell Blake* 'rises above the average novel. It is written in good, terse English, shows smartness in the observations, and is well knit and concentrated.' There were other favourable reviews, and the book went through several printings.

Lady Colin wrote no more fiction, but she composed a one-act play, *Bud and Blossom*, and with Clothilde Graves she shared the authorship of a full-length drama, *St Martin's Summer*, sub-titled 'A Play Written by Ladies for Ladies.' Both plays were performed in the West End, and *St Martin's Summer* starred the popular couple William and Maude Kendal.

[242]

Most of Lady Colin's post-trial writing consisted of newspaper articles and columns. She continued for a while to contribute to the *Saturday Review*, and her work also appeared in the *Pall Mall Gazette*, the *National Review*, the *Art Journal*, and *Lettres des Artres*. There were three journals, however, to which her name was principally attached: the *World*, the *Realm*, and *Ladies' Field*.

Edmund Yates, editor and founder of the *World*, became acquainted with Lady Colin after her divorce trial. He was impressed by her knowledge of art, music, literature, and foreign countries, and in 1889 he offered her the art editorship of his paper. She thus became the first female editor of a major London paper that was not specifically directed at women. She remained with the *World* until 1903, nine years after Yates's death.

For the *World*, Lady Colin wrote a weekly column of 2000 words, 'In the Picture Galleries,' signed 'Q. E. D.' Performing for the visual arts what her colleague George Bernard Shaw was doing for music, she reviewed exhibitions and commented on current events. Her columns were widely read and highly praised, and it is fair to say that she was among the best art critics of her time.

Lady Colin also wrote another column of 2000 words almost every week for the *World*. It was called 'A Woman's Walks,' and for this her pen name was Vera Tsaritsyn. 'A Woman's World' contained essays on places at home and abroad which Lady Colin had visited – from Venice to Brighton, from Switzerland to Scotland, from the Left Bank to Soho. This was travel literature at its best.

For most of the nineties and into the twentieth century, Lady Colin wrote 4000 words a week for the *World*. And there was more. Late in 1894, she and a friend founded a magazine to compete with the *Saturday Review*. It was called the *Realm* and appeared every Saturday, beginning on 16 November. The Newspaper Press Directory described it as 'a high class weekly review, conducted by Mr Earl Hodgson and Lady Colin Campbell, that pays especial attention to the movements of Society, to the affairs of state, to art, literature, music, and the drama, and to all learned topics of the day.' It continued through 1895, but its advertising, and presumably its circulation, fell off, and the last number appeared on 20 December. In addition to editing the *Realm*, Lady Colin wrote its weekly music column of 1500–2000 words, signed 'G. B.' Thus for thirteen months she was the co-editor of a weekly journal and the author of 5500–6000 words a week.

Lady Colin could not have been so prolific if she had led an active social life. She did a modest amount of entertaining in her drawing-room at Carlisle Mansions. She particularly enjoyed literary people, and her regular guests included Alice and Wilfred Meynell, George Meredith, Oliver Fry, and Henry James. She was not, howeever, in any danger of being distracted by social obligations.

The manner in which her *modus vivendi* had been altered by the trial may be illustrated by an incident occurring soon after she had joined the *World*. In Yates's office she met the visiting California writer Gertrude Atherton. The two women took a fancy to one another, and that night they attended the theatre together. At an afternoon reception two days later a woman took Atherton aside and said, 'I want to warn you, my dear, do not, I beg of you, be seen in public with Lady Colin Campbell. You are an American, very young, and so you don't know anything about her. I thought it my duty to warn you.'

'But I like her,' Atherton said, 'She is very clever and interesting, and her manners are impeccable.'

'She isn't so clever,' the English woman said, 'or she wouldn't be where she is today, an outcast from her own society, a declassé. Now, do take my advice and see no more of her.'

Although Gertrude Atherton ignored this advice, it was true that almost everyone in London society considered Lady Colin to be *persona non grata*. And so she had time to edit and to write.

During the principal year of the *Realm*, Lord Colin died. His widow was free to marry, but she seems never to have considered remarriage.

The last journal with which Lady Colin was connected was the weekly *Ladies' Field*. Established in 1898, it advertised itself as 'a high class illustrated paper for women of culture.' It contained articles on fashions, society, music, art, drama, and sports. In 1901, Lady Colin became its editor, and she held this position for two years. A later editor called her 'eminently fit to hold together the various interests of a journal concerned with whatever women did indoors and outdoors.'

In 1903, Lady Colin resigned from the *World* and from *Ladies' Field*. She had become a victim of what was then a painfully agonizing malady, rheumatism.

She could walk with difficulty until 1906, when she was confined to a wheel chair. She then led a semi-reclusive life until she died on the night of 1 November 1911 at the age of 53. Funeral services were held in a crowded chapel in Golders Green. Even in death she was ahead of her time. Her body was not buried. 'As the final prayers of the Reverend Dr McGowan were recited,' the *Morning Chronicle* reported, 'Lady Colin's coffin passed slowly into the crematorium chamber.'

Two weeks later the details of Lady Colin Campbell's will were noted in *The Times*. The total gross value of her estate, exclusive of death duties and debts, was £470.

Index

INDEX